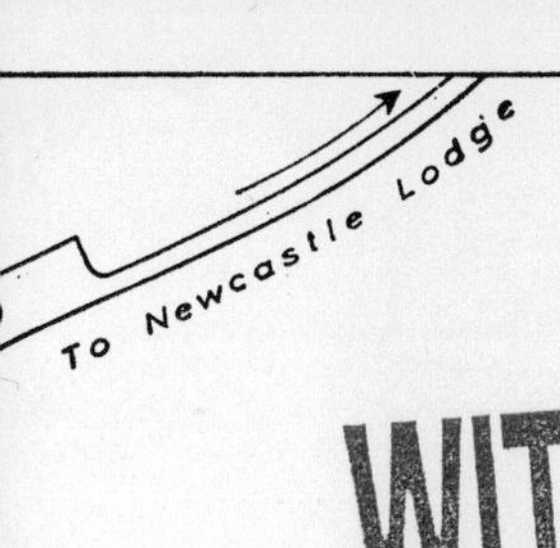

KEELE

Observatory

ES HALL

Observatory

Car Park

WOOD HALL

HORWOOD

SPRINGPOOL

A	Architects Department
B	Biology Department
C	Chemistry Department
CB	Chancellor's Building
CC	Computer Centre
Ch	Chapel
Cm	Communications Department
F	Finance Department
G	Geography Department
GL	Geology Department
KH	Keele Hall
L	Library
P	Physics Department
R	Refectories
Rr	Registry
S	Sports Centre
SU	Students Union
T	R H Tawney Building
W	Workshop
WM	Walter Moberly Hall
VC	Vice Chancellor's Residence
✠	Health Centre
▒	Staff Houses and Halls of Residence
▭	Annexes and other buildings

MAY GB 1971

Keele

An Historical Critique

THANKE GOD FOR ALL

Keele

An Historical Critique

Sir James Mountford

Formerly Vice-Chancellor of the University of Liverpool

Routledge & Kegan Paul

London and Boston

First published 1972
by Routledge & Kegan Paul Ltd
Broadway House, 68–74 Carter Lane,
London EC4V 5EL
and 9 Park Street, Boston,
Mass, 02108, U.S.A.
Printed in Great Britain by
Butler & Tanner Ltd
Frome and London

ISBN 0 7100 7237 6

Contents

Illustrations

Plates 2, 3a and 5 are by courtesy of the *Evening Sentinel*. The photograph of Dr H. M. Taylor (8c) by Walter Bird is reproduced by permission of Godfrey Argent. The end-papers were drawn by Mr G. Barber, cartographer in the Department of Geography.

TO DORIS

Foreword

A few years after Keele opened in 1950 we were invited by more than one publisher to write a book on the problems of founding a new university institution. We declined the invitation because we thought it would be a better book if we left the problems and some of the solutions to mature over a period of time. Similarly we were invited to write a series of handbooks arising out of the Foundation Year which would be texts for Keele students and a guide to any other interested people. Here again we declined because it was already clear that the Foundation Year was going to be modified and changed for many years to come, as a later study showed. Perhaps we were over-reticent, but I do not believe our decisions were wrong. In any case this book now makes it an academic argument.

Keele is the first of the post-1945 university foundations and it seems to us in our twenty-first year that we should examine its growth historically for five main reasons. First, to see how and why the ideas which led to its foundation and still inform its practice, were shaped. Second, to see how an institution comes into and maintains existence amid the political, social, economic and administrative cross-currents. Third, to discover how men and women take broad principles and breathe life into the body of knowledge and the organisational skeleton to make the spark and the fire of education possible. Fourth, to trace continuity and change in all these things both to encourage and to discourage the others as well as ourselves. Fifth, and humanly, to see if there is any cause for satisfaction in what has so far been achieved.

The kind of book we had in mind was a detailed critique of the development of Keele from its beginnings as the last of the university colleges, and the key to the whole enterprise was to find an author who could evaluate documents and opinions and who could make his own interpretation. Sir James Mountford was for many years Vice-Chancellor of the University of Liverpool (1945–63) and a former Chairman of the Committee of Vice-Chancellors and Principals (1948–9). In addition he has studied and written authoritatively on universities in Great Britain. When, to our very great pleasure, he agreed to write this book we knew that experience, integrity and lucidity would be brought to bear and that as we had hoped from the start the volume would be no exercise in pious history. We believed that such a book as this would be of interest to persons not connected with Keele as well as to those who knew it at first hand.

Sir James asked for a group of experienced people at Keele whom he might consult from time to time and whose comments he would seek on drafts of the final text. Both he and I are grateful to the following for having helped in this way: Professors A. G. N. Flew (Philosophy), A. R. Gemmell (Biology), D. J. E. Ingram (Physics), J. J. Lawlor (English), the Registrar (Mr J. F. N. Hodgkinson), the Librarian (Mr S. O. Stewart), Mr A. H. Iliffe (senior tutor), Mr P. J. V. Rolo (senior lecturer in History) and Mrs M. B. Broome (Information Officer). I know that Sir James has also consulted a number of other people to whom he is making his own acknowledgements.

The Leverhulme Trust deserves in this, as in so many other things, the University's gratitude, for it was their generosity which enabled us to invite Sir James to undertake this work over a period of more than two years.

Keele, June 1971 W. A. C. STEWART

Preface

The first purpose of this book is to put on record the background of educational endeavour which led to the concept of a College in North Staffordshire, the immediate circumstances and negotiations which led to its realisation, the stages by which the Keele curriculum came into being and was modified, and the general history of the twenty-one years of the existence of the College and University. Keele needs neither eulogy nor apologia; and the University has readily agreed that what was of importance was that as objective an account as possible should be presented. It is hoped that the book will be of interest not only to all who have an intimate knowledge of Keele either as students or as members of staff but also to many who have a concern for university education in general.

For access to and permission to use original documentary sources I am greatly indebted to the Registrar and Librarian of Keele itself, to the Town Clerk of Stoke-on-Trent, to the registrars of the Universities of Oxford, Manchester and Birmingham, to the Chairman and Secretary of the University Grants Committee, and to the Secretary of the Committee of Vice-Chancellors and Principals. Mrs Gladys Harris (*née* Malbon) most generously copied out for me excerpts from her detailed diaries and personal reports of meetings and provided documentation not otherwise available. Mr R. A. Lowe has very willingly allowed me to use material from his M.A. thesis (Keele, 1966) on adult education movements in the Potteries. Messrs. Chatto and Windus kindly gave permission to use the quotation from W. B. Gallie's book on p. 52 and Lady Stocks to use the quotation from her own book on p. 23.

As the chapters of the book were written, mimeographed copies were circulated to all members of the Keele group to whom the Vice-Chancellor refers in his Foreword; and the suggestions they made by way of additional material and comments have been invaluable. Furthermore I was fortunate in that all or most of the first six chapters were also read by Lady Scott, Dame Lucy Sutherland, Mrs Harris, Dr F. A. Vick, Professor A. E. Teale, Professor S. E. Finer, Professor T. Kelly, Mr R. A. Lowe and Mr P. Hibberd: their informed and pertinent criticisms have saved me from many errors of fact, interpretation and emphasis. There are many correspondents too who have given me the benefit of their knowledge about particular points on which I consulted them: to all of them, and particularly to those whose replies form the basis of Chapter 8, I am very grateful for their ready help.

There are two people in particular without whose support this book could scarcely have been completed. Mr J. R. B. Bosworth, appointed for the session 1969–70 as my personal research assistant, not only lightened my labours by his scholarly approach and by his initiative and assiduity in tracking down and assembling documentary material, but added still further to the debt I owe him by compiling reliable précis of innumerable minutes and memoranda and casting much of the material into an annotated narrative form. Mrs Doreen Brookes, as secretary to the enterprise throughout, must have found attending to a voluminous correspondence the least onerous part of the assistance she gave: she coped with my untidy drafts and deciphered the mosaics of script and afterthoughts with an encouraging patience; and she shouldered the very considerable burden of tabulating the answers received in response to the student questionnaire (see Chapter 8). No author could have had two more loyal and dedicated helpers.

In the planning of this book it seemed evident that a thematic treatment should in general predominate over the doggedly chronological. In so far as this means that a document, event or topic may occasionally appear in more than one context, cross-references in the footnotes and the index will, I hope, be of help to the reader. Since the evidence on which this book is based consists almost entirely of unpublished and confidential committee minutes, reports, memoranda, and official or semi-official correspondence, I have refrained from the pedantic luxury of quoting chapter and verse for every statement of fact. The kind of source on which I rely can generally be deduced from the context; to have burdened a book of this kind with hundreds of detailed references to material not easily accessible would only have annoyed the reader without putting him genuinely in a position to assess the evidence.

June 1971 JAMES MOUNTFORD

One

Introducing Keele

THE 'KEELE EXPERIMENT'

If you take a map of North Staffordshire you will find the small village of Keele (*cȳ-hyll*, 'cow hill') a little way beyond the westernmost fringe of the Potteries, five miles from the centre of the City of Stoke-on-Trent and just outside the boundary of the Borough of Newcastle-under-Lyme. It was here, in Keele Hall, a Tudor mansion extensively reconstructed in Victorian times, that the newly founded University College of North Staffordshire, the forerunner of the University of Keele, welcomed its first 157 students in October 1950.

There was no pageantry nor any great fanfare of publicity to mark the inauguration of the College; and even the academic world in general, which might have been expected to display a warm and welcoming interest, gave it little more than a grudging and sidelong glance. Yet the event was one of great importance in the history of English university education: the first part of a significant new chapter in that history was being written. This College was not simply the first institution of university standing to be established after the end of World War II, though that in itself would have been worthy of note. Keele was much more than one further 'University College' added to the list of similarly named institutions; for in a number of important ways it was quite unlike anything previously known in Britain. The manner of its founding was unprecedented and its educational programme was unique; its influence direct and indirect can be traced in much subsequent discussion of university education. From its earliest days the College and its curriculum were referred to as the 'Keele experiment'; and all those who were involved in the founding of the College—the persistent promoters of the project, the University Grants Committee (UGC) which had approved it and were providing most of the funds for its realisation, and the Universities of Oxford, Manchester and

Birmingham which agreed to act as 'sponsors' for it—all of them were conscious that they were committing themselves to a bold venture. Certainly later events have shown that the unusual financial and constitutional arrangements which were made when Keele was established decisively affected the patterns which were adopted in the further development of newer universities in the 1960s: after Keele, no university college of the older type was or could have been founded. Even more significant is the fact that after Keele had demonstrated that a new and unconventional university curriculum could be fashioned and implemented, a sense of freedom from established concepts of university education made it possible for the universities of the 1960s, even though they did not closely copy Keele, to plan exciting new degree structures of their own.

A brief glance at the history, status and educational framework of earlier university colleges will show how anomalous was the University College of North Staffordshire. The earliest of the provincial university colleges was Owens College in Manchester which opened in 1851; and between that date and the end of the nineteenth century nine others were founded in large centres of population in England: at Leeds, Bristol, Sheffield, Birmingham, Liverpool, Nottingham, Reading, Southampton and Exeter; and three were also established in Wales at Aberystwyth, Bangor and Cardiff. In the first half of the twentieth century three more were founded in Leicester, Hull and Swansea. The founding of each one of these colleges was the outcome of a desire for higher education in a particular locality; there was no concerted 'University College movement'; and in the cases of Manchester, Sheffield, Birmingham, Nottingham and Hull the turning point had been the practical and generous interest shown by an individual founding benefactor. How these colleges were to survive was in every case a nagging anxiety. For their income they depended on the interest accruing from such endowments as they possessed, on subscriptions and appeals, on subventions from Local Authorities, and on the fees from students; only rigid economy could make ends meet. The central Treasury made small grants to a very few of them from 1889; but it was not until the UGC was set up by the Treasury in 1919 that the serious financial troubles of university institutions as a whole were appreciably alleviated. By this time many of the university colleges had become full universities and the colleges in Wales had been federated in the University of Wales; all these were at once included in the grant list of the UGC. But Exeter had to wait until 1922 and Leicester and Hull until 1945 before they were judged to be of sufficient maturity and academic standing to be supported from government funds. Keele did not have to wait.

Until they were granted full university status by Royal Charter these university colleges had no power to award degrees; they offered courses of university content and quality, but could not themselves attest the achievement of their students. That these colleges were academically viable at all was due to the extraordinary nature of the University of London (founded in 1836) which for long had no teaching function of its own but was created to determine syllabuses, conduct examinations and confer degrees on students of 'approved institutions'. The university colleges all became 'approved' without difficulty and their students sat for what came to be widely known and generally respected as the 'London external' degree. The galling disadvantage of this system was that the academic staff of the colleges had no say in determining the syllabuses of instruction or in examining their own students. The one advantage was that the London degree afforded a recognised criterion for academic standards. But the often long drawn out apprenticeship which had thus to be served before full university status could be achieved was frustrating and inhibiting.[1] Keele did not have to serve such an arduous apprenticeship.

In North Staffordshire the idea of having a university of their own had been mooted from the 1890s onwards by a number of people. In fostering this idea an important part was played by those who were involved in the university extension movement and in the activities of the Workers' Educational Association. The local aspirations were encouraged and sustained also by prominent educational leaders from outside, particularly by R. H. Tawney, the distinguished economic historian, and by A. D. Lindsay, later Lord Lindsay of Birker, Master of Balliol and Keele's first Principal, both of whom had for a long time been deeply involved in adult education work in the Potteries.

[1] Even when Liverpool and Leeds became federated in 1884 and 1887 with Manchester in the Victoria University, and Aberystwyth, Bangor and Cardiff in the University of Wales (1893), they retained the title of 'university college' and their students took the degrees of the federal university. The individual Welsh colleges still have this status and title.

It was not until 1946, however, that circumstances proved to be opportune for the first effective steps to be taken towards achieving the long-cherished ideal; and even then four wearisome years were to pass before the College became a reality. Such is the brief outline; the unfolding of the whole story is the theme of later chapters. Meanwhile we turn to the distinctive features which made Keele so interesting a landmark in educational history.

The 'Keele experiment', though it brought in its train a number of constitutional innovations, was first and foremost a matter of educational philosophy and policy. The curriculum as we now find it has an appearance of homogeneity and structural consistency which gives no hint of the discussions which led up to it; for the scheme finally adopted is very different from some of the proposals which were current at various stages. Some of the earliest advocates of a College had only a narrow concept of what an institution of university standing should set out to do. The one thing they were clear about was that its work should be closely related to local industry and commerce; the study of ceramics and physical chemistry would, along with economics, be the main pillars. On the other hand, those whose educational creed was expressed within the adult education movements envisaged the future College as a much more liberal institution which would be 'a centre and focus of all higher education in the region' and would put particular emphasis on social studies.

A third element in the thinking about a new College was the feeling that a new approach to education at the university level was needed. The existing patterns of university curricula, it was said, were unsatisfactory in that they separated subjects from one another too rigidly into departments and, instead of broadening the outlook of students, led to ever narrowing areas of specialisation; and this malady, because of the inflexible entrance pre-requisites on which university departments themselves insisted, had spread down into the grammar schools and infected their teaching in the sixth forms.[1] The breaking down

[1] At the time the Keele curriculum was being planned, sixth form examinations did not yet offer even the minor palliative of papers in General Studies. A 'General Paper' was first made available by the Northern Universities Joint Matriculation Board in 1951 as an 'Ordinary' level examination intended for sixth forms. A 'General Studies' examination at 'Advanced' level was added in 1959.

of departmentalism and over-specialisation, however, was only one of the reasons for devising a new curriculum. A further consideration was of a more positive and constructive kind. Was there not in the modern world a place for a type of university education which by a radical re-planning would emphasise the concept of the unity of knowledge and inculcate and strengthen a sense of the whole scope of Western civilisation, both past and present? To weaken the stranglehold of departmentalism was not enough by itself; it was a new attitude to university study that was essential; a new focus should be created to give a new perspective; and that meant an entirely new kind of curriculum.

The most striking feature of the solution which was eventually worked out at Keele for the conflict between study in breadth and specialisation was the institution of a new type of first-year course called the *Foundation Year*. This course is planned to provide a wide survey of three main areas: the humanities, the social sciences and the natural sciences. For the student there is a clean break from the kind of specialisation either in arts or in science subjects which he has usually experienced in the sixth form; he is given this opportunity to widen his vision and discover his real aptitudes at the very threshold of his university course. The Foundation Year is compulsory for all students and there are no exemptions from any part of the course on the ground that a student has previously studied this or that part of the syllabus. It is intended to be, not a trivial 'survey course', but a carefully designed and disciplined integration of studies in a variety of fields each of which is significant in the world of today. Every member of the academic staff is involved in it in some way or another—a very important feature of the Keele system; and from the outset its content and methods have been under constant scrutiny. It imposes a considerable burden of serious work on the students; and on the staff a responsibility to control their personal enthusiasms in the interest of a common purpose.

After the Foundation Year has been satisfactorily completed the student embarks on a further three years of study before taking his degree; a shorter period than that would not be sufficient to equip him for whatever his chosen career might be. This of course means that the whole curriculum is necessarily spread over four years, in contrast to the three years which is usual for very many students elsewhere. An undergraduate training of this length is also part of the Keele experiment: it is costly in time for the student, it depends on the willingness of Local Authorities to finance the student, and it has its repercussions on the amount of residential accommodation which has to be provided.[1]

The three later years of the Keele curriculum, however, are not by any means along the lines of a first degree course in the older institutions. It would have undermined the whole spirit and purpose of Keele if the Foundation Year could have been regarded as a tiresome hurdle to be surmounted as an otiose preliminary to the serious business of getting back to one's specialisms. Consequently in these three years also there is an insistence on breadth of interest. This is achieved in two ways. In the first place, all students have to offer at least two principal subjects in their final degree examination and cannot concentrate on a single subject. To this extent, the Keele degree resembles the 'Combined Honours' available in other universities. But a second obligation placed on students is to offer either one principal subject or one subsidiary subject taken from an area clearly outside their primary fields. Thus the scientist has to present a subject from the humanities or the social sciences; and a student in the humanities or social sciences is required to select something within the field of the natural sciences. In other words, either as a principal or as a subsidiary subject, every student offers both a science and something which is not a science. It becomes obvious, therefore, that the Keele curriculum is to be assessed as a totality, not judged solely by its individual features: it is conceived as a whole from start to finish; and it is expected that the Keele graduate will be a different kind of educated person from one whose sixth form interests have never been assisted or encouraged to expand. One interesting consequence of the Keele concept of a university education is that every student is assumed to be taking a course of study within the same general framework, for which the appropriate goal is some class of honours degree; and a pass degree is awarded only if a student's achievement at the end of his course cannot be adjudged to justify the award of honours at all.

[1] What is here described is still the basic Keele pattern. A three-year course for a limited number of students is to be introduced in 1973; see p. 222.

Mention must also be made of the unusual residential arrangements which were adopted at Keele and contributed to its particular ethos. The older university colleges had been intended primarily to ensure facilities for higher education for the young people living within particular areas; and the provision of Halls of Residence for students coming from a distance did not become a really serious consideration until after World War I. By 1945, however, it had become axiomatic that it was a good thing on educational grounds for a student to go to a university or college away from home; and maintenance grants from public funds which were given in increasing numbers to university students took account of this. In their search for a suitable site for the College, the Stoke-on-Trent promoters of the project had always had it in mind that an appreciable number at least of the students would be in college residences. When Keele Hall and the surrounding land became available the opportunity was taken not only to convert existing structures so that all students could be accommodated but to provide housing also for the staff and their families within the clearly defined perimeter of the campus. For this there was no exact precedent. So it was not only studies which were integrated at Keele; staff and their young families and the students would at least see each other day by day and if proximity of residence could achieve it, Keele would be a closely knit community both academically and socially. Whatever transient personal stresses and strains there might be, this feature of life at Keele proved to be not only tolerable but successful; and the more recent modifications of it which have occurred have been due to practical difficulties rather than to any second thoughts about the underlying principle.

A College offering a curriculum of the kind we have outlined was far too exceptional to follow the path trodden by all other university colleges previously established. The requirements for the external degree of London, even though by this time London made special syllabus arrangements for individual colleges, could scarcely be stretched to include all the features of the Keele plan; and no serious enquiry along these lines was ever made by Keele. Freedom, complete and untrammelled, to experiment was inherent in the concept which the promoters of Keele, and especially their leader, Lord Lindsay, had formed of their educational pioneering. The only alternative, apart from immediate full university status, was to petition for the power to award their own degree of B.A., without seeking the right of awarding the full range of higher degrees. This was a constitutional innovation of the first magnitude. The precedent thus established, which broke once and for all the system of tutelage under the umbrella of the London degree, proved to be of great importance for the universities of the 1960s: for them, there was never any question of withholding degree-granting powers—and their privileges were not confined to the B.A. What had been unthinkable before Keele was founded was tacitly accepted as normal ten years later.

Nevertheless, there had to be some acceptable guarantee of academic standards; of this necessity the founders of Keele were well aware. At first there were thoughts that some sort of link with Oxford alone would suffice and could be achieved; but as early as 1946 a scheme was suggested whereby the three universities of Oxford, Manchester and Birmingham should jointly share in the role of 'sponsors' for the College. It was not easy to bring this scheme to fruition and at one stage negotiations almost foundered. What was eventually agreed was that the three universities should each appoint two members to serve on an Academic Council where they would be in a majority and have wide powers of approval for academic appointments and courses of study. In practice this plan worked well because the representatives of the sponsoring universities took their duties seriously and acted with sympathy and understanding. Here again Keele provided a precedent for the 1960s; for although the newer universities did not have the formal sponsorship of a limited number of other institutions, they were helped and their standards were guaranteed by Academic Advisory Boards or Committees whose individual membership was drawn from a wider range of universities: the broad principle, however, was the same as that which had applied at Keele.

In the matter also of government approval and financial support through the agency of the UGC the founding of Keele marked the beginning of a new epoch in university affairs. It is conceivable that some sort of a College could have been started in the same kind of fashion as the older university colleges had been: Articles of Association under Board of Trade regulations would have given it a legal status. But the Local Authorities in the Potteries were in no position to find anything like the necessary funds and there was no generous benefactor in sight. Circumstances at the end of the war, however, were propitious: additional public funds were to be made available for university development and the Stoke promoters seized the opportunity to put their proposals before the UGC. The upshot was that a Charter was obtained and adequate financial resources were promised. What was not widely appreciated in university circles at the time, was that the part played by the UGC in the matter of Keele was the first sign of a notable change in the relationship of that body to university institutions as a whole. On the one hand it was virtually impossible in post-war conditions for a new institution to be established without heavy reliance on government funds and that circumstance inevitably gave to the UGC the decisive voice when a new foundation was under consideration. On the other hand, the UGC's functions were deliberately widened in 1946 to include the duty of co-ordinating university developments in the light of national requirements, a duty which considerably enlarged the influence which the UGC could exert over a wide range of university affairs. Keele was the first College of any kind to be founded with this specific approval of the UGC; and, as we shall see later, that approval was not hastily given and then only subject to the fulfilment of certain conditions. Although the initiative did not come from the UGC, there was a sense in which Keele could be said to have been founded by the state.

To sum up the preceding paragraphs, the ways in which Keele broke new ground can be listed as follows:

1. a Foundation Year common to all students;
2. a four-year course for all students;
3. two principal subjects in the final examination;
4. a science and a non-science in the last three years;
5. no separate course for a 'pass' degree;
6. residence on campus for all students and staff;
7. a scheme of 'sponsorship' to guarantee standards;
8. the awarding of its own B.A. degree;
9. its foundation specifically approved by the UGC;
10. immediate financial support provided through the UGC.

The winning of approval for the scheme from the UGC, the success of negotiations for sponsorship, the granting of a Charter and the allocation of funds, these were the necessary preliminaries to the launching of the College. There were, of course, many practical problems to be faced. Keele Hall itself and other structures on the site had to be adapted in a hurry to academic and residential purposes; a staff of professors (thirteen) and readers (two) had to be appointed; innumerable administrative arrangements had to be worked out; the broadly conceived outline of a curriculum still needed to be fully discussed in considerable detail and schemes of study determined. It was on the shoulders of a relatively small group of people that the burden of these tasks fell; and in retrospect we can appreciate how great must have been the demands made on their time, energy, resolution and, above all, on their faith and confidence in the future. As a result of all these efforts it proved to be just possible for academic work to begin in October 1950, even though under conditions which involved major inconveniences and some positive hardship.

Mention was made at the beginning of this chapter of the attitude of other universities to the founding of Keele. This is a topic which will be dealt with in detail later on, but it has to be said at once that academic opinion as a whole was unfavourable and even resentful. All the available government grants (it was thought) could be better spent on the development of existing institutions and not frittered away on an intruder; the special privilege accorded to Keele of awarding its own degree was unfair to the other university colleges; the proposed curriculum was new-fangled and based on ill-considered educational assumptions; and a curriculum which would not allow students to concentrate on a single subject would be a crippling handicap for Keele graduates. Nor was the system of sponsorship clearly understood outside Oxford, Manchester and Birmingham. Many of the misunderstandings about Keele could have been more quickly dispelled had the Principal been a member of the Committee of Vice-Chancellors and Principals, where frequent contact with colleagues engaged in the discussion of matters of common university concern would have been of advantage; but the composition of that Committee at that time was such that only two of the Principals of university colleges (taken in rotation) had a seat thereon, and it was not until 1952 that anyone from Keele attended the meetings of the Committee. This unfortunate circumstance cut Keele off, at a critical stage of its infancy, from an important source of knowledge about general trends in university affairs. In this regard, as in so many others, the tripartite sponsorship was a life-line.

In addition to the coolness with which the inauguration of Keele was greeted, the College was dogged by misfortunes which only a malignant fate could have conjured up. The first Principal, Lord Lindsay himself, died before the end of the second session after the opening of the College; his successor also died after being in office only eighteen months; and the third Principal lived only long enough to see four sessions through. It needs little imagination to sense the shocks which these events caused in the struggling College and what a handicap it was not to have a firm and continuing leadership in the early formative years. During the three interregna which supervened—and one of them lasted almost two years—it was a different professor on each occasion who was appointed as Acting Principal. Two of the original thirteen professors who had strenuously participated in the building up of the curriculum and the formulation of academic policy left for posts elsewhere at the end of the first four years; and another left two years later. It must also be said that what proved to be an error of judgment was made in the appointment of the first head of the administrative side of affairs. An academic of distinction though he was, he had not had the right kind of experience for this particularly exacting post in a pioneer institution, and the conduct of even the routine business of the College faltered badly until the post of Registrar was assumed in 1953 by the present holder.

Yet, because of the dedication and determination of those who, from the Principal and his academic colleagues to the secretaries and porters, threw in their lot with Keele in its early years, and thanks also to the members of the Academic Council who came so regularly to Keele from the three sponsoring universities, Keele survived and flourished. Compared with other universities, even with some which are younger than itself, it is still—and largely by choice—one of the smaller institutions;[1] but it has continued to make a kind of contribution

[1] In October 1970 the total number of full-time students was 1,863, of whom 252 were postgraduates.

to English university education which is not paralleled elsewhere.

THE 1970–1 CURRICULUM

In view of what has been said above about the misunderstandings which existed—and may still exist—about the Keele pattern of university education, this chapter can appropriately end with a concise survey of the Keele curriculum as it is working out in practice in 1970–1.

The *Foundation Year* provides for every student the broad context of human knowledge in which his later studies will be set and introduces him to the scope, methods and interconnections of the main branches of university studies. The most novel feature of the instruction during this year is a course of 230 *lectures* to which all departments contribute. Two lectures are given each day at 9 a.m. and 11 a.m. throughout the session and a full list of them can be found in Appendix III. What is called the 'Main Thread' begins with a consideration of the earth as an object in space and proceeds in logical sequence to the development of man through Greece and Rome, the Middle Ages, the Renaissance and Reformation, and the Enlightenment right up to the present day with particular emphasis on the philosophical and political ideas, the social changes and scientific discoveries which characterised all these different periods. Within this dominant framework there are inserted from time to time small groups of lectures for the 'Discursive Treatment' of topics which have arisen in the main series; and for most of the session the lectures given on Friday are devoted under the heading of 'Recurrent Topics' to a consideration of themes which have a continuing significance and tie the main series together. Associated with the lecture course there are weekly *discussion groups* of six to eight students with a senior member of staff as chairman and two other members of staff from other departments to help; and during the session each student has to present a total of nine *essays* so chosen as to include topics from each of the three main groups of subjects: the humanities, the social sciences, and the natural sciences.

During the Foundation Year each student must also attend two sessional courses and three terminal courses. The *sessional courses* are pursued at weekly classes throughout all three terms and are intended, as part of a broadening process, to introduce students to serious work in subjects they have not studied before: no subject which has been pursued to the 'A' level in the sixth form may be taken as a sessional. The *terminal courses,* each taken in weekly classes for a single term only, are meant for students who have studied the subject seriously before and have it in mind to continue the subject in their degree course: but terminal courses are also available in some subjects not normally included in a school curriculum and so provide an opportunity of making at least a brief acquaintance with something quite new. In order to ensure breadth of interest, the sessionals and terminals must normally be distributed across the three main groups of subjects.

At the end of the session an examination is set on the topics covered in the lecture course; it consists of three essay-type papers, one in each of the three main groups of subjects; but students who have done sufficiently well in multiple-choice objective tests set during the session are exempted from it. Examinations are set also on the sessional courses; but terminal subjects are not formally examined. A special panel assesses the over-all performance of students at the end of the Foundation Year.[1]

For the *degree course* itself, pursued during the second, third and fourth year in the University, the division of subjects into three groups, each administered by a Board of Studies, is of importance. These groups are:

Group A (*humanities*): American studies, Greek, Latin, English language and literature, French, German, history, Russian studies, philosophy, music.

Group B (*social sciences*): economics, geography, law, politics, psychology, sociology, applied social studies, theory and practice of education.

Group C (*natural sciences*): biology, chemistry, geology, mathematics, physics, astronomy, computer science.

All subjects in groups A, B, and C may be taken either as principal or as subsidiary subjects except American studies, sociology and law which may be taken as principal subjects only; and music, astronomy and computer science which may be taken as subsidiary subjects only. A principal subject is studied

[1] At Keele the Foundation Year is popularly designated as 'FY' and the later years of the curriculum as P1, P2 and P3.

for three years. A subsidiary subject is studied for one year only. The normal degree requirement is that a student offers two principal and two subsidiary subjects,[1] with the very important proviso that at least one of the four must be chosen from groups A and B combined and at least one from group C: this ensures that some science and some non-science is studied at a serious level by everyone.

External examiners are involved in the assessment of work at both subsidiary and principal levels. The class of degree to be awarded is determined by strictly applied internal regulations. Each principal subject is assessed separately and to obtain a first, for example, a student must achieve a first class mark in one subject and not less than the minimum II(i) mark in the other, though if his mark in his weaker subject falls just below that normal minimum a good performance in both subsidiaries may be allowed to compensate. The doctrine underlying these regulations is that a first class chemist or historian is not necessarily a first class Keele graduate.

[1] In the rare cases when three principals are taken, only one subsidiary is required. The subsidiaries may be taken either together in the first degree year or spread over the first two years. There are special arrangements of courses for candidates who combine the degree with the Certificate in Education or the Diploma in Applied Social Studies.

Two

The Genesis of an Idea

THE EARLY BACKGROUND

The first really firm proposals for the establishment of a University College in North Staffordshire were made in the period immediately following the end of World War II when an Exploratory Committee, constituted in 1946, carried to a successful conclusion an intricate series of negotiations resulting in the granting of a Charter in 1949 and the opening of the University College of North Staffordshire in 1950. But this effort was not something suddenly conceived: it was the ultimate stage in the realisation of an idea which had been gathering strength for more than half a century. Intermittently from the 1890s suggestions had been made for the setting up of a college or university and though none of the earlier proposals came to fruition the concept was not lost sight of; and it is the main purpose of this chapter to give an account of the cultural and intellectual environment out of which the idea of a university institution in North Staffordshire emerged. The dominating factor from the last quarter of the nineteenth century was undoubtedly the growing strength of the university extension movement and later of the Workers' Educational Association in the Potteries.

It is of course not to be supposed that the university extension movement could itself have taken root in wholly virgin soil; and what was happening in the first half of the nineteenth century has some clear relevance to what came later. The earlier cultural and educational groupings and organisations however belong for the most part to the general history of adult education,[1] and only a very brief sketch of their development in the Potteries can here be given. But first, for readers who are unfamiliar with the area, a word should be said about the

[1] See T. Kelly, *A History of Adult Education in Great Britain.*

Potteries themselves. This name was applied from the Industrial Revolution onwards to a congeries of townships and smaller villages which, notably through the firm founded by Josiah Wedgwood (1730–95), became the centre of the ceramics industry, though coal mining and iron and steel working also occupied an appreciable number of the inhabitants. Few industrial areas have in consequence a more forbidding external appearance. In 1910, the six towns of Stoke, with Hanley, Burslem and Tunstall to the north and Longton and Fenton to the south were federated under the name of Stoke-on-Trent[1]; but Newcastle-under-Lyme to the west (which traces its existence to a document of 1173) remained outside. Each of these towns had its own strong traditions; and local loyalties vigorously persist to this day. The mosaic of educational history is on that account unusually complicated.[2] Mechanics' Institutes, circulating libraries for subscribers, 'philosophical' societies, and courses of lectures: all played their part in stimulating and satisfying educational and intellectual needs, particularly for the middle classes and to some extent for the ceramic designers who were the élite of the skilled operatives. By the beginning of the nineteenth century there was a subscribers' library at Hanley which in 1834 possessed over 3000 volumes. A similar library was started at Newcastle-under-Lyme in 1812. The Pottery Philosophical Society at Shelton (later part of Hanley), whose President and active patron was Josiah Wedgwood II, set up a library in 1820 and arranged lectures on 'natural, experimental and mental philosophy'. In 1826 the Potteries Mechanics' Institution was started at Hanley; it had a library and, with local industrial needs in view, from 1829 organised classes in chemistry, modelling and drawing. By 1830 a Socratic School was meeting monthly at the Wheatsheaf Inn in Stoke. At Newcastle-under-Lyme a Literary and Scientific Institution was founded in 1836; by 1851 the

[1] The name Stoke-on-Trent distinguishes it from Stoke-upon-Trent, one of the six towns.

[2] R. A. Lowe's unpublished M.A. thesis (University of Keele, 1966), 'The development of adult education in the Potteries with special reference to the founding of a university in the area', gives the fullest available account of the early cultural history of the Potteries and continues the story up to 1950. Both for this chapter and the two which follow, this admirable work has been invaluable for its references to original sources and for its assessments of their relevance.

annual issues of its books to subscribers had reached the 10,000 mark; and in 1853 it established a school of art. In Longton, after abortive beginnings, an Athenaeum and Mechanics' Institution was put on a firm basis in 1848; and about the same time Athenaeums came into existence at Stoke-upon-Trent (1846), Tunstall (1850) and Fenton (1853). At Burslem in 1869 the statesman W. E. Gladstone laid the foundation stone of the Wedgwood Institute which provided a library, reading-room, museum and school of art. Thus no township in the Potteries remained without its focal point or organisation for the encouragement of the intellectual or vocational interests of those who had the urge for such activities, the leisure to devote to them—and the means to pay the lecture fee or annual subscription.

The needs of the ordinary workers were less appreciated by the organisations just mentioned and the workers themselves were barely conscious of those needs. The adult schools movement of the early nineteenth century, which grew in part out of the Sunday schools and Methodist class-meetings and was concerned to a large extent with the elementary skills of reading and writing, did not take any firm root in the Potteries as it had done in places such as Bristol and Nottingham; and it was not until the middle of that century that we can observe the growth in North Staffordshire of working-class societies and clubs for mutual improvement and self-help. Such societies had only meagre resources and they were shy of middle-class patronage, but the zeal of those who became members was unmistakable; and once the possibility of thus securing some educational advancement had become apparent, the number of these societies, though individually small in membership, increased to such an extent that in 1861 a North Staffordshire Adult Education Society was formed 'to foster the work of night schools and similar efforts'. One source of strength in these societies was the fact that political discussion was not banned, as it generally was in the Mechanics' Institutes; and though it lasted only four years from 1850 to 1854, the People's Hall in Hanley with its magazine *The Lever* was outstanding for the way in which an educational programme was linked with fervour for social reform. In total, however, the number of members of such societies never reached a remarkably high level; they represented a leaven in the working class but did not of themselves lead to a widely popular movement. The Education Act of 1870 which led the way to compulsory elementary education lessened the need for such societies and the North Staffordshire Society itself went out of existence in 1892.

UNIVERSITY EXTENSION AND TUTORIAL CLASSES

The university extension movement, to which we now turn, was first put on a formal basis when James Stuart, a mathematical Fellow of Trinity College, prevailed upon the University of Cambridge in 1873 to make itself responsible for the organisation of courses of lectures in the larger centres of population. In the autumn of that year courses were begun in Nottingham, Leicester and Derby. London University followed suit with a similar scheme in 1876, Oxford (on the initiative of Benjamin Jowett, Master of Balliol) in 1878 and the Victoria University (Manchester) in 1886. As the work grew in volume and experience was gained, the courses came to include history, political economy, literature, art, natural science and philosophy. Printed syllabuses were circulated; and in association with the lectures, some students stayed on for discussion and were encouraged to do optional written work and to sit for an examination.

The success of this movement was due to a number of factors. First of all, the lectures were of serious intent and brought to the students a university approach and a sense of genuine scholarship in every subject which was treated in them. The lecturers were carefully chosen not only for their mastery of their subjects but also for their ability to expound in a stimulating manner; and many of them cheerfully faced a very heavy schedule of travel and lecturing. In 1885 Oxford led the way in providing boxes of books for use in its courses, a simple device but one of the utmost value. Furthermore, Oxford began in 1888 and Cambridge in 1890 to organise short summer schools in the University itself and so afforded over the years the opportunity for many extension students to live briefly in a university atmosphere: for them, and even for those who could not attend, the university was no longer just a place from which the intellectual 'missionaries' came. Good relations were also established with the Local Authorities who came to give financial help for the running of the courses and to students who wished to go to a summer school; and this willing and continuing co-operation was to be of the utmost importance in North Staffordshire when the founding of a College was being actively considered. Finally, the quality of the lecturers was matched by the enthusiasm and organising competence and drive of the people within the universities who acted as secretaries: (Sir) Michael Sadler (from 1885) and then (Sir) John Marriott (from 1895) at Oxford and R. D. Roberts at Cambridge and London were outstanding. No less important is the fact that such men were backed up by persons of similar calibre in the local centres; and the Potteries fortunately was no exception.

In some centres the contribution which the university extension movement made to the emergence of university colleges is unmistakable. Cambridge courses were of notable influence in Sheffield, Leeds, Nottingham and Exeter, as were the Oxford courses in Reading. Mark Firth was Mayor of Sheffield in 1874 when Cambridge was first invited to send lecturers there and he became so 'convinced of the benefits resulting from the lectures and classes' that he provided a site, a building and an endowment for the Firth College of Arts and Science which opened in 1879 and ultimately became the University of Sheffield. At Leeds the industrially-orientated Yorkshire College of Science began work in 1874; but it was the president of the local Extension Lectures Committee, (Sir) Edward Baines, proprietor of the *Leeds Mercury*, who in 1877 secured funds for the establishment of posts in classics and in modern literature and history; the College dropped the word 'science' from its title and was on the way towards university rank. The Cambridge lectures at Nottingham which began in 1873 were so successful that an anonymous donor offered to provide a 'University Extension' building to accommodate them; by the time it was ready, the town itself had provided additional funds and what was opened in 1881 was in fact University College. At Exeter an educational building was erected in 1865 as a memorial to the Prince Consort which later also housed extension lectures; these became so important a feature that in 1893 the city established the Exeter Technical and University Extension College, the forerunner of the present University. Reading's association, however, was naturally with nearby Oxford. The strong local centre for extension work which came into being in that town was encouraged by Jowett of Balliol[1] and a number of Fellows of Christ Church to aim at the establishment of a permanent home of its own; and in 1892 the University Extension College was established with the help of the town council.[2]

If, with these examples of success in mind, one asks how the extension movement fared in the Potteries, it must be admitted that it was very slow to strike any vigorous roots; and it was only at the third attempt that a thriving plant was reared. Between 1874 and 1876 Cambridge endeavoured to introduce systematic extension work in Hanley, Burslem, Stoke-upon-Trent and Newcastle-under-Lyme; but the response was disappointing and for the next eleven years the extension field in the Potteries was virtually fallow. Then from 1887 to 1892 Oxford, Cambridge and the Victoria University resumed the task. For four years Oxford had some success in Newcastle-under-Lyme and tried to re-open a centre in Stoke-upon-Trent; from 1890 Cambridge organised courses in Burslem, Hanley, Tunstall and Stoke; and Victoria tried its hand in Longton. All these efforts petered out; yet it was during this period, as we shall see, that F. E. Kitchener quite clearly mooted the idea of a University College.

The third, highly successful, stage in the development of extension courses in the Potteries began in 1898 when Oxford took up the work in Hanley which Cambridge had earlier had to abandon. By 1900 or 1901 Oxford centres were started or revivified in Stoke, Newcastle, Longton, Fenton and Tunstall. As in the earlier period from 1887 to 1892, the Staffordshire County Council gave financial help and their support was supplemented by grants from the education authorities of Stoke, Newcastle and Longton. But the essential personal drive was mainly supplied by A. W. Brown, a biologist by training and a recognised extension lecturer, who came to reside in the district as organising secretary. He was on the spot all the time, not a peripatetic and occasional visitor, but one who could

1 See W. M. Childs, *Making a University*, 1933, p. 7.

2 Plans for a university college in Bristol were well advanced in 1874 before the Extension movement had got under way; but it is worth noting that the incorporation of the College in 1876 was partly due to Oxford help; Jowett offered the co-operation of Balliol and some financial support, and persuaded New College to do the same.

encourage and indeed create opportunities for the expansion of the work.

Of all the centres founded in the Potteries at this time the one at Longton was the most lively and energetic; and this in large part was due to the activities of E. Stuart Cartwright, a young clerk in the Longton Education Offices, who in 1901 became secretary of the Longton class. For twelve years he was the most dynamic force in the adult education movement in the Potteries, organising courses, attending courses himself, maintaining close links with Oxford and supplying an all-embracing drive and energy. He was invited to Oxford in 1912 to become Secretary of the Oxford Tutorial Classes Committee but never lost interest in the Potteries.[1]

Longton has a particular claim to fame in relation to what came to be known as tutorial classes. By 1907 the extension students at Longton were discussing with the Reverend G. W. Hudson Shaw, one of the most outstanding of the Oxford extension lecturers, how they could pursue their studies to still greater depth. He mentioned to them that at Rochdale in Lancashire a group of Workers' Educational Association students had in mind a scheme for a course extending over two years (later extended to three), with twenty-four meetings each winter and spring, comprising lectures and discussions, together with regular written work; and that an important feature of the project was that the students themselves should have a predominant share in selecting the topic for study. It happened also that in connexion with the summer school in Oxford that year, which Cartwright attended, there was an important conference on the relationship between the universities and the working classes. This resulted in the setting up of the Oxford Tutorial Classes Committee on which both the University and the Workers' Educational Association (founded on a national basis in 1903 by Albert Mansbridge) were represented.

With Cartwright at hand, it is not surprising that the Longton Education Committee asked Oxford to provide a tutorial class; and on 24 January 1908 the class held its first meeting just one day before the opening of the Rochdale class.[2]

1 See H. P. Smith, 'E. S. Cartwright', *Rewley House Papers*, III, i, 1949–50, pp. 8–24.

2 That Rochdale should have been deprived of the honour of being the first tutorial class to begin work seems to have been due to the fact that Rochdale

The tutor appointed to conduct the class was R. H. Tawney, and the subject selected was 'The Industrial History of England in the Sixteenth and Seventeenth Centuries'—certainly not a topic for any but serious students. By 1910 some members of the Longton class founded the nucleus of a second class at Hanley (which later moved to Burslem); the Longton class itself asked for a continuation when its first three years were coming to an end in 1911; a third class began at Stoke in 1912, where twelve of the thirty-five students were miners; and in the same year preliminary steps were taken for the formation of a class at Tunstall with (Sir) Henry Clay as tutor.[1] Thus in the 1913–14 session, of the eighteen tutorial classes then organised by Oxford, four were in the Potteries; and it is not surprising that those people in Oxford who were interested in this work had a special and continuing regard for intellectual developments in North Staffordshire.

As compared with the extension lectures, a greater proportion of tutorial class students came from the working classes, many of them also being politically conscious. The classes thus developed a strong sense of social purpose and some individual members were active in the Labour movement. From 1911 there was discussion of the possibility of sending outstanding members of tutorial classes to Oxford as full-time students. The attitude of the classes themselves to this idea was a cautious one and it became acceptable only on the understanding that the purpose of sending such students to Oxford should be to equip them for eventual service as tutorial class teachers. This did not indicate that the students did not want a university education, but rather that they feared that any student who went up to Oxford would be lost to his social class.

The Longton class shared with the one in Rochdale the great good fortune of having Richard Henry Tawney (1880–1962) as its tutor. As a schoolboy at Rugby he formed a life-long friendship with the future Archbishop William Temple and as an undergraduate at Balliol he was greatly influenced by A. L. Smith, who was later Master of Balliol. With these men he

preferred to meet on Saturday afternoons rather than Friday evenings; and this also fitted in better with Tawney's travel arrangements.

[1] Clay was later an Oxford representative on the Academic Council of the University College of North Staffordshire, from 1950 to 1953.

shared a liberal and progressive outlook on education and social reform. After graduation his strong consciousness of social purpose took him for a time to the Toynbee Hall University Settlement in London and he was one of the earliest members of the executive committee of the Workers' Educational Association. In 1906 he accepted a part-time post at £50 a year as assistant to teach economics at Glasgow University. It was sheer dedication to a cause and certainly not the token fee which led him to undertake the conduct of the Longton and Rochdale tutorial classes: for he had to travel from Scotland on Fridays to meet the Longton class in the evening, go to Rochdale for the Saturday afternoon class there, and face a dreary Sunday journey back to Glasgow. During the six years which passed between January 1908 and the time he joined the armed forces at the beginning of World War I, he did not miss a single class meeting. He resumed his work in adult education in the Potteries for a time when the war was over; and it was a happy coincidence that more than twenty years later when he was Professor of Economic History in the University of London (1931–49), a Fellow of the British Academy (1935) and Honorary Fellow of Balliol (1938), he was also a member of the UGC (1943–8) just at the time when that Committee was discussing the North Staffordshire proposals for a University College.

> Tawney, though he spoke with the accents of Balliol and carried his head like a monarch of the glen, looked at times like a manual worker who had not bothered to tidy himself up for a collar-and-tie job. . . . He appeared impervious to physical discomfort and wholly devoid of worldly ambition. . . . He had a perception of human frailty which enabled him to detect insincerity, pompousness or greed, and a mastery of English so complete that he could pierce it with a single phrase of unforgettable elegance and sting. He did not, however, encounter insincerity, pompousness or greed among his working-class students, and his carelessness of outward appearance put them at their ease. He talked to them as man to man, neither claiming authority nor asking for unquestioned agreement. But as he talked, the breadth and quality of his mind and the meticulous accuracy of his scholarship reflected itself

> in the work of his students and established the standard of their thought. He will probably go down to history as the greatest adult education tutor of all time as well as what he later proved himself to be, a notable explorer of England's economic history and a writer of magnificent English prose.[1]

Not least of the activities of the Longton group was the part it played in the unusual story of the North Staffordshire Miners' Higher Education Movement. Though, as the pits were worked out, coalmining diminished in the Potteries themselves, it continued in a number of villages to the north and west. Distance and inadequate transport cut these miners off from the main stream of adult education; and in 1911 the Longton tutorial class was asked to help in a scheme to meet the miners' needs. E. S. Cartwright was eager to assist and made contact with Albert Mansbridge of the WEA whose co-operation was no less readily forthcoming. At a meeting in Stoke in May 1911, which was addressed by R. H. Tawney on the topic of 'Higher education considered apart from industrial training', the movement was inaugurated. In the autumn and winter of 1911–12 classes began in ten villages and the Longton tutorial class provided from amongst its own members eight out of the ten tutors. As the title of Tawney's address had indicated, the wishes of the miners and of their tutors had not been for industrial or vocational training; and the subjects of the classes, which were conducted along tutorial lines with discussion following the lectures, included: English History (Constitutional and Industrial), the History of Staffordshire, the Development of the English Parish, Geology, Astronomy, Literature, Botany and Physical Geography. As early as 1912 some students from the village centres went to the summer school in Oxford. By 1915, when the work had still further expanded and classes under the auspices of the Miners' movement were being held even in the Potteries towns themselves the need was expressed for a resident tutor on a permanent basis. This request for a tutor, 'preferably Mr. Tawney', was repeated in 1919 and the Chairman of the Oxford Committee, A. D. Lindsay, Fellow but not yet Master of Balliol, persuaded

[1] Mary Stocks, *The Workers' Educational Association: The First Fifty Years*, p. 39.

the Education Committees of Stoke and Staffordshire to provide the necessary funds for Tawney's appointment.[1] Not content with this, the Miners' movement set afoot the co-ordination of all adult education activities in the area and in 1920 entrusted its funds to the North Staffordshire Adult Education Association which it had been instrumental in establishing. From this point onwards not only was the development of adult education in North Staffordshire a history of expansion and consolidation, but the links binding the organisations together became increasingly strong. In 1921 the North Staffordshire district of the WEA came into being; in 1925 at the instigation of the WEA Oxford agreed to the establishment of a North Staffordshire Joint Advisory Committee with A. D. Lindsay, now Master of Balliol, as its chairman and E. S. Cartwright as its secretary. In 1944 this Committee was reconstituted under the title of the North Staffordshire Committee for Adult Education, with Lindsay still as its chairman and representatives of the Education Committees of Staffordshire, Stoke-on-Trent and Burton-on-Trent amongst its membership. From 1925 onwards closer and closer bonds were forged between Oxford, the organisers of adult education activities in the Potteries, and the local authorities of North Staffordshire whose interest and financial support underpinned the whole structure. But of special significance and importance is the fact that these co-ordinating committees brought together in the service of a common cause people of influence who got to know one another and came to share a common aspiration: that basically is why the foundation of a University College at long last became a feasible proposition. To that aspiration in its various and not always consistent manifestations, our attention can now be directed.

PROPOSALS FOR A COLLEGE

It is a mere oddity of educational history that the first proposal for a university in Staffordshire was made as long ago as 1814 by Charles Kelsall in his book *Phantasm of an University*. He was advocating a new kind of university composed of colleges which would each teach a separate subject i.e., Civil Polity

[1] Tawney held this appointment until 1923.

and Languages, Moral Philosophy, Fine Arts, Natural Philosophy, Agriculture and Manufactures, and Mathematics: 'For the situation of the new university, let a healthy and cheerful spot be chosen in the County of Stafford, and let the silver Trent meander at the end of the University Grove.'[1] This idyllic suggestion seems to have attracted no attention locally or nationally and it had no connexion whatever with later proposals. There is no evidence that Kelsall had personal associations with the Potteries and he probably had nothing more definite in mind than a central and pleasant location; but for Keele he has become something of a legendary progenitor.[2]

Serious history must take the 1890s as the effective starting-point for the idea of a university institution in the area. The impetus came in the first instance from the recognition of the need for further education in subjects related to local industries. Early in 1890 an address on this topic was made to the North Staffordshire Chambers of Commerce by F. E. Kitchener, Chairman of the newly-formed Staffordshire Education Committee, who had been one of the local secretaries for Cambridge extension courses. The occasion was one of importance and the speaker had knowledge and authority. As reported in the local newspaper[3] he pointed out the lack of facilities for further education in the district and contrasted North Staffordshire with Manchester, which had Owens College, and with Birmingham, which had Mason's College.

> If this neglect of providing higher education after school life was over was allowed to continue to the end of the century it must very sensibly affect the success of the district. He could not think that it was impossible that there should come a time when at Hanley, around the technical museum they were about to establish, there should be a University College with chairs for professors of chemistry and engineering.

[1] C. Kelsall, *Phantasm of an University*, London, 1814, p. 170.

[2] Kelsall's first appearance in the mythology of Keele is in the introduction to Sir George Barnes's *Annual Report 1956–7*, where the above quotation is printed without explanation or comment. By 1961 it was felt appropriate for the Petition for a Charter to begin boldly with this assertion: 'The desire of the inhabitants of Staffordshire [!] for a University was first noted in 1814 when a proposal for the establishment of a new university near the River Trent was made.'

[3] *Staffordshire Sentinel*, 13 February 1890.

Although Kitchener had threatened adverse effects if nothing were done by the end of the century, it was not until the century was almost over that the idea of a university college was revived; and the emphasis was still on the need for teaching in subjects related to the needs of local industries. In 1899 T. Turner, Director of Technical Instruction to the Staffordshire County Council, suggested that further provision should be made for higher education in the district. This time positive action followed in so far as a meeting of those interested was held at the Mayor's Parlour, Hanley, and a Committee of Enquiry was formed to draw up a report. This Report[1] explained exactly what the promoters meant by the term 'University College':

> by the words 'University College', the Committee has not understood an independent College aiming at the standing of a University, but a local College working in connection with or affiliated to one of the great Universities, specially equipped to meet the needs of the district and supply teaching of the University standard in such subjects as it undertakes.

The main reason advanced for a university college was the economic well-being of the area; but the range of teaching suggested by the Report was not to be entirely restricted to those subjects which had an immediate bearing on local industry. The training of teachers was stated to be 'of special importance' and in view of later developments it is interesting to note that it was suggested that a Day Training Department for elementary teachers should be affiliated to the College. It was proposed also to offer teaching in literature and the classics 'such as would supply culture to the general public, and help to meet the needs of teachers in primary and secondary schools'. Subjects which would add to 'general culture' were suggested and the teaching of history would have a place as being of value to the working men who 'served on the various governing bodies in the Potteries'. Finally—and even in 1971 this point has an exasperating significance[2]—whilst a medical faculty was not specifically proposed, it was noted that the area had: 'a

[1] *A University College for North Staffordshire: Report of a Committee of Enquiry*, Hanley, 1899.

[2] See pp. 202–6.

fully equipped and well-staffed infirmary, which could, if necessary, offer exceptional advantages to medical students.' All in all, the Report had a more liberal outlook than its opening paragraphs might have led one to expect. The disclaimer of independent status for the college was, in the circumstances, prudent; and the alternative of 'affiliation' had more than an ephemeral attraction.

The Committee which drew up the Report was realistic enough, however, to recognise that the full scheme might be too expensive for the district. They estimated that a less ambitious scheme, providing only for instruction in 'higher Applied Science', would require an initial outlay of only £6,000 whereas the full scheme would cost £20,000. Even so, it is worth emphasising that, though it was recognised that 'it is not probable that all the subjects in which higher education is desirable could be undertaken from the start', the Report stressed that the fuller scheme was 'most strongly to be recommended;' and the hope was expressed that it might be possible to raise sufficient funds for it if some individual were to pave the way by a donation of, say, £10,000.

How then came it about that the institution which, fifteen years later, could trace its origins to the 1899 Report was not a university college but a school of science and technology? It is a story of waning ambitions and of the triumph of practicable possibilities over idealism. The immediate consequence of the Report was that a Provisional Committee was set up to consider 'what steps could be taken to carry out the recommendations'. This committee soon enlarged itself to become the Council for the Extension of Higher Education in North Staffordshire, a body which aimed, first, to provide a local organization for the extension lectures of the University of Oxford and secondly, as the ultimate goal, to bring about the foundation in the area of a College which would be the coping stone of the educational structure. It was hoped to achieve this second aim by means of the first and so follow the example of Reading where a College had been developed from a university extension centre. The setting-up of the Council for the Extension of Higher Education was thus a significant moment in the development of the idea of a university institution in the Potteries; and it was the adult education movement which was to keep alive the university idea when the demand for technical instruction, which had initially given birth to it, was satisfied by the foundation of a School of Science and Technology.

At first the Council for the Extension of Higher Education showed commendable energy. In July 1900 it appointed as its organising secretary A. W. Brown, whose work in connexion with extension lectures has already been mentioned.[1] The Chairman of the Council, A. S. Bolton, privately purchased a suitable site in Victoria Road, Stoke-upon-Trent, for the projected college and offered it to the Council; but his death at the end of 1901 halted the scheme. It also turned out that A. W. Brown himself was cautious; for in his Report to the Oxford Delegacy in 1902 he expressed the view that

> a complete University College is neither necessary nor desirable in this district at present, though an advanced scientific college is very badly needed. The district is a poor one and would be quite unable to build and support a full college.

Brown therefore proposed a less ambitious 'composite institute'. This still provided for instruction in subjects other than those of immediate use to local industry; for, in addition to a mining department and a school of pottery, there was to be a joint pupil-teacher centre and a university extension department. Yet the idea of a University College was not forgotten, since Brown saw his institute as being 'the element out of which a full University could grow'. But he recognised that there were still difficulties in the way of this more limited scheme: 'There are seven very jealous municipalities to deal with. The people of the district are conspicuously lacking in any real interest in education. Progress is bound to be slow.'

Though nothing came of Brown's scheme in 1902, the Council for the Extension of Higher Education carried the matter further early in 1905 when they submitted to the County Council a detailed scheme for a College on the lines laid down in Brown's plan. It was about this time too that the Duke of Sutherland offered his house at Trentham for use as a college.[2] The County Council's sub-committee on North

[1] See p. 20.

[2] Though the River Trent flowed through the grounds, Trentham was hardly the 'healthy and cheerful spot' on the banks of the 'silver Trent' which

Staffordshire supported the view that a college was 'very necessary to meet the educational needs of the district, especially the need for the training of teachers and pupil-teachers': but all that emerged (in December 1906) was a scheme for a Mining and Pottery Institute to be built on the site which had been bought by A. S. Bolton. Even this came to nothing, since the stipulation that half the total cost of the scheme, £6,500, should be raised locally could not be met; and the Council for the Extension of Higher Education itself went out of existence in 1906. The death knell of the university idea seemed to have been sounded when in 1908 the Staffordshire Director of Education, (Sir) Graham Balfour, reported to his Committee that there was no appreciable demand for an institution of 'higher general education' in the district: 'So far, therefore, as the establishment of any University College in North Staffordshire is concerned, the movement is at any rate indefinitely suspended.'

The story draws towards its end in 1910, when the federation of the Potteries towns seemed to have removed one of the obstacles to local co-operation. Francis Bolton, the son of A. S. Bolton, offered his father's site to the newly-formed Stoke-on-Trent Education Committee on condition that within two years there was built a Pottery and Mining Institute which was also to offer advanced instruction in physics and chemistry. The result was the building of the Central School of Science and Technology which was opened on 20 April 1914.[1] The bulk of the cost of £30,000 was borne by Stoke-on-Trent and Staffordshire. In effect what had happened was that that part of public opinion which wanted provision for technical education was now satisfied and the local Councils, having largely financed one scheme of further education, must have been less able and less willing to contemplate another.

But the idea of some sort of a University College persisted, particularly in the ranks of the adult education movement; and proposals relating the need for a College to the expansion

Charles Kelsall had envisaged in 1814. The problem of sewage in the river was forcing the Duke of Sutherland to look for a way of disposing of his house!

[1] In 1926 the title was changed to the College of Technology. It is now a constituent part of the North Staffordshire Polytechnic.

in adult education did not take long to re-emerge. When reporting in 1911 to Oxford about the foundation of the Miners' Higher Education Movement, E. S. Cartwright, the Longton class secretary, wrote: 'That the movement may prove to be the germ of a Working Men's College for the teaching of humane subjects (such a college to be connected with the old university of Oxford) is an ideal some of us have in view.'[1] The proposed College was to grow out of the adult education movement and was to reflect its character by teaching non-vocational subjects and by maintaining the link with Oxford. Cartwright was optimistic about the chances of such a college. In May 1911 he wrote from Oxford to Harry Jenkins, secretary of the Longton tutorial class, that the Oxford Tutorial Classes Committee were interested in North Staffordshire, 'and there is no reason why before you die you shouldn't be Chairman of the Governing Body of the University College of Stoke-on-Trent'. Nor was Cartwright alone in promoting the idea of a College. In May 1911 Albert Mansbridge was writing to him concerning the practical problems of finding money and a location for a College: an appeal must be launched. Two years later, in his book *University Tutorial Classes,* Mansbridge developed his ideas. He mentioned the link with Oxford and particularly the fact that many students went to summer schools there. This was[2]

> a connection fraught with many possibilities because it is certain that, sooner or later, the increase in the number of classes will necessitate the construction of some definite centre which may be a great Staffordshire College working in affiliation with the University of Oxford.

Again the College was seen as growing out of the adult education movement; again it was seen as being influenced by that movement's links with Oxford; again affiliation was assumed to be the natural relationship.

All this had been speculation. But a definite and public proposal for a University College was made after World War I. A letter from the secretary of the Longton tutorial class

[1] Quoted in H. P. Smith, 'E. S. Cartwright', *Rewley House Papers,* III, i, 1949–50, p. 20.
[2] *University Tutorial Classes,* p. 91.

and six others appeared in the *Staffordshire Evening Sentinel*[1] suggesting that a University College would be a suitable war memorial. It could be created by expanding the Central School of Science and Technology. It would have both a science and an arts side. The need for the former had been demonstrated by the work of the School of Science and Technology, but only too evident were the needs of those who, 'for professional or other reasons require a university education and either have to forgo it or seek it outside the district.' The peculiar needs of Stoke-on-Trent, 'one of the twelve largest towns in the Kingdom', as the centre of the pottery industry are prominently mentioned: a University College would help the city's industrial and commercial progress as well as add to its dignity and status. But: 'Equally important with the healthy progress of economic activities is the constant development of an enlightened and instructed citizenship, in the face of the growing complexities of modern life.' The idea was welcomed by a few *Sentinel* readers; but no editorial support, which could have injected life into the scheme, was forthcoming. In spite of the 1910 federation, local jealousies were still a great obstacle. At a meeting held at Longton to discuss what form a war memorial should take, the federation was described by one speaker as a 'hideous mistake' and it was said that 'Longton was determined to have its own effort'.[2] It is not surprising therefore that each of the Potteries towns built its own separate war memorial.[3]

It was now almost thirty years since F. E. Kitchener in 1890 had broached the concept of a University College and apart from the Technical College there was in practical terms little to show. Another quarter of a century was to pass before

[1] 30 January 1919. This influential newspaper will be referred to subsequently under the brief title of *Sentinel*.

[2] *Sentinel*, 7 February 1919.

[3] In Leicester a very similar suggestion was brought to a highly successful conclusion. In November 1917, long before the end of the 1914–18 war was in sight, the *Leicester Daily Post* urged that something more than 'artistic' memorials was required and advocated a university college as a highly desirable scheme; a year later, on the day after the armistice was concluded, the first donations for a college as a war memorial were announced; soon afterwards a generous benefactor provided a site; and by 1921 University College, Leicester, was fully in being. The full story can be found in Jack Simmons, *New University* (1958), pp. 61–81. Information about what was happening in Leicester may have prompted the Longton proposals of January 1919.

circumstances arose which made it feasible to launch a scheme which proved to be acceptable. But though little was done overtly between 1920 and 1945, the idea of a University College was far from being forgotten. From time to time there were public pronouncements which had more than a passing importance. The first of these was a speech made in Stoke by A. D. Lindsay in November 1925 when the Joint Advisory Committee was inaugurated.[1] He said [2] that the adult education movement

> had got to such a size that they ought to dream dreams and see visions about it. He wanted to see the movement become what it was already almost, a University. In the last 20 or 30 years there had been, he thought, eight universities started in England, but they had all been of one kind. Why should they not in North Staffordshire say they were going to start something new—a real people's university?

Lindsay went on to outline the work which this University would carry out:

> It would be a case of their general teaching in the tutorial classes, the teaching of the WEA, and their adult education generally swallowing up the technical and science education of the new universities. Theirs would primarily thus be a people's university. The University would have to be such that a man would be able to go in and at once get something. There would be more elementary classes, and then they would go on to the more systematic and higher work of the tutorial classes.

No university was a real university unless it undertook research, so this one would have 'special research students'. Lindsay continued:

> They could begin by calling it a University College, but it would be the core of that adult education which they could trace from that Longton class in 1908. He told them from his University that they were wanted to do that, and the University would give them all the help they could in order to achieve their aspirations.

[1] See p. 25.
[2] *Sentinel*, 16 November 1925.

Lacking in precision though these remarks may be, it is evident that in Lindsay's mind the proposed University College was at this time not only closely linked with the adult education movement but was to be the 'core' of that movement—an idea which recurred again in 1946 when it was proposed that the University College should be 'a centre and the focus' of adult education, a 'real people's university'. It is typical of Lindsay's enthusiasm that he should, even as a rhetorical flourish, seem to commit his own University so far.

On two occasions at least, influential local dignitaries lent their public support to the idea. In 1934 at the Venison Feast held in his year as honorific Mayor of the Ancient Corporation[1] of Hanley (1934–5) E. N. Scott, who was editor of the *Sentinel* from 1926 to 1947, made a speech in which he called for a large-scale and comprehensive planning of Stoke-on-Trent and included a College within his scope, but one related to local needs: 'We are not too optimistic . . . in visualising some years ahead a University of North Staffordshire, a University having special application to our ceramic and mining industries.'[2] More significant in its timing was the plea for a College made by Alderman W. H. Kemp on the occasion of his installation as Lord Mayor of Stoke-on-Trent in November 1944. Surveying the list of 'post-war tasks', as a prominent member of the Education Committee he put education high in his priorities:[3]

> But . . . we cannot give our children what London, Manchester, Liverpool, Birmingham, Nottingham and Leicester can give them, because we are a city without a university. Leicester and Nottingham are about the size of Stoke-on-Trent. How long are we going to lag behind? . . . At the end of the last war memorials were erected all over the country, including Stoke-on-Trent. Would not the finest expression of our gratitude to those who have served us be the firm resolve to found a new university—not in

[1] Not the Borough of Hanley, which was created in 1857 and ceased to exist on federation in 1910. J. S. Crapper, *The Ancient Corporation of Hanley*, revised ed., 1901, says that Hanley, not having a royal charter, 'made its own charter of corporation' and held an inaugural feast in September 1783. The Ancient Corporation continued to exist as a social fellowship without any local government functions.

[2] *Pottery and Glass*, April 1952: obituary notice.

[3] *Sentinel*, 9 November 1944.

> the dim and distant future, but now, when the need is greatest.

The *Sentinel*,[1] now more positive in its approach than it had been in 1919 to a similar proposal, welcomed this 'constructive, inspiring and enterprising proposition'.

> There is almost ready found a medical teaching school at the Royal Infirmary, with fine equipment and good buildings and medical, surgical and specialist staffs of particularly high and outstanding attainment. . . . Again, we have a Mining School and a Pottery School, which are of eminence in national estimation. The Pottery School, in many respects is unique because of the location here of the great traditional English pottery industry.

The newspaper returned to the topic two weeks later very much along the same lines of thought, stressing ceramics, mining and a medical school, but adding:[2]

> Our own superior educational establishment, which could develop into a university college (hitched on to Birmingham and Manchester to begin with) and, given great endeavour and enterprise, into a university, must have a special purpose or purposes and have individuality and unique character.

The reference to Birmingham and Manchester suggests that affiliation was still in mind—but not with Oxford.

Alderman Kemp himself was in office during the closing months of the war, was Deputy Lord Mayor during the next municipal year, 1945–6, was appointed as a member of the 1946 Exploratory Committee, and served on deputations which visited the UGC. His public commitment to the idea of a University was an important source of strength in the negotiations which ensued.[3]

Meanwhile, during the years between the two World Wars,

1 10 November 1944.
2 28 November 1944.
3 Alderman Kemp was the leader of the Independent group in the City Council. In November 1945 the Labour party gained control of the Council under the leadership of Alderman the Reverend T. Horwood, who assumed the chairmanship of all the major policy committees and consequently became the key figure on the City side in the negotiations for the establishment of a College.

the work of the adult education movement went steadily ahead, keeping alive the broader concepts of education. From 1921, when it was formed, the North Staffordshire District of the WEA took over the work of organisation which had previously been done voluntarily, and notably by members of the Longton class. This reorganisation in turn enabled further expansion both in the number of tutorial and non-tutorial classes; and further students were reached through organisations which had affiliated themselves to the WEA. A significant part of this expansion was in the number of students who attended summer schools at Oxford and elsewhere. In 1921 fifteen students from the Potteries attended the Oxford summer school; in 1928 fifty-two students from the WEA District attended summer schools at Oxford, Cambridge, Bangor and Arley Castle. In 1931 twenty-seven students attended the first week of the first Continental summer school and fifteen students the second week; and in the same year sixty-six students attended summer schools at Oxford, Cambridge, Bangor and Saltburn. The popularity of these courses over the years indicates that North Staffordshire students felt that the universities had something to offer them; and a climate of public opinion was slowly being created in favour of a university institution nearer home.

It is not surprising, therefore, that when, after World War II, the demand for a University College was revived, the impetus came from people who had been involved in the adult education movement; and it was this movement which had brought together organisations and people whose co-operation was to be of great importance in the subsequent negotiations for a University College.

First there was the University of Oxford, which had been involved in adult education in North Staffordshire virtually from the start. It had provided the extension lecturers, who had operated in the area continuously from 1899, and the tutorial class tutors. Its contribution had also included the provision of financial grants and of summer school places. Local recognition of its contribution was clearly to be seen in those suggestions for a University College which assumed that the proposed College should be affiliated to Oxford. Even after the foundation, in July 1921, of the North Staffordshire

District of the WEA, the link with Oxford was still regarded as vital; and it was this feeling which had led to the setting up in 1925 of the North Staffordshire Joint Advisory Committee. The co-operation of Oxford and the WEA on this Joint Advisory Committee proved to be very fruitful; for the Committee surveyed the whole sphere of work in the WEA District and shaped the planning of class programmes. The WEA too was strengthened thereby in its negotiations with other bodies. For example in October 1926, Lindsay, the Committee's chairman, successfully requested the Stoke Education Authority to allow the use of the Central School of Science and Technology for weekend courses. So, for more than twenty years before the 1946 University Exploratory Committee was set up, a number of bodies whose representatives were to play an important part on that Committee, had been involved in close and valuable co-operation. Also, the Chairman of the Joint Advisory Committee from its foundation was A. D. Lindsay, Master of Balliol. As we have seen, he had made known his ideas for a University College at the time of the Committee's first meeting; and, through the Joint Advisory Committee he was henceforth to be continuously associated with the area.

Also of long standing was the co-operation of Local Authorities with both the local organisers of adult education and Oxford University. This tripartite co-operation had been seen as early as 1902 when the Longton Education Authority had financed the extension courses provided by Oxford. In 1919 Staffordshire County Council agreed to contribute £350 and Stoke-on-Trent £250 per year to finance the costs of a resident tutor; and these same two authorities, together with that of Burton-on-Trent, had co-operated closely with the District Secretary of the WEA, George Wigg,[1] in the planning of adult education for wartime at the start of World War II. This long tradition of co-operation was formalised when the Joint Advisory Committee of Oxford and the WEA was joined in 1944 by the Local Education Authorities of Stoke, Staffordshire and Burton to form the North Staffordshire Committee for Adult Education.

Like the Joint Advisory Committee, the North Staffordshire Committee for Adult Education undertook much valuable

[1] Later, Lord Wigg. He joined the armed forces in 1940 but continued his help and was officially secretary of the WEA District until 1946.

work. It helped to bring about the opening in February 1945 of the Wedgwood Memorial College at Barlaston[1] which made possible an increase in the provision of weekend and summer courses; and it helped to supervise the opening in 1947 of Cartwright House, the new administrative centre for the WEA District. But more important, as it proved, for the future of the University College proposal was the fact that the Committee now included the three Directors of Education for Staffordshire (F. A. Hughes, succeeded in 1947 by J. H. P. Oxspring), Stoke-on-Trent (J. F. Carr) and Burton-on-Trent (A. H. Blake), who by their professional knowledge and wise sympathy were to be of importance later when the University Exploratory Committee was set up. Associated, too, was Miss Gladys Malbon who in 1939 had come to the Potteries as a full-time tutor on the staff of the Oxford Tutorial Classes Committee and helped also with the work of the WEA District. Subsequently she represented the WEA on the Exploratory Committee where her energy and devotion to the proposals for a College were unceasingly and most effectively deployed. She prodded laggards into action, arranged meetings and conferences and generally co-ordinated the activities of the Exploratory Committee with the help of Harry Taylor, Town Clerk of Stoke-on-Trent. Even after she left in 1947 for a post in Exeter she continued to be a very active member of the Exploratory Committee.[2] But there was one person above all others who was the natural and acknowledged leader: A. D. Lindsay, Master of Balliol; and it is to him that the concluding paragraphs of this chapter are most appropriately devoted.

A. D. LINDSAY[3]

Alexander Dunlop Lindsay belongs to a seemingly endless succession of Scots of outstanding ability and character who have deployed their talents to the enrichment of English academic and administrative life. Born in Glasgow in 1879, he was the son of T. M. Lindsay, D.D., Principal of the United Free Church College whose *History of the Reformation* had set

[1] This was the first residential college to be set up under the 1944 Education Act.

[2] In 1966 she became an Honorary M.A. of Keele.

[3] See Drusilla Scott, *A. D. Lindsay: a Biography* (1971). Lady Scott is the daughter of Lindsay.

the seal on his scholarly reputation. From Glasgow Academy, the young Lindsay went first to the University of Glasgow where he was one of the first candidates in the newly-founded special honours schools. Surprisingly he achieved only a second class degree in classics but was elected to an open scholarship at University College, Oxford, where, in addition to being President of the Union in 1902, he crowned his work with a first class both in Classical Moderations and in Greats. In 1904 he accepted a post in Manchester as Assistant Lecturer to the distinguished and stimulating Professor of Philosophy, Samuel Alexander. Balliol in those days was not prone to choose 'outsiders' for its Fellowships; and it was therefore a notable tribute to Lindsay's quality and growing reputation that he was elected to a Fellowship there in 1906 and to the Jowett Lectureship in Philosophy in 1910. During the 1914–18 war he served overseas with the Labour Directorate, was mentioned in despatches, rose to the rank of lieutenant-colonel and received the CBE. His former University of Glasgow invited him in 1922 to the Chair of Moral Philosophy but two years later, on the death of A. L. Smith, Balliol recalled him to succeed to the office of Master and for a quarter of a century he not only presided over his College but became an increasingly dominant figure in Oxford, particularly in the years 1935 to 1938 when he was Vice-Chancellor. In 1945 he was elevated to the peerage and took his seat in the House of Lords as the First Baron Lindsay of Birker of Low Ground in the County of Cumberland. Though he played a critical part in the discussions which led to the founding of the College in North Staffordshire, it was neither his wish nor his expectation that he would become its first Principal; yet when his acceptance of the post was virtually the only way of saving the scheme from foundering, despite ill-health, he courageously agreed and in 1949 left his beloved Balliol and Oxford for the harsher climate of the North Midlands and all the exasperations and problems of setting a new institution on its feet. The task took its toll of him and he died on 18 March 1952.

The sheer amount of work that Lindsay achieved as teacher, preacher, writer, administrator, committee man and public figure is impressive by any standard. It is as a teacher and educator above all else that he quite clearly would have wished to be remembered; even as Master of Balliol he continued to take his share of college tuition in addition to the lectures he delivered on Plato, Kant and topics of moral and social philosophy; and he was a frequent preacher in the college chapel and elsewhere. He found time also to write; and amongst the books which he thought worth mention in works of reference we may single out *Karl Marx's 'Capital'* (1925), *The Nature of Religious Truth* (a volume of sermons, 1927), *The Essentials of Democracy* (1929), *Christianity and Economics* (1933), *Kant* (1934), *The Moral Teaching of Jesus* (1937), *The Two Moralities* (1940), and *The Modern Democratic State* (1943), which last was his major published contribution to political philosophy. He also generously penned many introductions to the works of other writers. As Master of his college during a long reign he was jealous for its reputation in scholarship and learning in a period when social changes, as he was glad to see, were perceptibly altering the composition of an expanding student body. As Vice-Chancellor of the University, his conduct of affairs was such as to win the respectful admiration not only of all his colleagues but of the professional administrators too. He had played a prominent part in the planning of the new School of Philosophy, Politics and Economics (PPE, or Modern Greats) when it was being instituted in the early 1920s; and—what is significant in view of later events at Keele—he advocated a combination of philosophy with the principles of natural science. Similarly, as Vice-Chancellor, he immersed himself in the plans for the new Nuffield College. He was also one of the most active supporters of the movement to extend women's education in Oxford. Outside Oxford—too frequently, some said—he was in great demand up and down the country for addresses to every kind of organisation concerned with adult education and with such requests he readily complied; he constantly gave his advice on educational matters to the inner councils of the Labour Party and the Trades Unions Congress; he interested himself in the welfare of the unemployed notably in South Wales; as an Independent Progressive candidate in October 1938 he unsuccessfully contested a Parliamentary election for the Oxford City seat against Mr Quintin Hogg when the question at issue was the 'Munich settlement'; he visited India as a member of a mixed East–West Commission to review Indian Christian Colleges; he made several educational trips to the USA of which the most important was in 1943; he was the only British representative on the German Commission on University Reform in Germany which reported in 1949; and after his elevation to the peerage he often contributed to debates in the House of Lords. Such a record speaks for itself.

Yet what sort of man was this whose energies were exercised in so wide a field? The answer cannot be simple or complete. Few prominent men of his generation were more liable to be misunderstood by unsympathetic associates, or more unpredictable to those who took no trouble to sense the driving force. It is symptomatic of the controversial nature of Lindsay's life and work that W. B. Gallie's book about him and Keele[1] was written to rebut a comment that Lindsay 'just missed being a great man'. So let us first very briefly summarise some of the criticisms levelled against him. He dissipated his efforts (the critics say) and did nothing as well as he could have done with more concentration; he lacked depth as a philosopher and often appeared to be 'a messy thinker'; he was a bit of a humbug, if not a charlatan; he often lost his moral touch and compromised on issues when he should have stood firm; he was an opportunist and a power-seeker who could brush aside opposition too brusquely; he acted as if he were 'an instrument of the Lord' when he wanted his own way; he was too credulous in support of those who claimed to be advancing causes of which he approved; he shifted his ground disconcertingly and could not be relied on even as an ally; and yet, it was alleged, he had a strong conspiratorial streak in his nature.

Grouped thus together, these charges make up an incredible picture which must be hopelessly out of perspective. They cannot, however, be explained on the simple ground that Balliol though admired was not always loved or that a Master who proclaimed himself an adherent of socialist doctrine was an affront to the prevailing conservatism of Oxford. The plain truth is that Lindsay had severe critics whose sincerity could not be doubted and relentless enemies whose ill-will could not be disguised; but he was not the man to concern himself overmuch with refuting his critics or placating his enemies. Any sane assessment of him must take account of three things which moulded his character and influenced his actions: he had a Presbyterian upbringing; he had from early years a strong social conscience; and by temperament as well as by training

[1] W. B. Gallie, *A New University: A. D. Lindsay and the Keele Experiment.*

he was a philosopher. What he owed to his father and to his mother remained with him throughout his life not as identifiable doctrinal tenets but rather as a sense of an over-riding power in the universe working through men for their good. What he saw as a young man of the poverty and squalor of Glasgow made a lasting impression on him and directed his thoughts and emotions towards social reform and the creation through education of what he called 'social democracy'. It is an important facet of his mind that as a philosopher his interest was focused almost exclusively on ethics rather than logic or metaphysics, that he preferred Plato to Aristotle and Kant to Hegel, and that he had little patience in his later years with the Cambridge school or with logical positivists. His mind was vigorous and capacious; his reading was extensive in many fields which engaged his interest; and his contacts with people of all classes of society from Cabinet ministers to working men were unusually wide and influential. 'Burly, florid, and farmer-like' in his later years, he could not be unnoticed in any assembly; and when he was moved his utterances had an impressive fervour. Yet he was not always easy to understand and the train of his thought not always easy to follow: that is how he was; and the unsympathetic and the impatient too readily wrote him off and ignored the vision and the message. Lindsay's intellect was supple and flexible; he disliked rigid formulas, clichés and uncompromising slogans. The truths about education and social reform to which he held were many-sided and according to what he judged the circumstances demanded he placed the emphasis now here, now there. The totality, not the bits and pieces, was the real Lindsay, firm and basically consistent despite apparent falterings, and motivated by the deep conviction that, however his words or his actions might appear to others, all he did and said should be directed and was in fact being directed to the enrichment of the 'new democracy' in which he passionately believed.

In the following chapters we shall see something of Lindsay at close quarters in a particular context. Meanwhile, to fill in some details of the picture, we may with advantage cite a few responsible testimonies to his qualities.

> The eagerness of his vision and his longing that theory should result in action made him something of a prophet;

but he had the austerity, not the severity of a prophet, and the simplicity of his character, free from any assumption or affectation, endeared him even to those who differed most from him.[1]

Lord Lindsay would not best be described as a great scholar, though no man is elected Master of Balliol unless he is highly regarded by scholars. But he was a great administrator of scholarship, a great educator. He brought into the academic world a profound sense of social conscience; he was perhaps the most representative voice in the world of the thoughtful, practical idealism of the moderate left.[2]

Not infrequently the initial impression was of the complete academic, remote and somewhat cold. His manner as a lecturer or speaker added to rather than dispelled this impression. Whereas he was lucid and precise as a writer, in speech he tended to be hesitant as if he were doing his thinking aloud—rejecting dogmatic statement, interpolating conditions, groping for the right expression with many an enclitic 'as it were'. For all that, he was a gifted teacher. His coldness, too, was more apparent than real and those who knew him well were surprised that he should create such an impression.[3]

The outline of all he did must give a false impression of what he was. He was informal and unconventional; he did not like ceremony and he could be unceremonious. Being a strong man, he sometimes did not trouble to do what other people expected of him; but he was accessible, unassuming and ready with help for anyone who asked it. Self-confident, and sometimes over-confident, in relations with strangers he never overcame a kind of shyness; but the best of the good things that he did were done to and for the people that he knew.[4]

Politically Lord Lindsay was to the left, and this, although it roused opponents, was nationally to the good. He foresaw and welcomed increased control by the state, but he was for maintaining centres of independence under the

1 *The Times*, 19 March 1952.
2 *Manchester Guardian*, 19 March 1952.
3 *Birmingham Post*, 19 March 1952.
4 *Oxford Magazine*, 8 May 1952 (signed 'G.N.C.', presumably Sir George Clark, Provost of Oriel).

state—as, for instance, the universities and, inside them, the colleges. He shared his colleagues' feeling for democratizing education, but he was equally influential in representing to them the necessity of preserving quality. He was, in fact, an ideal man to have about when the tide of equalitarianism in education was flowing strongly.[1]

[1] *Times Educational Supplement*, 21 March 1952.

Three

The Founding of a College

NATIONAL PLANNING

It was a matter of national prudence that, even when the issue of World War II was still in doubt, attention should have been directed to the reconstruction of civilian life when peace returned. Housing, health, education, the social services and industry all came under scrutiny and in some fields planning was well advanced before the end of the war. Thus, within the sphere of education a new Education Act received the Royal Assent in 1944 and radically transformed the framework of primary and secondary education; a committee appointed in 1942 under the chairmanship of Sir Arnold (later Lord) McNair to consider the training of teachers and youth-leaders completed its task in 1944; and in 1944 also Lord Eustace Percy and his committee began their examination of the needs of higher technological education on which they reported in 1945.

During these same difficult years the universities themselves and the UGC were applying their minds to the problems of the future.[1] Two related matters were involved: finance and the expansion of student numbers. As early as June 1943, Sir Franklin Sibley, Vice-Chancellor of Reading University, wrote to Sir Walter Moberly, chairman of the UGC, on behalf of the Committee of Vice-Chancellors and Principals (the 'VCs' Committee') asking for a 'review of the financial implications of the expansion which national policy would require the universities to undertake'. In response to this request the UGC invited universities to indicate their proposals for development during the first post-war decade with estimates of the cost. The outcome was that in January 1945 the UGC recommended and the Treasury approved an increase from £2,149,000 to £4,149,000 in the annual grant for general recurrent purposes for each of

[1] See *University Development: 1935–1947* (Report of the UGC published 1948), *passim*.

the first two post-war years; and an assurance was given that there would be further substantial increases later on. It was during the early part of 1945 also that the University Colleges of Leicester (founded in 1921) and Hull (founded in 1928) were for the first time put on the list of institutions eligible to receive grants from Treasury sources. The determination of the needs for capital expenditure had to wait a little longer. In January 1947 the UGC assessed these needs as £40m. over the years 1947 to 1952, a figure which the Chancellor of the Exchequer accepted in principle, though in view of the shortage of materials and restrictions on works of new construction he included only half that amount in the estimates he laid before Parliament.[1]

The size and consequently the number of universities and colleges also came under discussion.[2]

> Two independent trains of thought pointed directly to a policy of expansion. In the first place the hard experience of war had demonstrated plainly in many fields the essential value to the community of university trained men and women. It was clear that the need for the services of such people would not become less with the end of the war. The other part of the case for university expansion was based upon the general sense that the equality of sacrifice which the nation demanded in times of tension and danger ought to be matched by a much greater measure of social and educational equality than had existed before the war.

In their 1943 proposals for development the universities had not neglected the question of size and the indications they gave pointed to a student population of 70,000 (as compared with the 50,000 of 1938–9) within the first post-war decade. Such was the estimate current when in December 1945 a Committee on Scientific Manpower was set up by the Lord President of the Council under the chairmanship of Sir Alan Barlow of the Treasury. Their Report[3] appeared in May 1946 and amongst other things they recommended that the immediate aim should be to double the existing output of graduates in science and technology at the earliest possible moment and that there

[1] Experience proved that it was not possible to achieve even the £20m. of building work during the period.

[2] UGC: *University Development: 1935–1947*, p. 26.

[3] *Scientific Manpower*, May 1946 (Cmd. 6824).

should also be a substantial increase in the number of students in the humanities. Thereupon the UGC asked universities for revised estimates of the numbers they could cope with by the end of ten years; and their revised total figure of 88,000 was within striking distance of the 90,000 the UGC now had in mind.[1] Knowing only of earlier lower estimates, however, the Barlow committee had also proposed that 'early consideration should be given to the foundation of at least one new University'; they 'believed that such a proposal would receive warm support from informed opinion and the general body of the public'.

This proposal, however, was far from being acceptable to 'informed opinion'. A few weeks after the publication of the Barlow Report a pronouncement was made by the VCs' Committee. In their *Note on University Policy and Finance in the Decennium 1947–56* (6 July 1946), prepared for presentation to the UGC, the Vice-Chancellors very firmly declared themselves against a new institution in the immediate or even the near future:

> If there were enough money, constructional material and equipment, and constructional man-power to spare for making a new University, in the national interest these had much better be spent in expanding the existing institutions properly. After the decade, if by then production from the present foundations proves to have reached what is hoped, and if there are still man-power, materials and money, the founding of a new University outside some suitable city or town would become reasonable, and would then receive the warm support from informed opinion which, the Vice-Chancellors venture to say, would not support it any earlier.

These were strong words;[2] and they came from a body to whose opinions the UGC was accustomed to attach great weight. When

[1] The desired doubling of the number of students in science and technology was almost completed in *two* years; and the total number of full-time students was already 85,241 by the autumn of 1949.

[2] The same argument against a new university was advanced in December 1946 in a pamphlet, *Universities and the Increase of Scientific Manpower* issued by the Parliamentary and Scientific Committee, an unofficial group of members of both Houses of Parliament and representatives of certain scientific and technical institutions whose President was Sir John Anderson (later Lord Waverley). *N.B.* This Committee also recommended the 'up-grading' of certain technical colleges, including (by name) the one at Stoke.

the UGC had before them the later estimates from the universities of attainable numbers, they too came to the conclusion that the kind of situation contemplated by the Barlow Committee did not arise:[1]

> In these circumstances the establishment of new institutions could no longer be regarded as a necessary means to the policy of expansion, and we have acted on the opinion that, in present circumstances, with shortages of qualified staff and with restrictions on building, greater progress could be made by concentrating the limited men and materials upon the development of existing institutions than by scattering them over a wider field. . . . We have listened with sympathy to deputations from several localities which aspire to become centres of university life and we hope that, in the easier times which the future may bring, some at least of these aspirations may be realised. In the meantime we have made one exception. . . .

That exception was the University College of North Staffordshire at Keele.[2]

APPROACH TO THE UGC

How came it about, then, that the hopes of North Staffordshire should at this particular time have found fulfilment while those of places like Brighton, Norwich and York were dashed? There would seem to be three reasons. First, tentative and restricted though the original proposals from Stoke undoubtedly were, they gave promise of a venture which was both unusual and worthy of support; secondly, as we have seen, the activities of the North Staffordshire Committee for Adult Education[3] had brought together more closely than ever before the leaders of the adult education movement in the Potteries, the Local Authorities and representatives of the Oxford Delegacy, and

[1] *University Development: 1935–1947* (UGC) pp. 41–2. Though this statement on policy was not issued until 1948, the underlying principle must obviously have influenced the thinking of the UGC from the summer of 1946.

[2] At first the project was called simply 'The Stoke proposal(s)'; the more formal designation came into use as the scheme progressed. From 1950 'Keele' was a convenient brief appellation and was officially adopted in the Charter of the University (1962).

[3] See pp. 37–8.

so there was ready to hand an influential group of people who understood each others' ideas and were poised for action; and thirdly, there was in the person of Lord Lindsay a man who was not content to take the chair at meetings and offer benign advice but who, when the need arose, energetically undertook the real hard work of giving shape to emergent ideas.

The sequence of events between the end of the war and the opening of the College in 1950 is easy to trace in broad outline, intricate though some of the details may be;[1] and the story is not without its moments of drama enacted against a background of tedious and faltering negotiations. There were two main strategic operations: the first was an approach to the UGC and the gaining of provisional approval; the other was the winning over of three universities which would act as academic sponsors. These two stages overlapped one another; but it will make things clearer for the reader if they are treated separately. Within this framework other important matters also began to claim attention: the drawing up of a provisional Charter, the acquisition of a site and the appointment of staff. And all the way through there were continuous discussions about the curriculum, a topic which is so vital to the whole history of the foundation and development of Keele that a separate chapter (4) must be reserved for it.

The prospective post-war increase in Treasury grants for universities was announced in Parliament in February 1945 and in the early summer R. H. Tawney, who was now a member of the UGC, E. S. Cartwright and Gladys Malbon were already talking amongst themselves about reviving the idea of a College in North Staffordshire. They at once enlisted the interest of Harry Taylor, the Town Clerk, and of J. F. Carr, the Director of Education for Stoke-on-Trent; and by the autumn they were assured of the enthusiastic support of Alderman the Reverend Thomas Horwood, leader of the City Council, and of

[1] For the period 1945 to 1950 the chief original sources used by R. A. Lowe (M.A. thesis, 1966) were the Keele and other local archives (including files of the *Sentinel*) together with private correspondence and papers at Rewley House, Oxford. Most of these sources have been re-examined and Mr J. R. B. Bosworth has collected additional evidence from the records of the UGC and the Universities of Oxford, Manchester and Birmingham. Mr P. Hibberd, research assistant to the senior tutor at Keele, placed at the author's disposal his own account and assessment of the material available to him; and the informed comments he has made on this and the two following chapters are gratefully acknowledged.

Dr (later Sir) Barnett Stross, M.P. for Hanley. The main initiative at this stage was clearly centred in Stoke; and in February 1946 Miss Malbon wrote to the UGC on behalf of the Stoke group asking for a date when a delegation could come to London to discuss the project. But it was evident that the influential help of Lord Lindsay would be invaluable if the approach to the UGC was to be fruitful. Lindsay, of course, was aware, particularly through Miss Malbon and E. S. Cartwright, of the hopes that were being entertained in Stoke; he readily promised his assistance and discussed the project in some detail with people from Stoke and with some in Oxford also.[1]

27 March 1946

A first meeting with the UGC was fixed for 27 March 1946. A fortnight earlier as a preliminary to the meeting Lindsay himself had written to Sir Walter Moberly, the Chairman of the UGC:[2]

> Would it be possible to consider whether we could make in the Potteries a University College on new lines, or at any rate not just a repetition of Southampton, Exeter, etc. It might be possible to get this University to take a special interest, help to conduct examinations and get rid of the London external degree. I should like to get hold of half-a-dozen people, *e.g.* Cole and Mannheim,[3] who have been thinking of the problem of Modern Universities, and get them to use their imaginations on this matter, before we go too far.

At the meeting itself a delegation from Stoke met Moberly, Tawney and H. A. de Montmorency (Secretary of the UGC) in London. The Stoke representatives consisted of the two local Members of Parliament (Ellis Smith, M.P. for Stoke and Dr Barnett Stross, M.P. for Hanley) with J. F. Carr and Miss

[1] This summary is based on Miss Malbon's diaries.

[2] Born 1881, Fellow of Lincoln Coll., Oxford, 1906–21, Professor of Philosophy, Birmingham, 1921–4; Principal Univ. Coll., Exeter, 1925–6, Vice-Chancellor, Manchester, 1926–34, Chairman of UGC 1935–49.

[3] G. D. H. Cole, the well-known Oxford economist and writer on politics; Karl Mannheim: Professor of Sociology, Frankfurt-am-Main 1930–3; lecturer in Sociology, LSE, 1933–46; Professor of Education, London Institute of Education, 1946–7.

Malbon; why Lindsay himself was not present is not known. A memorandum which Miss Malbon had sent in for discussion contained some significant proposals: to avoid 'exam-cramming' for London degrees there should be concern with other work besides that for external degrees and there should be 'specialisation in a few selected faculties'; there should be no attempt to rival 'national universities' and a special contribution could perhaps be made by the development of the study of ceramics and by those aspects of history, economics and sociological studies which had received attention in adult classes; the advantages derived from a residential university life should be recognised from the first; and the strong and vital connexion between the University of Oxford and North Staffordshire should be maintained. Moberly was sympathetic and 'thought it possible that the Committee [UGC] might be willing to give financial support to a new college from the outset if they were satisfied that it enjoyed a really strong measure of local support'.

Thus encouraged,[1] Carr and Miss Malbon turned their energies in the direction of the City Council whose approval and financial backing would be of prime importance. The dominant person on the Council was now Alderman the Reverend Thomas Horwood, Vicar of Etruria,[2] leader of the ruling Labour group and chairman of the finance committee; and he played so important a part in the founding of Keele that we must here recall something more of this remarkable figure who became Lindsay's staunch ally and was the first Chairman of the College Council. Born in 1875 in a small Buckinghamshire village, he left school at the age of eleven and after working as a farm labourer joined his father in the building trade. Realising that the Church was his vocation, he went to evening classes to make up for his lack of formal education and was tutored in Latin and Greek by an Aylesbury vicar. To raise money he built up a painting and decorating business and by the time he was twenty-seven he had sufficient funds to take him to Cambridge where he gained his B.A. in Theology. A London curacy led to his appointment to the Crown living in Etruria in 1914

[1] Despite the cautious words 'possible', 'might be', 'if', there was at any rate not a flat rebuff.

[2] An area near Hanley, so called from a model village provided by the Wedgwoods for their workmen who made china in the Italian style.

and thereafter the Potteries were his home. As a member of the Stoke-on-Trent City Council from 1929 onwards he was always in the thick of controversy, but managed to combine the duties of the pulpit and the enticements of the political platform without losing public esteem.[1] This is how he impressed two Keele professors:

> It would have needed a Rembrandt to do justice to his almost entirely bald, domed head, his yellow, parchment-like skin, the almost Oriental quiescence of his mouth in repose and the thoroughly Anglo-Saxon passion that gleamed from his liverish eyes and bright lips when he was roused. When the university college came into being . . . he was evidently past his best. . . . He now walked with painful hesitancy; his energy was fitful, his voice weak, his memory for numbers not all that it might have been . . . There was nothing pathetic or pitiable about the obvious signs of his physical decline, they only served to make more obvious the force of will that was keeping him alive. . . . He was still very much a power in the land. In the dark and dismal vestry of his church, where he was reputed to eat and sleep as well as work, he received an almost unending stream of visitors. . . . By now his main passion had become the university college.[2]

> 'The Vicar', as Lord Lindsay used to call him, was a born fighter. A small figure, impish, cherubic, and utterly determined—this is the image that will stay in the memory. One and the same thing made him both formidable and endearing—the fact that he knew what he fought for better than any other man. . . . His anger was reserved for vanity, and he was implacable in his aversion from that empty language in which refusal of understanding so readily cloaks itself. . . . The North Staffordshire University College was the work of many men, and Horwood was the first to remind listeners of what others had done to bring it about. But it is extremely doubtful whether what so many hoped for would have been realized in 1950 without the unflagging energies of 'The Vicar'. . . . No-one

[1] Manchester conferred on him an Honorary M.A. in 1953 and Keele an Honorary B.A. in 1954 at its first graduation ceremony.
[2] W. B. Gallie, *A New University*, p. 49.

understood the poor student, and what is rarer in universities, the student of limited intellectual abilities, better than he did. . . . On the first day the new college opened its doors, Horwood was invited to speak. He stood silent for a moment, conscious as he was of all that the occasion meant. Then, leaning forward, the familiar smile came with the words: 'It did not come from Heaven, you know. And now we've really got to work to keep it.' [1]

April/May 1946

After the meeting with Moberly at the end of March, little time was lost. On 17 April J. F. Carr, as Director of Education, presented a memorandum to the General Purposes Committee of the City Council and the resolutions then passed were confirmed by the Council itself on 2 May. The provision of a University College for North Staffordshire[2] was 'approved in principle' and a special committee was set up 'to investigate the whole matter'. The local nucleus of this committee which called itself the Exploratory Committee[3] met a few days later on 10 May, and co-opted additional members from the other Local Authorities, two from the WEA (Miss Malbon and Mr T. L. Hodgkin),[4] Miss F. A. Farmer, who had been a founder member of the Longton tutorial class, as 'a person with wide experience in education', and 'one representative from Oxford University'.[5] Who was to be the Oxford representative? Lindsay

1 J. J. Lawlor in the *Sentinel*, 19 December 1956. Horwood had died on 18 December in his eighty-second year.

2 Whether the college was to be 'for', 'in' or 'of' North Staffordshire was as yet a triviality.

3 Within a few months the name was changed to 'University College Committee'; but we shall find it convenient to use the earlier one.

4 Secretary to the Oxford Delegacy for Extra-mural Studies, 1945–52; formerly Staff Tutor in N. Staffordshire for the Oxford Tutorial Classes Committee (1939–45); Senior Research Fellow at Balliol since 1965.

5 Quite normally and properly the City Council made the proviso that members of the Council should always be in the majority. But the *Sentinel*, which on 11 April had already welcomed 'any practicable and well-founded plan', was enraged. The Council was Labour controlled; so, asked the *Sentinel*'s 'Observer', 'must it be assumed that the University College must be run by Socialists, for Socialists, and propagating chiefly Socialist education?' (20 April), and 'none but the Socialist-elect need apply . . . to the new Socialist-founded, Socialist-governed, and Socialist-minded University' (30 April). This was no passing flurry around the parish pump. The slander persisted to the extent that when the College opened bus conductors stopping at its gates called out 'Moscow' or 'Kremlin'.

wanted A. H. Smith, Warden of New College, to serve since he was not only interested in adult education but—an important point—was a member of the Hebdomadal Council at Oxford and so might enlist the interest of Oxford at the highest level; but when Smith declined nomination, Lindsay himself agreed to serve and at the second meeting of the Exploratory Committee (23 July) was inevitably appointed as its chairman.[1]

25 July 1946

A second delegation from Stoke, consisting of Lindsay, Dr Stross, Alderman Kemp,[2] Miss Malbon and J. F. Carr met Moberly and five of his UGC colleagues on 25 July. This conference discussed in considerable detail a factual memorandum on the existing educational provision in the Potteries from Mr Carr, a statement on academic courses and constitutional points prepared by 'a representative of Oxford University',[3] and a statement on policy, constitution and finance from Miss Malbon and Mr Carr. It was now envisaged that a Principal should be appointed in 1947 and that the College should open in 1948. The proposals were much more ship-shape than those of 27 March; and though the UGC members did not commit themselves to any clear expression of approval, at least a revised and comprehensive document was asked for by October. The questions still to be discussed were the scope of the syllabuses in science, technology (ceramics) and social studies, the running costs, and the matter of the London external degree, to no single one of which could a quick and easy answer be given.[4]

19 November 1946

The revised consolidated document was not ready, however, until 11 November 1946, but this time it achieved the dignity

1 Lindsay almost always chaired the main Committee and several of the later sub-committees; failing him, Horwood took over. At the third meeting of the Exploratory Committee (30 July, 1946) a second Oxford representative joined: Mr J. S. Fulton (now Lord Fulton), Jowett Fellow of Balliol and tutor in Politics.

2 See pp. 34–5.

3 This document is unsigned. See p. 99n.

4 Following this meeting with UGC members, Mr Carr arranged a Conference for *9 September 1946* with the Ministry of Education when the possibility of recognising the College for the training of teachers was discussed.

of print; it had a wide circulation, and in subsequent discussions it became a cardinal point of reference.[1] The deputation from Stoke was impressive, including not only Lindsay, Dr Stross and J. S. Fulton, but Alderman Kemp, Miss Malbon and J. F. Carr, F. A. Hughes the Director of Education for Staffordshire, Alderman W. Hutson of Burton-on-Trent, and the Town Clerk and the City Treasurer of Stoke-on-Trent.[2] Moberly had with him three members of the UGC and a representative of the Ministry of Education. Was the college going to be of a viable size, would the scope of the courses fit in with the requirements for the training of teachers, how would other university colleges be affected if special arrangements were made for Stoke, what form of 'apprenticeship' would be acceptable: such were the main topics surveyed. It was agreed that there was 'distinct promise' in the scheme; but, though under pressure from Lindsay, Moberly would go no further than to encourage Stoke to consult with possible sponsoring universities on the understanding that the UGC itself would not try to influence those universities and would reserve its general position.

3 December 1946

At long last the Stoke proposals came before the full UGC on 3 December. Some members of the UGC who had not been involved in the earlier discussions raised independently a number of the criticisms of the scheme which had been made previously; and one cannot but admire the skill with which some goodwill and many misgivings were subtly combined in the resolution which, with the support of Moberly and Tawney, was eventually agreed upon:

> that the Committee would consider sympathetically an application for financial assistance in respect of a new University College in North Staffordshire provided that the basis of studies in Science and Arts be adequately broadened. If the scheme is to include the conferment of degrees by the College, the Committee will wish to be satisfied that adequate arrangements have been made for sponsorship by a university or universities and that the

[1] For details of this document, see pp. 69–70, 101–3.

[2] As on 25 July, Horwood was not a member of the delegation.

proposal can be brought into line with university policy for the country as a whole.[1]

The Exploratory Committee was well satisfied for the present by this expression of the UGC's attitude and at their next meeting on 18 December 1946 they took several steps forward: Lindsay and Fulton were asked to work out details in relation to the first part of the UGC resolution; Oxford, Manchester and Birmingham were to be asked to sponsor the Stoke scheme; arrangements were to be made to discuss things further with Moberly; and Fulton was asked 'to consider the whole scheme' and 'to take whatever steps he considers desirable to draft the constitution of the University'.[2]

But 1947 was to prove to be a year of disappointments.

January–December 1947

During the first four months of 1947 there were two informal conferences between Moberly himself and a small local group from the Exploratory Committee consisting of Horwood (as leader), Alderman Hutson of Burton-on-Trent, Mr J. F. Carr, Miss Malbon and Mr Harry Taylor, the Town Clerk of Stoke-on-Trent. At the first of these meetings on *24 January 1947*, the question of appointing a Principal for the college was rather inconclusively aired, though it was generally felt that there

[1] The last eight words are clearly related to the 1946 revision of the UGC's terms of reference (announced in Parliament on 30 July 1946) which now included the duty 'to assist, in consultation with the universities and other bodies concerned, the preparation and execution of such plans for the development of the universities as may from time to time be required in order to ensure that they are fully adequate to the national needs'.

[2] The *Sentinel* was being far from helpful. On 30 November 1946, in an editorial 'University in a Hurry' they criticised the Memorandum of 11 November, deploring that no mention was made of a medical faculty and that little stress was laid on the training of teachers. 'It will be a School for Socialists.' On 9 December 1946, an editorial, 'Technical College Upgrading', declared: 'The North Staffordshire University Scheme has "gone with the wind" as inevitably must a proposition so impracticable, so useless to the needs of the area, so politically-minded, so regardless of the valuable institution which exists and which is capable of extension. . . . There is reasonable prospect of the Technical College being upgraded and accorded University status.' This last remark, of course, refers to a recommendation of the recently issued Report of the Parliamentary and Scientific Committee (see p. 47n). When news of the UGC's resolutions percolated, the *Sentinel* (12 December 1946) did little more than stress 'the need for study, training and research applicable to the ceramic and mining industries . . . obviously with the Technical College . . . integral and basic'.

were only two suitable people who might be interested.[1] On the same day the deputation, joined now by Mr J. S. Fulton, went to the Ministry of Education where they gained general approval for their proposed curriculum so far as the training of teachers was concerned. The same local group again met Moberly on *28 April 1947*, to report on plans for 'sponsorship' and to discuss the setting up of a governing body for the college. But none of these three meetings was in any way decisive; the drama of the period had other settings.

Sir Walter Moberly was nothing if not judicious and cautious in handling deputations; and those who had ears to hear would have noted that on at least one occasion he had hinted that the opinion of other universities was something the UGC would want to take into account. Both prudence and courtesy pointed in the same direction: existing universities should be apprised officially through the VCs' Committee of what was afoot at Stoke. What Moberly asked the VCs was not whether they approved, but what were the implications of the Stoke proposals for university policy for the country as a whole: it was not, and could not have been, suggested that they were in a position to impose a veto. The matter first came up at the VCs' Committee on 31 January 1947; a sub-committee was asked to report and did so after a meeting (on 11 March) with Lindsay himself.[2] Amended and expanded, this report was finally adopted by the VCs' Committee on *25 April 1947* and sent to the UGC; copies were also furnished to the three universities in negotiation with Stoke. Even though it did not significantly affect the course of events, this VCs' *Note on the Stoke Proposal* is most important as showing the state of feeling in universities at the time and the opposition with which the Stoke promoters had to contend. The VCs drew attention to the view they had expressed in their *Note on University Policy and Finance* of July 1946.[3] It was still true, they felt, that

> there is no prospect of gain from new institutions which would justify the diversion to them of human and material

1 Not mentioned by name in the report of the meeting.

2 The chair was taken by Mr Ifor Evans (Principal of University College, Aberystwyth); the others present were Sir Richard Livingstone (Vice-Chancellor of Oxford) and Professor W. J. Pugh (Manchester).

3 See p. 47.

> resources which could be employed with greater advantage to the national interest in enabling the existing university institutions to fulfil the programmes on which they have already embarked. . . . The present Universities and University Colleges can well accommodate more than the number of qualified entrants likely to be forthcoming for a considerable period of years. . . . The suggested basis [of academic studies] seems to provide not a new type of University institution, but a new type of Technical College; and in the view of the Vice-Chancellors such an institution could not be given even limited degree-granting powers without serious detriment to the whole University system. . . . The main argument for the proposal is that the alternative, a College whose students are candidates for 'external' degrees, is under a certain academic disability. . . . Yet it must be recognised that this 'external' system has been the usual, and empirically a not unsatisfactory way of approach. . . . A period of probation under an external examination system does not preclude, possibly even does not retard, growth towards the assumption of full University responsibility. . . .[1]

To this *Note on the Stoke Proposal* there was an Appendix in which the opportunity was also taken to draw attention to a letter the Chancellor of the Exchequer (Mr Hugh Dalton) had sent to the Deputy Chairman of the Parliamentary and Scientific Committee.[2] As reported in *The Times* of 10 March 1947, Mr Dalton himself shared the view of that Committee on the inadvisability of founding a new university at this stage.[3]

This adverse attitude of the VCs' Committee was not the only disappointment which had to be faced. A second one was in regard to the appointment of a Principal. At the meeting with the Stoke delegation on 24 January 1947, Moberly had agreed

1 The Vice-Chancellors' 'Note' was approved by them on Friday, 25 April 1947. It appears that Sir Hector Hetherington, Principal of Glasgow University, who was Acting Chairman of the Vice-Chancellors' Committee, had sent Moberly a copy of the draft 'Note' early in April; and consequently Moberly knew of the line the Vice-Chancellors were taking when he received the Stoke delegation on Monday, 28 April.

2 See p. 47n.

3 Mr Dalton also expressed considerable doubts as to the advisability of upgrading certain technical colleges, a view which could not have pleased the *Sentinel* (see above, p. 56n).

that such an appointment should be made as soon as there was a legal body capable of making it. The Exploratory Committee took action at its next meeting on *31 March 1947*, and agreed to recommend to 'the Governing body of the new University' [1] the appointment of Mr J. S. Fulton, M.A., of Balliol College, Oxford, as Principal. Fulton, as we have seen, was a member of the Committee[2] and had been active in the academic and constitutional planning for the proposed college. He felt himself unable, however, to accept the invitation; and on 2 May he informed the Town Clerk of Stoke, the secretary of the Committee, that he had accepted an offer of the post of Principal at University College, Swansea.[3]

What was now to be done? In vivid terms W. B. Gallie[4] recounts the story the Reverend Thomas Horwood told him of how, without consulting anyone else on the Committee, he took train to Oxford to see Lindsay and prevailed on him, there and then, to become their Principal despite the fact that, as Lindsay explained, his doctors had said he had only about three years to live: 'Master . . . it was you we always really wanted . . . Come to us for those three years.' This is a splendid story; but Miss Malbon's diaries make it clear that in chatting with Gallie the Vicar may have been letting his phantasy build on a defective memory. The facts are as follows. On 25 April Fulton let Miss Malbon know informally that he would be going to Swansea; two days later the Stoke deputation[5] which was going to meet the UGC on 28 April went in the Lord Mayor's car as far as Oxford, saw E. S. Cartwright and others, but had no formal discussion with Lindsay. A meeting, however, did take place in Oxford between Lindsay and the Stoke delegation on 22 May and in preparation for it Miss Malbon herself sent Lindsay a letter indicating 'what she and the Vicar and others had in mind': that the Master should be the Principal and be strongly supported on the administrative side. The Master told the

1 No such body as yet existed.

2 See p. 54n. Fulton was not at the meeting of 31 March.

3 Lindsay had known privately from early in 1947 that Fulton, whom he would have liked to see as Principal of the new College, was interested in the Swansea post. The Exploratory Committee's recommendation of 31 March looks like a bold bid on Lindsay's part to force the issue and save his nominee for Keele. For a time Fulton, as he promised, was able to continue his interest in Stoke and was present at the important meeting of 'sponsors' on 10 June 1947 (see p. 72).

4 W. B. Gallie, *A New University*, pp. 54–6.

5 See p. 57.

delegation that he would think further about the matter and 'discuss it with Mrs Lindsay'. The first indication of his decision is a remark he made in a letter of 3 July to Sir Richard Livingstone: 'I have said that when my time here comes to an end I will try and give the Stoke experiment a start for a year or so.' If there was a private intervention by Horwood it must have occurred between 22 May and 3 July; yet after the full discussion on 22 May there was no need for high drama; and no one involved at the time finds the Horwood story more than remotely credible.

Formally, things took a good deal longer. Fulton's decision could not be communicated to the Exploratory Committee until its next meeting on 23 July 1947, when a sub-committee was set up to consider future proposals for the principalship; it was not until 23 September 1947, that Lindsay was formally invited to become Principal 'for a period of three years'; and it was not until 19 February 1948,[1] that he personally informed the sub-committee that he was prepared to accept the offer. 'He stated, however, that he had been asked to extend his services as Master of Balliol College, Oxford, for another year and he would not, therefore, be able to give his full time as Principal until 1950, but in the meantime he would be able to devote part-time to University matters.'

By the summer of 1947 the Stoke proposals had really made very little progress. There had been a polite reception of the idea by Sir Walter Moberly on 27 March 1946, a rather more serious conversation on 25 July 1946, and some consideration of a full-scale document from Stoke on 19 November 1946. The first discussion of the matter by the full UGC on 3 December 1946 had resulted in an expression of sympathetic interest to which, however, there were attached three quite vital conditions regarding the basis of studies, the safeguarding of standards and conformity with national policy. On the other hand, the VCs' Committee and the Chancellor of the Exchequer had stated their opinions that the setting up of a new university at this time was inadvisable. Furthermore, the negotiations for

[1] This date is two weeks subsequent to the UGC's crucial resolutions of 5 February 1948. But presumably it was not so much uncertainty about the UGC's attitude as the arrangements he had to make in Oxford which explain Lindsay's delay in announcing his formal acceptance.

sponsoring which had been entered into with the Universities of Oxford, Manchester and Birmingham had, as we shall see, run into rough water. Lord Lindsay, however, was not to be daunted by coolness towards the Stoke proposals or by opposition to them and on *14 May 1947*, he initiated a debate in the House of Lords 'to call attention to university education in this country'.[1] He urged the Government to appoint a Departmental Committee, on which the UGC would be largely represented, to look into university education which, as he pointed out, was confined to a small proportion of the population: 1 in 1,013. The doubling of numbers would be a revolution in our university system. There was need for scientific research, for more teachers in schools, for professional men, for specialised instruction not leading to a degree, and for adult education. The increase in numbers could perhaps be achieved by expanding existing institutions or by having some new ones: and if new ones, of what type should they be? And so he came skilfully to Stoke:

> I myself have had something to do with the proposed experiment at Stoke-on-Trent. Ever since I first knew it—about 30 years ago—the city of Stoke-on-Trent has hoped to have a university college. When . . . there was a prospect that this dream might be realised, the promoters of the scheme sat down to ask themselves what kind of university college they ought to have. They took the view—I think rightly—that a local university college should have a close relation to the distinctive characteristics of the locality it serves. The distinctive characteristics of Stoke-on-Trent are the pottery industry and a quite extraordinary development of social services and adult education. Therefore, if it is to have a university college, it should have a Chair of Applied Ceramics and first-class teaching in physical chemistry; that is not to say that it should not have sections dealing with the sciences. On the other side, it should give special emphasis . . . on what we may call sociology—social studies, economics, social organization . . .
>
> Further is there a place in this country for the equivalent of what is called the American college; that is, the small

[1] Hansard, *House of Lords Debates*, 14 May 1947, pp. 695–742.

> college giving only a Bachelor's degree and not the higher degrees? These colleges have done some very interesting things.

In his reply the Lord Chancellor, Viscount Jowitt, said in effect that the newer terms of reference for the UGC[1] already enabled that body to survey and co-ordinate university education as a whole and that it was not opposition to the idea of new universities so much as shortage of materials which was, for the time being, guiding the UGC's policy. He did, however, quote the UGC's resolutions of 3 December 1946 and made what from so high a source could not but be regarded as an encouraging comment[2]

> Here is a new experiment—that the North Staffordshire people should have the right of setting their own examinations, if they do so in consultation with and by obtaining the benefit of the advice and experience of some of the older existing universities—I think they are here called sponsoring universities. Might that not be an experiment worth making?

But so far as the gaining of a firmer pronouncement from the UGC itself was concerned, the year 1947 was a period of doldrums.[3] Lindsay kept in touch with Moberly, but his main anxieties were now about the sponsoring universities. Everybody, as he said, seemed to be waiting for everybody else to make a move. One of the conditions laid down by the UGC was that adequate sponsoring arrangements should be secured but the UGC would give no lead to the universities concerned; and those universities in their turn, apart from having qualms about

[1] See p. 56n.

[2] There was a bitter tang towards the end of the Lord Chancellor's reply: 'I wish I could give him equal satisfaction with regard to building, but that assurance I cannot give.' It is interesting to recall that Lord Calverley seized the opportunity of this debate to put forward the claims of Bradford for a university, a desire which was not fulfilled until 1966 when Colleges of Advanced Technology were given university status.

[3] In November 1947 an article by the Reverend T. Horwood was published in the *Universities Quarterly* (pp. 77–81) entitled 'A new University College: a proposal for North Staffordshire'. It expounded the aims of a proposed curriculum, outlined a scheme for sponsorship by three named universities and quoted the UGC resolutions of 3 December 1946, together with Lord Jowitt's remarks in the House of Lords debate. Though signed by Horwood, the article was approved and partly written by others. It was in fact a carefully planned bid to enlist academic sympathy and support on a wide front.

the proposed curriculum and other matters, wanted to know where the UGC really stood before they made up their minds. As 1948 dawned there was gloom in Stoke, but still no lack of determination.

5 January 1948

The one ray of hope was that out of an informal conference between Lindsay, Moberly and A. E. Trueman, the Deputy Chairman of the UGC, there had come a suggestion that before the UGC formally came to a decision about the scheme, a Stoke delegation should meet the UGC or a representative portion of it. In preparation for such a meeting, Lindsay as Chairman of the Exploratory Committee sent a formal letter addressed not to Moberly alone but to the members of the UGC. It is an important document, especially as showing a critical shift of emphasis in the scheme of studies.[1]

> We are more concerned with providing a curriculum for the B.A. which will include both Science and Arts and break down the departmentalism which we think is so harmful in much modern University teaching than with concentrating on special subjects in either Science or Arts which are specially suited to the region. We would indeed rest our claim for special consideration on the importance for general University policy of this attack on departmentalism.

In this letter also the difficulties which had arisen about sponsoring were squarely faced and the awkward question of the position of other university colleges was put into what Lindsay now regarded as the true perspective.

> We had always assumed that it would be open to other University Colleges to adopt the 'sponsoring plan' if they so desired and that their adopting or not adopting it would be entirely without prejudice to their claims of priority for full University status. . . . This is a proposal for a new, and we think a better, form of apprenticeship. It is in no way an attempt to 'jump the queue'.

The meeting took place in London in the afternoon of 5 January 1948. It was, to judge by every available account of it,

[1] See chapter 4, pp. 103–7.

a tense and at times an emotional occasion. Lindsay realised how much might depend on the outcome and had brought with him a strong phalanx of supporters: Aldermen Horwood, Kemp, Leason and Barnett Stross, M.P.; the Town Clerk, Director of Education and Chief Architect of Stoke-on-Trent; Alderman W. Hutson to represent Burton-on-Trent, Alderman L. Davies from Stafford County, and Miss Malbon. On the other side Moberly was accompanied by more than a dozen members of the UGC.

Moberly began with a lengthy and pessimistic speech indicating all the difficulties which had been experienced. A new institution which had the right to give degrees would have, to that extent, an advantage over the existing colleges; it was felt that there should be an apprenticeship through external degrees; the new system would be very difficult to work; the VCs' Committee was opposed to it; two of the proposed sponsors had thrown the matter back to the UGC; if the UGC accepted the Stoke scheme it would be in opposition to general university views.

In his reply Lindsay went right to the heart of the matter. He had raised the question in the House of Lords where the Lord Chancellor had made it clear that national policy for universities was the concern of the UGC. It was emphatically not to be decided by the VCs' Committee. If the UGC did not take a decision itself, who would do so? In effect he was asking whether the UGC were abdicating from their responsibilities—a telling stroke of advocacy. As regards sponsorship, was not this also a form of apprenticeship, and indeed a better one? Was there never to be any change in the universities? The Exploratory Committee was broadening the scope of the curriculum; the problem of getting staff would be eased if they postponed their opening, as they were now willing to do, until 1950;[1] and as for buildings, Keele Hall was available.

Such a summary may suffice as a record of Lindsay's line of argument; but it conveys nothing of the tremendous impression he created: unshakeable on all his main contentions, shrewdly countering every objection, reasonable in appreciating the difficulties other people might find in his proposals, vigorous to

[1] At one point R. H. Tawney asked whether North Staffordshire would be willing to postpone the proposals for five years until university policy had been decided, and the deputation was unanimous in answering 'no'.

the point of banging the table when something needed to be rammed home. The scene was one which still lives vividly in the memory of those who were there.

5 February 1948

At their next regular meeting in February the UGC debated the Stoke proposals in the light of the January encounter with Lindsay and his colleagues. Moberly, it is said, agreed that departmentalism was an evil and was impressed by the Stoke attempt to deal with it; he regretted a divergence of view between the VCs' Committee and the UGC, but he was impressed by Lindsay's arguments; and he had come to the conclusion that the experiment ought to be tried and that a rigid rule which tied all colleges to the London degree for all time was not desirable. In this opinion he was eventually supported by almost every one of his colleagues[1] and the following resolutions were approved by a very decisive twelve to one majority of the members.[2]

> 1. That the Committee, having considered very carefully the proposals submitted to them for the establishment of a University College in North Staffordshire with the power of granting a B.A. degree under conditions of effective external sponsorship, are of the opinion that it is in the interests of university education for an experiment on these lines to be carried out.
> 2. That if the promoters of the scheme are able to enter into the necessary arrangements for effective sponsorship with one or more universities and to obtain a Royal Charter for the establishment of the College, the Committee will be prepared to recommend the provision of such financial assistance from the Exchequer as may from time to time appear to them to be required.

[1] Lindsay himself was aware that for some time one of the strongest and most outspoken supporters on the UGC of the Stoke proposals had been (Sir) Peter Noble, Professor of Humanity in the University of Aberdeen and later Principal of King's College, London (1952–68). His interventions in the debates about Stoke carried great weight.

[2] In some quarters there is a piece of folklore current to the effect that the major issue depended on the Chairman's casting vote. Nothing could be further from the truth. There was indeed a casting vote but it related to the less important (but not negligible) issue of whether 'two universities' should replace 'one or more' in the second resolution.

The nettle had been firmly grasped. The question whether the Stoke scheme was to be adjudged to be in line with national policy was definitely answered and what had so far been a serious obstacle to progress was removed. What Stoke wanted to do was 'in the interests of university education.' Nor was the sponsorship requirement onerous, since the phrase 'one or more universities' clearly allowed for considerable flexibility in the arrangements which Stoke might be able to make. The UGC could not now turn back.[1] But the question whether Oxford,

[1] Robert O. Berdahl, *British Universities and the State*, pp. 142–3, writes: 'I was told (though I received some reports to the contrary from other sources) that the UGC's decision in 1947 [*sic*] to support the foundation of the University College at North Staffordshire in the face of open opposition from the Vice-Chancellors' Committee stemmed directly or indirectly from the personal intervention of Hugh Dalton, the Chancellor of the Exchequer at that time. According to this version, the plan for an experimental college proposed by Lord Lindsay . . . would not have survived the opposition of influential university figures (whom the UGC is usually anxious not to offend) had it not been for Dalton's action.' A cruder version of this story is that Lindsay 'got round' Dalton who put pressure on Moberly to force the project through the UGC.

In assessing the credibility of this allegedly conspiratorial episode the following points ought to be considered:

(i) (a) Mr Dalton on 10 March 1947 was not in favour of founding a new university (see above, p. 58); (b) he resigned his office on 13 November 1947 and thereafter was not in a position to exert pressure on anybody; (c) the Stoke proposals were not on the agenda for a full formal meeting of the UGC at any time in 1947; (d) the decision of the UGC on which everything depended was not taken until 5 February 1948.

(ii) The UGC was directly responsible to the Treasury and its operations were the only sphere in which the Chancellor was himself a 'spending department'; though it was established custom that he should (and did) refrain from interference in regard to the allocation of funds placed at the disposal of the UGC, it would be proper for him to manifest an interest in major matters of broad policy; and no sinister implication can be drawn from any such interest.

(iii) The story is not consonant with Moberly's handling of the Stoke proposals or with the recollections of people who were members of the UGC at the time. Until 5 February 1948, Moberly showed no marked warmth towards Stoke, did not help them round awkward corners, and was impressed by the views of the VCs' Committee. If he had been under pressure of the kind suggested he would have realised: (a) that if he told his colleagues or if they sensed it (as they did not), there would have been an unholy rumpus not confined to the UGC; and (b) that if he had been minded to play a lone hand in the UGC, his very independent-minded colleagues could not have been persuaded, bludgeoned or tricked into something of which they did not approve.

(iv) Miss Malbon in a letter to the author says: 'There is no mention in my papers about Lindsay seeing Dalton or Cripps.' There was little or nothing about the Stoke negotiations that Miss Malbon was not told or did not find out.

(v) What part did Dr Stross play? He was a very assiduous member of the

Manchester and Birmingham—any or all of them—would cooperate had still to be resolved.

THE SPONSORS

It had always been evident to those who were interested in the setting up of a college in North Staffordshire that such an institution would have to depend in some way on the interest of existing universities. The earliest assumption was that there would be an affiliation with Oxford which through the university extension movement had special links with the Potteries. The 1899 Hanley Committee of Enquiry had mentioned this; E. S. Cartwright in 1911 and Albert Mansbridge in 1913 had reiterated it; and Lindsay himself in 1925 had a similar idea at the back of his mind.[1] When serious proposals were being made to the UGC in 1946, Lindsay's first thought was that Oxford might be induced to 'take a special interest' and the

Exploratory Committee and as MP for a North Staffordshire constituency it would be proper for him to discuss formally or informally the Stoke project with the Chancellor. Stross certainly sent a copy of the Memorandum of 11 November 1946 to Dalton and discussed it with him; but the evidence shows that Dalton then acted with entire propriety and made enquiries about the UGC's view on it. After a meeting with the sponsoring universities on 10 June 1947, at which he had been present, Stross again let Dalton know how affairs stood. By the end of September 1947, the Chancellor was said to be 'taking a keen personal interest in the proposed college'. Yet however busy Dr Stross himself may have been behind the scenes, the available evidence about his activities does nothing to support the thesis that the Chancellor's 'personal interest' amounted to putting pressure on Moberly.

(vi) After the meeting with the UGC on 5 January 1948, it appears that Lindsay had it in mind to go and see Dalton's successor, Sir Stafford Cripps; but no such meeting took place. Sir Stafford, however, did send to Lindsay and to Stross a letter indicating his approval of the UGC's resolutions of 5 February 1948; but this surely was a matter of courtesy and not any indication that Cripps had assumed the rôle assigned to Dalton in this piece of folklore.

(vii) The Manchester representatives on the Joint Committee of the three sponsoring universities stated in their Report of 3 March 1949; 'We have no evidence supporting the view (which has had some currency) that the encouragement and seeming priority given to the Stoke scheme was political in origin.'

(viii) How did the story arise? Was it from some ill-considered, mistaken and boastful remark made by somebody at some stage, such as 'I think we've got Dalton on our side'? Or was it a figment of imagination or even a spiteful deduction on the part of someone who disliked Lindsay or Dalton or both of them?

[1] For these pronouncements, see pp. 27–8, 31, 33.

memorandum sent to Moberly in March 1946 looked to the fostering of a vital connexion with that University.[1] How affiliation would work was never discussed in detail; but what was emerging was a firm conviction that the London external degree system would not be a suitable or even possible arrangement for a college which wanted freedom to experiment with its own curriculum.

By July 1946, however, the concept of 'sponsorship' by one or more universities had taken the place of that affiliation: the sponsor(s) would be a public guarantee of standards.[2] This line of approach to the problem was in principle acceptable to the UGC; what needed to be done was to secure the assent and co-operation of the sponsors—and no one could have foreseen what a soul-searing task that was to be. From the autumn of 1946 to the spring of 1949 negotiations dragged on. It was a jungle of hesitations and delays, misgivings and misunderstandings, conferences, and committee after committee within the three universities concerned: Oxford, Birmingham and

[1] See p. 51. No emphasis seems to have been placed on the possible precedent of St David's College, Lampeter, whose Charters (1852 and 1865) empowered it to award its own degrees of B.D. and B.A., but provided for a board of examiners appointed by Oxford and Cambridge, with which Universities St David's was affiliated in 1880 and 1883. It is now a constituent institution of the University of Wales.

[2] Sponsorship was not quite a new idea, and its genesis is interesting. In the UGC's first published Report (February 1921), the Chairman, Sir William McCormick, had written in connexion with the University Colleges of Nottingham, Reading and Southampton: 'dependence on London external degrees is educationally unsound and is unsatisfactory and unfair both to teachers and to students. . . . What is needed is a system whereby University Colleges may be recognized as a grade of University institution free from their present disadvantages. . . . A scheme has been proposed as a solution of the difficulty. . . . It is suggested that the University Colleges might be given the privilege of granting a first degree on courses, curricula and examinations prescribed by themselves, but approved and supervised by a patron University to which they were attached for this purpose.' This scheme—which is Keele in embryo—was a brain child of (Sir) Hector Hetherington, Principal of the College at Exeter (1920–4) and was conceived at the time when Exeter was applying for admission to the UGC grant list in the early 1920s. The idea of such an external academic supervisory Board was informally well received in Oxford, the prospective 'patron'; but there was so much opposition elsewhere that no more was heard of it. Hetherington, however, was Lindsay's successor in the Chair of Moral Philosophy at Glasgow and was Chairman of the VCs' Committee 1943–7 and 1949–52 and Acting Chairman for part of 1948 and 1949. It may well have been he who first suggested the idea of 'sponsorship' to Lindsay and he certainly corresponded with Lindsay about it. See Hetherington's *The University College at Exeter*, Exeter, 1963.

Manchester. There were two separable themes running through all the talk. The first was educational: what exactly was it to be that the universities were being asked to sponsor? This will be dealt with in chapter 4. The second was constitutional: what would be the precise function of the sponsors and how would they be exercised? In the course of the discussions Keele agreed to many modifications of its first proposals, particularly as regards curriculum. Oxford was the most sympathetic of the three universities, Manchester the most recalcitrant and Birmingham an eventual whipper-in. The position of these universities was, of course, far from easy. Apart from internal divergencies of opinion in each university, they all had a strong sense of loyalty towards existing university colleges, and they were very conscious as negotiations proceeded of the collective views of the universities about new institutions as expressed by the VCs' Committee.[1]

July–December 1946

'The Master of Balliol stated that the link proposed with a University need not be limited to Oxford, but that Manchester and Birmingham might be united with Oxford in carrying out the scheme.' So runs a Stoke report of that informal but important meeting which took place with some members of the UGC on 25 July 1946.[2] It was the first mention at a serious level of tripartite sponsoring.[3] During the summer the idea was considerably elaborated and the Memorandum of 11 November 1946 (which was discussed with the UGC members on 19 November) set out clearly two alternatives:

> (a) That the new College should be empowered to award degrees subject to the inclusion in its charter of a provision whereby one or more (not exceeding three) existing universities would sponsor the College and vouch to the

[1] See p. 54.

[2] On this occasion R. H. Tawney suggested that it might be wise, in view of difficulties that might arise with other university colleges, to get started first with a London external degree and go on later to a sponsoring scheme. In July 1946, this was not an acceptable idea; but it seemed less obnoxious by June 1948 (see p. 75).

[3] The *Sentinel* (28 November 1944) had previously groped towards an association with the two nearest universities; see p. 35.

interested public for the maintenance of adequate standards of work.

The machinery suggested for this purpose would be the appointment by each of the sponsoring universities of two academic advisers. The academic advisers thus appointed would form an academic advisory council whose functions would be:

(i) To approve all higher appointments to teaching posts;
(ii) To approve external examiners for the degree examinations;
(iii) To receive an annual report from the examiners on the standard reached on the degree examinations, and to forward this report with their comments to the Governing Body of the College.

(b) That degrees should be awarded by an existing University after examinations based upon the curriculum of the College. This would imply that the degree awarding University was satisfied with the content of the degree courses; that it should appoint examiners to conduct, jointly with those from the College, degree examinations, and to agree for each candidate the class of honours to be awarded.

The Stoke delegation made it quite clear that they preferred the first of these alternatives, which, with some extension of the functions of the academic advisers, proved to be the scheme incorporated in the Charter of 1949; and, so far from objecting, Moberly gave them some encouragement to enter into negotiations with universities which might be concerned. Indeed sponsorship was made one of the conditions for the award of degrees by the College in the formal resolutions passed soon afterwards by the UGC on 3 December 1946. It is a little surprising, however, to find that by the end of 1946 Lindsay was already writing to Moberly to say that favourable replies had come from Birmingham and Manchester but there would be a delay at Oxford. This is typical of Lindsay's disconcerting readiness to believe that other people had said the sort of things he wanted to hear.[1]

[1] On 17 December 1946 Miss Malbon had been to see Sir John Stopford, Vice-Chancellor of Manchester, who had expressed some general and personal willingness to help. Unfortunately, apart from the minutes of Council and Senate, documents and correspondence relating to Stoke cannot now be

January–June 1947

Lindsay met a specially appointed sub-committee of the Hebdomadal Council at Oxford in mid-January and had an initial success, his rather ingenuous line of argument being that what was being asked for was no more than had been done for Reading or Bristol.[1] But the Council itself refused to commit itself to any expression of approval for the scheme and agreed only that the Vice-Chancellor should consult with Manchester and Birmingham.[2] Meanwhile the Exploratory Committee at Stoke was hard at work, considering how the curriculum might be broadened and what should be the functions of the academic advisers. To the three functions they had set out in their Memorandum of 11 November 1946, they now added a fourth and important item which would give the advisers much greater influence over general policy

(iv) To make representations from time to time to the Governing Body about the general progress and development of the College.

By the end of May, when the comments of the VCs' Committee on the Stoke Proposal were already well known, Stopford at Manchester was feeling serious doubts about the Stoke project and did not think sponsorship would work; and Priestley's informal communication to his Senate in Birmingham had elicited a largely unfavourable response.[3]

Nevertheless, the three Vice-Chancellors met the Exploratory

found in the Birmingham archives; but the reaction of Sir Raymond Priestley when he first heard accidentally of the Stoke project in October was that his university would lose the financial support they had from Stoke! (See also p. 73n). But at neither university had Senate and Council been consulted and neither Vice-Chancellor would be in a position to commit his university. At Oxford, Lindsay's letter was referred to a committee of the Hebdomadal Council.

1 Reading's connexion with Oxford had been largely on a personal basis. H. J. Mackinder, Student of Christ Church and reader in geography at Oxford had for many years been a part-time Principal of the College and there were others from Oxford who went to Reading to give lecture courses. Reading students sat the examinations for Oxford diplomas, but not for degrees. The College itself was loosely affiliated to Oxford from 1899. See W. M. Childs, *Making a University*, 1933. For Bristol see p. 20n.

2 The three Vice-Chancellors did in fact have an informal meeting with officials of the UGC on 30 January 1947.

3 Amongst the few who took a more sympathetic line was Professor Roy Pascal (see p. 77). The Vice-Principal, Sir Norman Howarth, Professor of Chemistry, was strongly opposed.

Committee in Stoke on *10 June 1947* and every aspect of the proposals was very fully and frankly discussed, Manchester stressing in particular that the members of what was now being called the Academic Advisory Council would have to spend a very great deal of time and attention to their duties. Lindsay himself did most of the talking and was well satisfied with the day's work. He gave Moberly (who thought his letter 'a little tendentious') a sanguine account of what had happened and (not without guile) said that the opinion was that the UGC should now make up its own mind; to which Moberly firmly replied that agreement on adequate sponsoring arrangements was a prerequisite for the UGC's full approval of the Stoke scheme.[1] Stopford too thought it 'very naughty' of Lindsay to say that they were all prepared to recommend sponsoring to their governing bodies. The truth of the matter seems to be that Lindsay, whose experience of the civic universities was limited to a junior post at Manchester some forty years earlier, never quite appreciated the difficulties which Stopford and Priestley might have to face in their own universities and tended to interpret *any* interest in Stoke, even if critical, as willingness to champion the project through thick and thin.

July–December 1947

After the meeting of 10 June a revised and printed version (dated 20 June) of the proposals was circulated to the three universities and Lindsay concentrated now on getting the three universities to accept the rôle of sponsors; presumably he hoped that if he could produce his sponsors he would force the hand of the UGC to come to a favourable decision on the question of 'national policy'. Little could be done during the long vacation; but on *10 October 1947*, Lindsay again met a sub-committee of the Hebdomadal Council and secured agreement (which the Council itself confirmed on 20 October) that Oxford was in favour of the experiment and would sponsor it if Manchester and Birmingham came in, though it was made clear that Oxford would not wish to find itself in conflict with other universities on the matter.[2] This was no mean triumph. But something

[1] Satisfactory sponsorship was still an important proviso in the UGC resolutions of 5 February 1948. See p. 65.

[2] Though the Hebdomadal Council accepted the recommendation on 20

approaching disaster was at hand. On 19 November 1947, the Senate at Birmingham accepted a resolution:[1]

> That, until decision on the national needs for university expansion has been made and guidance given by the Government Authorities charged with this responsibility, we are unable to give advice on the proposal to establish a degree granting University College at Stoke-on-Trent.

At Manchester feeling was equally hard, as is shown by the Senate's resolution of 11 December 1947:

> . . . the University is deeply concerned that the interests of existing University Colleges should not be overlooked. The University also wishes to emphasise that the proposed scheme of sponsorship raises problems of a serious and far reaching nature and recommends that a decision on the University's participation in any such scheme should be deferred until a satisfactory assurance is received that the Stoke proposal is in line with University policy as a whole.

It is no wonder that Lindsay was despondent: 'It is most disappointing. It is the worst we have had. . . . I do not think the game is up, but I feel less hopeful than I have ever done before.'[2]

January–June 1948

Almost two years had gone by since the first small delegation had waited on Moberly in March 1946, and still there was little

October the formal Decree accepting the obligations of sponsorship was not presented to the Congregation at Oxford until May 1949. Untroubled by constitutional niceties and perhaps not unfairly, Lindsay conveyed the impression to the other two universities from the autumn of 1947 onwards that Oxford's sponsorship was quite certain if they came in; but Manchester certainly thought that they had been misled.

[1] The universities were not being asked by anybody to 'give advice'. An amendment moved by Professor Pascal, which was rather more sympathetic, was decisively rejected.

[2] Letter to H. Taylor, 20 December 1947 (quoted by R. A. Lowe, M.A. thesis, 1966). How desperate people in Stoke were feeling is also shown by J. F. Carr's letter to Horwood of 15 December 1947 in which he suggested an additional grant of £500 each to Birmingham and Manchester for the coming year: 'This would give us an argument with the UGC that instead of quarrelling with Birmingham and Manchester because of our own scheme, we are still ready to help more than in the past. I am proposing really "a sprat to catch a whale".' (Quoted by R. A. Lowe.)

sign of encouraging progress. Yet a strong shaft of light pierced the gloom when the UGC on 5 February 1948, declared its opinion on the Stoke proposal to the effect that it was 'in the interests of university education for an experiment on these lines to be carried out'. Lindsay's spirits revived and he lost no time in pointing out to the three universities the significance of what the UGC had now said and suggesting that they should reconsider their attitude.[1] By the end of February, Birmingham and Oxford were willing to have a meeting of representatives of the three universities to discuss the situation; indeed Oxford, which would not itself act as sole sponsor, went so far as to express a hope that Birmingham would agree to become a sponsor.[2] It was Birmingham in fact which took the initiative in arranging a meeting in that city for *22 April 1948*. Not influenced on this occasion by any personal advocacy from Stoke, the representatives of the three universities drew up a precisely worded report of exasperating coolness:

> On the basis of the documents before the committee it would not be possible for the members to make a clear recommendation to their respective universities either for or against sponsorship. It was unanimously agreed to recommend to the Hebdomadal Council of the University of Oxford and to the Senates of the Universities of Manchester and Birmingham that they should each appoint four representatives who would together form a Committee

[1] It is indicative of the efforts being made at this juncture that J. F. Carr sent to Oxford a resolution passed on 19 February by the North Staffs. Committee for Adult Education (see p. 37): 'That the . . . Committee trust that the University of Oxford will become the sponsoring university for the proposed University College in North Staffordshire.' In March, Miss Malbon approached Lady Simon, wife of the Chairman of the University Council at Manchester, to enlist her support and arrange a meeting with Stopford (which took place on 19 April)—a clear sign of how far relations between Stoke and Manchester had deteriorated: a direct approach to Stopford was no longer easy.

[2] In February, Lindsay wrote to Horwood: 'We are not quite out of the wood as we have got to get this sponsoring arranged. I am trying [through Livingstone?] to get Oxford to withdraw their condition. . . . Oxford does not want to do it alone, but I am hoping to get them to say that they will do it on the understanding that we are approaching Manchester and Birmingham' (quoted by R. A. Lowe, M.A. thesis, 1966).

Oxford discussed the situation with Cambridge on 16 April 1948, at one of their normal joint meetings, when it was stated that Cambridge was being asked whether it would be prepared to sponsor a university institution at Norwich. (The Town Clerks of Stoke and Norwich had corresponded already in October 1947.)

> to discuss the proposal further with the Exploratory Committee or other body appointed by those interested at Stoke and report back to the three Universities which would, after considering the Report of the Committee, decide individually whether they can undertake sponsorship under conditions agreed between the Stoke authorities and the Universities' Committee.

At least the bogey of 'national policy' had been exorcised by the change in the UGC's attitude in February 1948, and qualms about unfairness to the other university colleges were seemingly allayed; but further delay was inevitable: representatives had again to be formally appointed and a date for a meeting arranged despite 'the inability', noted by the Manchester delegates, 'of the representatives of the University of Oxford to attend either in or out of term'.

There now occurred a manœuvre which almost passes credibility, so unexpected was it and so out of keeping with everything which had previously been proclaimed. The minutes of a sparsely attended meeting of a section of the Exploratory Committee of 9 June 1948, simply record that Lindsay had interviewed Moberly and that Sir Walter: 'had agreed with him that the Committee should now proceed with the acquisition of Keele Hall and the preparation of the Charter, and not to wait until the sponsorship of the University College had been finally settled.' It is what was not recorded that is significant. It so happens that Miss Malbon took her own notes at this meeting and sent a copy to Horwood: they are invaluable for the light they throw on what had occurred:

> The Master then reported on a private discussion with Sir Walter Moberly and the Deputy Chairman of the UGC (Dr A. E. Trueman) . . . After consultation with Alderman Horwood he had asked whether the attitude of the UGC would be changed should the North Staffs. Committee decide to take a London External Degree for the first few years: this would only possibly happen if the negotiations about sponsorship had not been brought to a successful conclusion by 1950. Sir Walter had stated that this would not prejudice the attitude of the UGC in any way.

It had been one of the cardinal doctrines of the Stoke promoters that they must be free to experiment with their own curriculum and therefore must not be tied to the London external degree; and when Tawney at a crucial meeting with UGC members had suggested that London links might be a good thing for a few years, his argument was vigorously rejected.[1] Why then were soundings being taken about this very proposal in the summer of 1948? The obvious explanation is that Lindsay, urged on by Tawney,[2] now wanted an insurance against the complete breakdown of the negotiations for sponsorship and a guarantee that a college of some sort would definitely start in 1950. The assurance he received from Moberly would have been a boomerang had he tried to use it with the reluctant sponsors to extort agreement; and (somewhat to their chagrin) the three universities were in fact not told about it until 15 February 1949 when negotiations were in much calmer waters. We must assume of course that Lindsay had not missed any subtle nuance in Moberly's remarks. Even though the other members of the UGC would have been taken aback had sponsorship been abandoned and freedom to experiment consequently been placed in jeopardy, they could scarcely at this stage have rejected a London solution. We have no idea of how Lindsay thought such an arrangement would work in the particular context of the Stoke curriculum. London had for some time been sympathetically accommodating about the syllabuses of existing university colleges and since the war had entered into special relationship with a number of new colleges in the underdeveloped parts of the Commonwealth. Perhaps they could have digested Stoke as well. But at no time was the question put even in the most tentative form to the University of London itself.

July 1948–July 1949

The new 'inter-university' committee whose establishment was recommended on 22 April 1948, eventually met privately under the chairmanship of Dr W. T. S. Stallybrass, Vice-Chancellor of Oxford, on *21 October 1948*. The whole of the summer, however, had not been wasted. At Stoke itself great progress was

[1] See p. 64.

[2] In June 1948 Tawney was still pressing on Lindsay and Miss Malbon the view that 'an interim arrangement with London might be a possibility in case of necessity'.

made with the drafting of a Charter, now that Lindsay's talk with Moberly (reported on 9 June) had cleared the air; and one of Stoke's champions at Birmingham, Professor Roy Pascal, had begun work on a memorandum dealing both with the constitution and the curriculum of the college. On 21 October the whole day was spent on the Charter which although already lodged in draft form with the Privy Council on 6 August 1948, could still be—and was very drastically—amended. The sponsoring universities were now, after all their hesitancies and misgivings, taking the whole matter very seriously and doing all they could to help.

A further meeting took place in Birmingham under Pascal's chairmanship on *15 February 1949*.[1] This proved to be the real turning point. After a morning of private discussion, the universities' representatives were joined by Lindsay, Miss Malbon, Dr W. A. Jenkins (the recently appointed Registrar), and the Town Clerks and Directors of Education for Stoke, Burton and the County Council. It was now not only the Charter which was examined, but revised proposals for the curriculum; and it was evident that Lindsay and his colleagues cordially welcomed the assistance they were being afforded. By nightfall all but the final hurdles had been surmounted and before leaving for home the representatives of the three universities agreed amongst themselves that they would: 'recommend to their appropriate governing bodies that those bodies should accept the obligations of sponsorship and proceed to the appointment of sponsors.'

What now ensued can be briefly told. By an odd quirk of timing it was first at Manchester, where opinion had been so markedly unfavourable, that the Senate approved the recommendation for sponsoring on 10 March 1949; on 9 May, the Hebdomadal Council at Oxford approved the enabling Decree to go to Congregation; and finally the Senate at Birmingham agreed on 18 May. The sponsors' representatives were appointed and held their first meeting with Lindsay and some others at Stoke on 23 July 1949.[2]

[1] Lindsay at this time was just recuperating after an operation for appendicitis.
[2] Until professors were appointed and a Senate was in being, it was not possible for there to be a properly constituted Academic Council (see p. 80); but there was urgent business to be done somehow; and it is interesting to note that at this informal meeting in July 1949, a wide range of topics came up for discussion and decision: the first year course and examination, the

Oxford was represented by *Sir Henry Clay*, the Warden of Nuffield College, who at one time had conducted tutorial classes in the Potteries and had held Chairs of Economics in Manchester; and *Miss Lucy Sutherland*, Principal of Lady Margaret Hall and formerly tutor in history at Somerville College. From Manchester there were *H. B. Charlton*, head of the department of English literature and recently Chairman of the Joint Matriculation Board; and *Graham Cannon*, Professor of Zoology and Pro-Vice-Chancellor—two of the outstanding members of the Senate, forthright in their opinions and vigorous in their expressions whether of assent or dissent. The representatives of Birmingham were *J. G. Smith*, Professor of Finance and something of a 'king-maker' in his own university; and *L. J. Russell*, Professor of Philosophy. However difficult it had been to secure the assent of the sponsoring universities, there could be no doubt that those universities were now determined to give all the help they could by appointing as their representatives persons of distinction who carried great weight within their own institutions and outside.[1]

On 30 June 1949, the Charter was approved by the King in Council and was formally sealed on 11 August. The Earl of Harrowby was named therein as the first President of the College and Lord Lindsay of Birker as the first Principal. At long last the University College of North Staffordshire had come into existence.

THE 1949 CHARTER AND STATUTES

Since the awarding of degrees is a privilege deriving from the Royal Prerogative, it was necessary for the promoters of the proposed new College to submit to the Privy Council a Petition

advisability of a further three years of study, the subjects in which professors and heads of departments were to be appointed, the terms of such appointments and the information on policy which should be supplied to candidates.

1 There seems to have been no kind of consultation by the universities concerned in regard to the way in which subjects were represented by the sponsor members of the Academic Council. Consequently Professor Cannon was the only one who could advise expertly on the science side. This weakness, particularly in the physical sciences, was remedied in 1953 when Professor M. Stacey (chemistry) succeeded Professor Russell as a representative of Birmingham. When new universities were founded in the 1960s this problem of balance of subjects on advisory committees was solved in a different way (see pp. 287–8).

and a draft of a Charter and Statutes. The earlier university colleges which could not award degrees had in general been governed either by the terms of a Trust Deed or by Articles of Association registered with the Board of Trade. For Keele there was no clear precedent and the task of drafting a new type of constitution with provision for sponsoring was not an easy one. The professional members of the Exploratory Committee, Town Clerks and Directors of Education, had no direct experience of what was needed for an institution of university rank; and the constitutional arrangements at Oxford were so different from those which had by now proved suitable elsewhere, that Lindsay himself was very willing in the later stages of drafting to accept all the help he could get from the sponsoring universities. The final drafting, however, was largely the work of Mr Harry Taylor, Town Clerk of Stoke-on-Trent, to whose interest and wisdom the College continued to be greatly indebted.

The early proposals for a Charter need not delay us long; but there are a few points of interest to be mentioned. The broad pattern was to be the structure familiar in civic universities and university colleges: a Court as the supreme governing body, a Council as the executive authority, and a Senate for academic affairs. But, in addition to provision for an Academic Council, there were two matters in which a marked divergence from common practice was suggested without any comment on their novelty or argument in their favour; and in both of them we may see the influence of the academically autonomous and democratic element in the organisation of the University of Oxford. First, it was proposed that 'a majority of the Council should consist of academically qualified persons'—and whatever precisely the last three words may have been taken to mean, they would leave small place on the Council for representatives of local authorities.[1] Secondly, Senate would consist not solely of professors but would include 'Readers, senior lecturers and representatives of the junior staff'—an idea well in advance of the times.

The greatest interest of the Charter and Statutes lies of course in the powers they confer on the *Academic Council* through which the sponsoring universities were enabled to

[1] This proposal was already in the 'Oxford' document discussed with UGC members on 25 July 1946 (see p. 54).

exert their influence. The Charter provides that the approval of the Academic Council is required for:

(a) the curriculum and organisation of studies for the Bachelor of Arts degree and other studies;
(b) the nominations for the appointments of the Principal (other than the first Principal), the Professors and the Senior Lecturers;
(c) the nominations for the appointment of external examiners.

That these three requirements and no others should be embodied in the Charter itself emphasises their basic importance: the Academic Council is to have the effective voice in what is to be taught, who is to teach it, and who is to assess the standard of students' achievement.

It is the Statutes which define the composition of the Academic Council and rehearse their powers in detail. It is to consist of:

(a) The Principal.
(b) Six members to be appointed as under: (i) two by the University of Oxford, (ii) two by the University of Birmingham, (iii) two by the University of Manchester.
(c) Three members of the Senate appointed by the Senate.
(d) One member of the permanent teaching staff who is not a Professor or Head of a Department, appointed by such staff as prescribed by Ordinance.

The important points to notice are: the representatives of the sponsoring universities are in a majority; only the Principal is a member *ex officio*;[1] neither the Court nor the College Council has any say in the appointments under (c) and (d); and provision is made for the views of non-senatorial staff to be heard as of right and the staff concerned is entirely free in selecting its representative.

The powers and duties of the Academic Council are to be:
1. To approve or initiate proposals for the whole curriculum and courses for the Bachelor of Arts Degree and other

[1] As late as April 1949 this point was under discussion. The Vice-Principal had also been included *ex officio*; but both Lindsay and the UGC were strongly in favour of the structure finally adopted.

studies and to make representations with regard to new posts and new departments.
2. To initiate discussions or approve proposals on academic administration, the establishment and functions of Faculties, Boards of Studies, or other academic bodies of the College.
3. To approve nominations for the appointment of the Principal (other than the first Principal), the Vice-Principal, Professors, Readers, Senior Lecturers, Registrar (other than the first Registrar) and Librarian of the College.
4. To approve nominations for the appointment of External Examiners.
5. To receive and consider an Annual Report from the External Examiners on the standards reached in the degree examinations and to forward such report with their observations to the Council of the College.
6. To consider the Annual Report of the Principal and to forward it with such comment as they think fit to the Council and to the Sponsoring Universities.
7. To appoint three representatives of the Sponsoring Universities to be members of the (College) Council.

If these powers are compared with those suggested in the Memorandum of 11 November 1946 and the addition made in the spring of 1947,[1] it will be realised how much thought had been devoted to making the Academic Council a really effective body with powers not only of approval and report but of initiation also. If the UGC and the other universities were looking for safeguards of academic standards, they were there in full measure so far as a written constitution could guarantee them; everything would depend on the rigour with which the Academic Council exercised its powers.

The other statutory bodies whose composition and powers are prescribed by the Charter and Statutes are the Court, the Council and the Senate. The *Court* requires no special comment. Like similar bodies elsewhere, it is the supreme governing body, consists of some 200 persons representing a wide range of public bodies, together with members of Council and Senate, and normally conducts its main business of receiving reports and appointing certain officers of the College at a single Annual

[1] See pp. 69–71.

Meeting. What the composition of the *Council* should be was a topic about which the sponsoring universities had strong and prevailing opinions, fearing as they did that too large a proportion of local authority representatives could involve the College in political dissensions and, by unwise financial pressure, could thwart or skew its academic policy. It was eventually agreed that the Council of thirty-three members should comprise: six *ex officio* members (including the Principal), six appointed by the Court, ten local authority representatives (four from Stoke, four from the County, two from Burton), five appointed by the Senate, one non-senatorial representative of the staff, one from the WEA, one from the Extra-Mural Delegacy at Oxford, and three from the sponsoring universities. In practice this meant that one could count on ten members who were clearly academic, a proportion which was markedly more liberal than at that time would be found elsewhere—though far from the suggestion made in the Memorandum of 11 November 1946. The inclusion of the WEA and the Oxford Delegacy among the appointing bodies gratifyingly preserved the links with the adult education movement.

As the executive authority within the College, the Council (in addition to exercising financial control) made appointments, but those of an academic nature had to be on the recommendation of the Senate and with the approval of the Academic Council. Any proposals for Statutes drafted by the Council had to be discussed by the Senate and all Ordinances affecting academic affairs had to be recommended by the Senate. These checks precluded authoritarian actions by the Council. On the other hand, collective senatorial folly could be stopped by a proviso which appears in most similar Charters to the effect that the Council could 'review amend refer back or disallow any act of the Senate required under these Statutes to be reported to the Council'; and there was also the quite usual power of the Council to 'review the instruction and teaching of the College'—whatever in practical terms that might be asserted to mean.

The composition of the *Senate* was entirely academic: the Principal, the professors, independent heads of departments, the Librarian and 'at least two representatives' of the non-senatorial teaching staff appointed on a yearly tenure. Its main powers were to control the admission of students, regulate courses of study and examinations, and promote research and appoint internal examiners. Its organisation of the curriculum, however, and its recommendations for external examiners were subject to the approval of the Academic Council. In these respects the Senate had less freedom than the Senate of a full university, but was much less hampered in working out its own schemes of academic development than a college bound by the requirements of the London external degree.

There are three matters in which the Charter and Statutes are oddly nonchalant. First there are no separate statutory provisions for the composition or functions of Faculties or Boards of Studies; they are mentioned only as bodies which it is within the powers of the Senate and the Academic Council to establish. Secondly, the Students' Union is not embodied in the constitutional instruments except in so far as one representative has a seat on the Court and a short Statute states that Ordinances shall prescribe the constitution, functions and privileges of such a Union. Thirdly, the graduates of the College are ignored except that an otherwise undefined Association of Past Students has a right to elect a single representative to the Court. This was in marked contrast to the civic universities where a formally established body of graduates called Convocation[1] elects a large number of members to the Court and some to the Council as well; and in London and Manchester this body enjoys even wider privileges and powers. The 1962 Charter, however, gave to the Association rights of representation similar to those accorded elsewhere—a sensible change, since graduates have a clear interest in the welfare of the institution and particularly in the maintenance of the standard of the degrees which they have been awarded.[2]

[1] Historically the according of certain rights to graduates is derived from the Oxford and Cambridge constitutions. Students of university colleges who took external degrees were eligible for membership of the Convocation of the University of London. Not least among the privileges of members of a Convocation was the right to a parliamentary vote in university constituencies until they were abolished by the Representation of the People Act of 1948.

[2] Two special provisions were made in the Statutes for an interim period: (a) in regard to procedure for academic appointments prior to the first Academic Session; and (b) to confer power on the Principal prior to the first session and for three months thereafter 'to take such action as he thinks fit to bring the College into existence and to carry on its activities'. Despite some minor misunderstandings and hurt feelings, these arrangements worked well.

Coat of Arms

The design of a coat of arms for the College was in the main the work of Mr J. H. P. Oxspring, Director of Education for Stafford County. In non-technical language the main features of the shield are: a chevron with an open book on it to indicate a place of learning; in the lower part, a scythe taken from the arms of the Sneyd family of Keele; and in the upper part a Staffordshire knot, flanked on the left by the fleur-de-lys of Burton-on-Trent and on the right by the fret of Stoke-on-Trent. For the crest, above the shield and helmet, there is a representation of Rodin's 'Le Penseur'. The motto on the scroll beneath the shield caused some controversy. The bilingual pun[1] *qu'ils apprennent*, 'let them learn' was finally rejected in favour of the Sneyd motto 'Thanke God for All'.

THE SITE

The problem of finding a home for the College was not an easy one to solve at a time when there could be no hope of erecting new permanent buildings for academic purposes; the best that could be achieved would be to adapt something already in existence. The first proposal was to acquire Meaford Hall and its seventy-three acres of land at Stone, mid-way between Stoke and Stafford; and it was this solution which was put forward in the Memorandum of 11 November 1946, for the consideration of the UGC. The Hall could accommodate fifty residential students in single study-bedrooms, together with common rooms and some teaching rooms, and other temporary buildings could be constructed in the grounds. By the summer of 1947, however, negotiations for this property had fallen through, the temporary transfer of a Corporation site at Hanchurch intended for a sanatorium was considered and dismissed and the military camp at Trentham Park which might have been suitable was acquired by the National Coal Board before the Exploratory Committee could get far with their own negotiations for it. By September 1947 the one remaining possibility was Keele Hall, just outside the boundary of Newcastle-under-Lyme.

1 The neatest motto of this kind is *Lampada ferens*, 'bearing the torch (of learning)', which Hull adopted with reference to their benefactor T. R. Ferens.

After protracted negotiations with the owner, Colonel Ralph Sneyd (1863–1949), and with a number of Government departments, a contract was signed in April 1949 by the Stoke Corporation for the purchase of the Hall itself, the Clock House and Lodges with 154 acres of land at a cost of £32,675 and the conveyance to the College was completed in May 1950.

Keele Hall itself was built about 1580 by Ralph Sneyd[1] whose family resided there for well over three centuries. The west front was added in the early nineteenth century, a fire destroyed the west wing in 1835 and the whole was extensively reconstructed in the 1850s. The Clock House near the Hall (now the official home of the Vice-Chancellor) was built in the 1830s to provide stables and residences for the coachman and head-gardener. At the height of its glory, the Hall was handsomely panelled and sumptuously furnished; its well laid out ground and gardens with vineries and peach and orchid houses were famed afar. But as the fortunes of the family declined at the beginning of this century, it was rented to various tenants including the Grand Duke Michael of Russia, and from the early 1930s was left unoccupied. At the outbreak of World War II it was requisitioned for the training of British troops, then for the American forces, and after being a transit camp, it was finally occupied as a Polish Army camp.

At the time the College obtained possession, it was a picture of the utmost desolation and disrepair.[2] On three sides the land slopes determinedly downwards towards Keele Hall and the lakes beyond. This configuration shelters the Hall from the north and north-easterly winds but creates unrelenting problems of drainage. More than seven years of occupation by the military had churned the estate, where it was not overgrown by untended shrubbery, into a vast expanse of mud. The place was littered too with Nissen huts made of corrugated iron for the troops and wooden huts on brick foundations (a few of which are still in use in 1971) for the non-commissioned officers. On the north side fronting the Newcastle road there was—and still is—a forbidding eight-foot stone wall, a mile or so in length, outside of which one had in those days of uncertain transport to trudge towards civilisation. This was the place where a College was to

1 See J. M. Kolbert, *The Sneyds and Keele Hall*, 1967.

2 The classic descriptions of the scene are to be found in W. B. Gallie's *A New University*.

begin; it required nerves of steel, patience and persistence beyond compare and blind and unshakeable optimism in the future to face such a prospect. The staff who came in early 1950 and the students who enrolled in October were built in heroic mould—and none was more heroic than the septuagenarian Lord Lindsay, recently Master of Balliol.

From the spring of 1949, a 'Keele Hall sub-committee', under the chairmanship of Horwood and with the assistance of Mr J. R. Piggott, the City Architect of Stoke-on-Trent, faced the task of subduing chaos into some sort of order. Mechanical equipment coped with the all-pervading mud and the encroaching brambles; building contractors refurbished the Hall and the huts; the Principal and the recently-appointed Registrar allocated the space in the Hall for offices, a library and classrooms,[1] and various huts were reconditioned for student residences, a refectory and common rooms. For a time from the summer of 1949 Lord Lindsay resided in the Lodge nearest to Keele village until the Clock House was ready for him at the end of the year. It was possible to put in train permanent living accommodation for the academic staff only through the generosity of the Local Authorities who with the agreement of the Ministry of Health surrendered to the College twenty-one of their precious licences for the building of houses.[2] It was no paradise to which the first students came: that they could be found places at all to eat and sleep and study was in itself a triumph.

THE STAFF

One of the matters which had seriously exercised the minds of the UGC members, the VCs' Committee and the sponsoring universities when they were considering the 'Stoke Proposals' was the feasibility of obtaining suitably qualified academic staff for a new College.[3] During the war there had been a

[1] The departments of chemistry and physics, for example, each began its work in a large bedroom of Keele Hall. Until the Hall was available, the City of Stoke provided office accommodation for the College administration.

[2] Stoke provided fifteen licences, the Borough of Newcastle five, and the Newcastle Rural District Council one. Twelve houses of 2,000 sq. ft. each and nine of 1,500 were erected, but pending the completion of some of them and to provide additional accommodation some army huts also were converted into bungalows.

[3] H. J. Perkin, *New Universities in the United Kingdom*, says Keele made 'an

continuous drain on the staff of existing universities. Many had joined the armed forces and almost as many had been taken into the service of various Government Departments. Those who remained within the universities could just about cope with the depleted student numbers. But when peace was restored, there was a large intake of ex-service students. Furthermore, for six years very few promising young people had been receiving the kind of postgraduate training which would fit them for posts in universities. As Stopford told Lindsay on 10 June 1947, it would be three years at the very least before any improvement in the situation could be expected; and even if everything else went favourably, it would be impossible to open the College in 1948 as had at first been hoped. The protracted negotiations with the UGC and particularly with the sponsoring universities were therefore not wholly to the disadvantage of the College.

The two first appointments to be made after the UGC had given its general approval to the scheme and Lindsay had accepted the Principalship, were those of the Registrar, *Dr W. A. Jenkins*[1] who assumed office on 1 January 1949, and the Librarian, *Mr S. O. Stewart*,[2] who took up his duties on 1 October 1949. As soon as the Charter and Statutes were approved in June 1949, steps could be taken to make appointments to the academic staff.[3] By this time it had been agreed

avoidable mistake' in paying its professors salaries £200 lower than the basic rate elsewhere. There is a misunderstanding here. In June 1949 the UGC approved a range of professorial salaries of £1,600 to £2,500. To allow for a 'spread' between these limits each university was given a separately calculated sum for supplementations above the basic £1,600. Keele at first was given no supplemental sum and had to make all appointments at the minimum of the range.

1 W. A. Jenkins, C.I.E., D.Sc., LL.D., a graduate of Sheffield, had spent many years in the Indian Educational Service. In 1952 he transferred from the office of Registrar to become Director of Studies and resigned in 1953 to become Vice-Chancellor of the University of Dacca. He died in 1958.

2 Mr Stewart, a graduate of Glasgow, had been Deputy Librarian at the University of Liverpool.

3 All the applications for the first group of Chairs vanished and a further advertisement had to be issued asking applicants to re-apply. Ribald guffaws rippled through College common-rooms: 'that new place at Stoke is odd anyway!' Who achieved the feat of losing so much paper was never ascertained; was it the Registrar, the Principal, or a visiting grandchild addicted to the making of paper boats?

There was trouble too about the selection committees. The Statutes contained special provisions for appointments made prior to the first academic session; they were to be made by the Principal (not the Council) on the recommendation of a committee consisting of (a) The Principal, (b) that there should be thirteen Chairs and two readerships; applications for these posts were invited in the summer and early autumn of 1949; a sufficient muster of professors was available to enable the first meeting of the Senate to be held on 12 February 1950—a Sunday; and from then onwards, until the College opened in October, Lindsay and his academic colleagues gathered, sometimes for whole weekends, to discuss and decide upon the detailed content of the first year course and to map out a general plan for the later years of the curriculum.

It was these first fifteen members of the Senate who under the leadership of Lord Lindsay shouldered the task of organising the academic work of the College and conducting its teaching; and it is fitting that their names should here be recorded. In the order in which they appeared in the first Prospectus of the College, they were as follows:

J. J. Lawlor, Professor of English; graduate and senior demy of Magdalen College, Oxford; lecturer in English at Brasenose and Trinity Colleges, Oxford, and university lecturer in English.

W. B. Gallie, Professor of Philosophy; graduate of Balliol College, Oxford; senior lecturer at Swansea; left Keele for a Chair at Belfast in 1954; Professor of Political Science, Cambridge since 1967.

A. E. Teale, Professor of Moral and Political Philosophy; graduate of Leeds and Oxford (B. Litt.); research student at Balliol, then lecturer in Philosophy at Manchester; retired in 1968.

J. W. Blake, Professor of History; graduate of King's College, London; senior lecturer at Belfast; official War Historian to the Government of Northern Ireland; Acting Principal at Keele,

three representatives of the University Committee of North Staffordshire, and (c) two representatives nominated by each of the Vice-Chancellors of the sponsoring universities (who thus had a majority voice). The 'sponsoring' members were chosen variously according to the subject of the particular Chair concerned and did not necessarily have any knowledge of the background of Keele's foundation. Since there had to be one meeting for drawing up a short-list and another for interviewing candidates, and there were fifteen senior posts to be filled in a short time, it was not easy to arrange dates convenient for everybody. Some selectors took umbrage at what they considered to be Lindsay's high-handed and autocratic procedures; and at one time some even suggested that Oxford should withdraw from sponsorship since (it was said) the University was being used only to give a spurious prestige to the College. All of Lindsay's diplomacy was required to soothe the hurt feelings.

1954–6; left Keele in 1964 to be Vice-Chancellor of the University of Botswana, Lesotho and Swaziland.

W. W. Chambers, Professor of Modern Languages; graduate of Glasgow, Paris and Munich; lecturer in German at Leeds; left Keele for the Chair of German at Glasgow in 1954.

B. R. Williams, Professor of Economics; graduate of Melbourne; lecturer at Adelaide and Belfast; left Keele for a Chair at Manchester in 1959; Vice-Chancellor of Sydney from 1967.

S. E. Finer, Professor of Political Institutions; graduate of Trinity College, Oxford; lecturer and research fellow of Balliol; left Keele for a Chair at Manchester in 1966.

S. H. Beaver, Professor of Geography; graduate of University College, London; reader at London School of Economics.

W. A. C. Stewart, Professor of Education; graduate of University College, London; schoolmaster, assistant lecturer at Nottingham, lecturer at Cardiff; Acting Principal at Keele, 1960–1, and Vice-Chancellor since 1967.

I. N. Sneddon, Professor of Mathematics; graduate of Glasgow and Trinity College, Cambridge; lecturer at Glasgow; left Keele for a Chair at Glasgow in 1956.

F. A. Vick, Professor of Physics; graduate of Birmingham; lecturer at University College, London and senior lecturer at Manchester; Acting Principal at Keele, 1952–3; left Keele in 1959 for Atomic Energy Research Establishment (Director from 1960); Vice-Chancellor of Belfast from 1966.

H. D. Springhall, Professor of Chemistry; graduate of Lincoln College, Oxford; senior demy of Magdalen College, Oxford, Commonwealth fellow, senior lecturer at Manchester.

A. R. Gemmell, Professor of Biology; graduate of Glasgow; Commonwealth Fellow; lecturer at Glasgow and Manchester.

F. W. Cope, reader in Geology; graduate of Manchester; principal geologist at Geological Survey; Professor at Keele from 1953.

J. M. T. Charlton, reader in Classics; graduate of Manchester and St John's College, Cambridge; lecturer at Reading; Professor at Keele from 1953.[1]

Of these fifteen men not a single one had reached his fiftieth

[1] In addition, R. B. Henderson was appointed as lecturer in Religious Knowledge, Miss Mary H. Wilson as Warden of Women's Residential Hall, and R. N. Rayne as Warden of Men's Residential Hall.

birthday and twelve of them were under forty; the two youngest were thirty-one. Lindsay, it is said, did not want the new educational experiment to be thwarted by old men set in their ways:[1] there was no patent ossification in this group. They had taken their first degrees at a number of different universities: four at Oxford (of whom only one had been an undergraduate at Balliol), three at Glasgow, three at London, two at Manchester, and one at each of Leeds, Birmingham and Melbourne; Teale had gone on to Oxford, Sneddon and Charlton to Cambridge, and Springall and Gemmell to the USA. Their collective teaching experience included not only Oxford but London, Glasgow, Belfast, four civic universities and two colleges in Wales. In departmental administration and the formulation of academic policy most of them had not yet had much responsibility: one had been a reader and four had been senior lecturers. Between 12 February 1950, when the infant Senate first met and the following October when the students arrived was all too short a time. Mostly unknown to each other, only a few of them previously acquainted with Lindsay, the majority of them still rather uncertain about what it was, apart from a broadening curriculum, that Keele was intended to achieve, they and their families came to a bleak and uninviting campus to accomplish what they could with their eagerness and energy and the stimulus of an educational experiment. And while they were fashioning their courses, it was Lindsay who bit by bit inspired them—or most of them—with his own sense of educational purpose, expounded his intuitions about the way things should go, and discussed with them individually and as a group the details of their own proposals. It was in those eight months, more than at any other time, that Lindsay stood forth as the founder of the College.[2]

A NOTE ON FINANCE

How the College was to be financed was a matter which the promoters of the scheme had in mind at an early stage in their

[1] In October 1949, however, he had suggested to the Academic Council the possible appointment of distinguished professors who had retired under the normal age limit from other universities and mentioned an immediate possibility for the social science department. Nothing further was heard of this idea.

[2] In benign moments he was liable to exhort the Senate as 'my children'.

negotiations. At the first meeting with Moberly and Tawney on 27 March 1946, both Dr Stross and J. F. Carr had said that they thought the City of Stoke would accept responsibility for finding £300,000 or £400,000 for buildings. Rather more precise proposals were contained in one of the memoranda discussed with members of the UGC on 25 July 1946: Stoke should raise a loan for capital costs of not less than £250,000 apportioned between the three local authorities concerned;[1] running costs should be met from students' fees, local revenue, and grants from the Ministry of Education for teacher-training, plus help from the UGC itself.

The Exploratory Committee's important Memorandum of 11 November 1946, invited the guidance of the UGC under three heads: (a) capital costs for buildings, (b) capital for endowment, (c) maintenance and running costs. At this time it was expected that the College would open in 1948 with 200 students and that the number would rise to 500 or 600 by October 1950. Tuition and examination fees would bring in £10,500 in 1948–9, £20,500 in 1949–50, and £31,500 in 1950–1; the expenditure which could be foreseen for those years was £40,120, £50,000 and £61,500; in each year, therefore, there would be a gap of between £29,500 and £30,000 to be made good by Local Authority and UGC grants. Moberly, quite naturally in the circumstances, made no kind of precise promise about the sort of amounts the UGC might contribute: there was a long way to go before the College became a reality.

Nothing of significance on the financial side now happened until April 1948, when the three Local Authorities formally agreed to participate, as they had done previously in adult education affairs, on the basis of 45 per cent from Stoke-on-Trent, 45 per cent from the Staffordshire County and 10 per cent from Burton-on-Trent; and part of the agreement was that these proportions should apply not only to financial responsibility but also to representation on committees and governing bodies[2]

[1] Newcastle-under-Lyme, being a Municipal (not County) Borough and therefore not a Local Education Authority, could have no part at this or any later stage in the financial arrangements. Their Education Officer was a co-opted member of the Exploratory Committee but he seems to have held only a watching brief and had no share in the work of the important sub-committees or conferences or delegations.

[2] About this time the membership of the Exploratory Committee was enlarged to make this balance of representation possible.

and to the sharing of educational facilities.[1] In December 1948, a sub-committee was appointed to prepare estimates which were sent to the UGC early in 1949 and formed the basis for many technical discussions with officials of the UGC in the months that followed. The most interesting and important feature of these estimates is that it was now assumed that the UGC would bear the whole cost of purchasing and renovating Keele Hall, adapting other structures on the site, and providing books for the library and scientific and other equipment; no further mention was made of the raising of a loan for such purposes by the City of Stoke. Capital expenditure arising before 31 July 1949, was estimated as £100,000 and for the ensuing twelve months as £233,000; for recurrent purposes the estimate for the period up to 31 July 1949, was put at £5,000 and for the next twelve months at £20,000. The provision of residential accommodation for members of the staff was quite outside the functions of the UGC and the building of houses and the supplementary conversion of huts was eventually financed by a direct loan from the Treasury which was to be repaid over the years from the rents received by the College.[2]

It would be tedious, however, to follow in detail all the negotiations which took place. In 1947 the UGC had resumed its usual practice of making block grants to universities for recurrent purposes to cover a whole quinquennium and so special arrangements had to be made for Keele until the next quinquennium began in August 1952. The Local Authorities for their part agreed to make total annual grants in the agreed proportions, starting at £2,000 for 1948–9 rising to £8,000 for 1949–50 and £16,000 for 1950–1, and then by an additional £4,000 a year up to a maximum of £32,000;[3] the one proviso was that the grant for any one year should not exceed 25 per cent of the College expenditure. How the finances of the College worked out can be judged from Table 1 which summarises the major items from 1949 to the end of the 1947–52 quinquennium.

[1] This proviso assumes that most students would be coming from North Staffordshire.

[2] An application was made in July 1949 for a loan of £62,625 for houses; and in October 1949 for £20,000 for conversion of huts for bungalows, plus a further £52,500 over the next three years for additional houses.

[3] At the request of the College, the Local Authorities in fact stepped up their grant for 1950–1 to £20,000 which became the base line for the annual £4,000 increments.

Table 1 Income and expenditure 1949–50 to 1951–2[a]

	1949–50	*1950–1*	*1951–2*
Capital expenditure (£)			
UGC grant	54,481	235,464	378,080
Recurrent account (£)			
UGC grant	25,500	48,500	65,000
Local Authority grants	6,058	20,000	24,000
Fees, etc.	271	7,151	13,479
Total income	31,829	75,651	102,479
Expenditure	24,502	77,079	112,626
Surplus	7,327	—	—
Deficit	—	1,428	10,147

[a] The figures for the 1949–50 Recurrent Account include (a) payments of £5,500 from the UGC and £895 from Local Authorities and (b) disbursements of £3,580 for salaries and incidentals, all made prior to the granting of the Charter in August 1949.

In his interim Report for the session 1948–9, the Treasurer of the College[1] presented estimates also for the two following years and made some significant comments.

> The financial picture which I have presented to you shows a balance in the recurring accounts for 1949–50 to be carried forward to next year, the probable exhaustion of that balance by the end of 1950–51, and the necessity for economical and controlled expenditure in 1951–52 if we are to end that session without a deficit. Our estimates do not include any item for emergencies, and while in a well established institution it may be possible to foresee and provide for all likely demands, it is very desirable that particularly during our first years we should have a reasonably large balance upon which we can draw for unforeseen but necessary expenditure. That is not likely to be the case for some time to come, and indeed in 1951–52 the amount available for such an essential development as the appointment of additional staff to cope with the additional work consequent upon a further year's

[1] Mr A. P. Walker, City Treasurer of Stoke-on-Trent. As Treasurer of the College and University he gave notable service until 1968.

> intake of students is very small.[1] Whether the minimum requirements consistent with academic efficiency can be met has still to be worked out, but it is clear that a considerably greater increased recurring income will be required from 1951–52 onwards if the College work is to develop according to its agreed plans.

The University College of North Staffordshire had been safely launched; the hard realities of academic life in the 1950s had now to be faced.

[1] A year later in his Report for 1949–50 Mr Walker remarked: 'The appointment of the additional staff—to meet the needs of a further year's intake of students—has been kept to an absolute minimum.' An Appeals Committee was set up early in 1950.

Four

From Ceramics to Foundation Year[1]

THE 'LOCAL' CONCEPT

The way in which the Keele curriculum took shape is a topic of unusual interest because this is the first instance in Britain of an entire university scheme of study being deliberately formulated on the basis of a consciously accepted set of educational principles. It would be a mistake, however, to suppose that these educational ideas were the result of any sudden flash of insight into the solution of a single clearly defined problem. The Keele programme was, so to speak, the residual precipitate of discussions spread over several years.

In broad terms the history of the fashioning of the Keele programme of studies can be regarded as a case study of the progress from a concept of a local college providing higher education for young people of the area and concentrating its attention very markedly on the manufacturing and mercantile needs of the area, towards a wider vision of what a college should aim to do. In the narrative which follows we can trace the history of a whole complex of ideas and proposals, some of which were not long persisted in, while others emerged at a relatively late stage and proved to be of enduring significance. We can, for example, trace the fate of ceramics, mining and engineering; the prospect of a medical school; the fluctuating place of adult education and of social studies; the attention paid to the training of teachers and social workers; the range of subjects to be offered; the question of pass and honours degrees; and, above all, the hammering out of the Foundation

[1] For this chapter, see: G. Malbon, 'Adult education in North Staffordshire and the foundation of the University College of Keele', *Rewley House Papers*, III, iii, 1954–5, pp. 34–49; A. E. Teale, 'The origin of the Keele experiment', *N. Staffs, J. of Field Studies*, Vol. I, 1961, pp. 101–14; R. A. Lowe, 'Determinants of a university's curriculum', *Br. J. of Educational Studies*, Vol. XVII, No. 1, 1969, pp. 41–53.

Year. Several stages in the development of ideas about a college and its curriculum are clearly discernible. At first the Exploratory Committee paddled its own canoe; discussions with the UGC, the Ministry of Education and the sponsoring universities led to broader schemes which were more acceptable; the informal Academic Council evolved a still firmer framework; and finally the Senate itself filled in the practical details.

Local pride and emulation of Manchester and Birmingham played some part in the earliest proposals for a College in the Potteries; but it was the satisfying of local needs which was the dominant note. F. E. Kitchener's plea for a College in 1890[1] did not look further than Chairs of Chemistry and Engineering. The Hanley Committee of Enquiry in 1899,[2] while advocating scientific instruction related to local industries and 'economic teaching of the first order', went further in envisaging also a Day Training Department for elementary school teachers, other subjects which would add to 'general culture', and a medical faculty. A. W. Brown's 1902 scheme[3] included a mining department, a school of pottery and a pupil-teacher centre—all of local importance; he did not repeat the proposal for a medical school but he advanced the idea of a university extension department. With the establishment of the Central School of Sciences and Technology at Stoke in 1914, some part of the needs of industry and commerce was satisfied; but already in 1911 E. S. Cartwright[4] was directing attention to a 'working men's college' for the teaching of humane non-vocational subjects; this was the pure gospel of the adult education movement. The abortive proposal made in 1919 that a University College would be a fitting war memorial[5] had as its basis an expansion of the school of science and technology by the addition of an arts side which would put its emphasis on non-vocational adult education and the 'development of an enlightened and instructed citizenship'. At the time, this was about the only way in which a College could have been set on its feet.

Lindsay's first public reference to a College,[6] made in 1925, was much closer to Cartwright's idea than to the 1919 war memorial scheme. The phrase he used was 'a people's university' which would be 'the core of adult education work'. It would,

[1] See p. 26. [2] See p. 27. [3] See p. 29.
[4] See p. 31. [5] See p. 32. [6] See p. 33.

Plate 1 Lord Lindsay of Birker, first Principal of the University College of North Staffordshire (1949–52)
(*from a painting by Lawrence Gowing*)

W. A. C. Stewart F. A. Vick J. W. Blake A. R. Gemmell S. H. Beaver
S. E. Finer B. R. Williams A. E. Teale H. D. Springall S. O. Stewart (*Librarian*)
J. J. Lawlor W. W. Chambers W. B. Gallie
Miss Bailey (*Registrar's Secretary*) I. N. Sneddon W. A. Jenkins (*Registrar*)
Lord Lindsay H. G. Cannon (*Academic Council*) Mrs Morton (*Principal's Secretary*) Mrs Cannon

Plate 2 The Professors of the University College (February 1950)

Plate 3a At the Official Opening of the College (17 April 1951)
The Reverend Thomas Horwood H.M. Queen Elizabeth Lord Lindsay

Plate 3b Keele Hall from the north-west

Plate 4a Aerial view of the campus (1967)

Plate 4b The Senior Common Room, Keele Hall (1971)

of course, be unfair to subject to critical analysis the *obiter dicta* uttered by a speaker on a somewhat emotional occasion such as the first meeting of the North Staffordshire Joint Advisory Committee presumably was; Lindsay's purpose clearly was to inspire his hearers to further efforts; he was not there and then defining the goal with any precision. But what is significant is that at this early date he pointed out that the recently chartered universities had all been of one kind: 'why should they not in North Staffordshire say they were going to start something new.' The urge to experiment was already there.

Between 1925 and 1945, however, public references to the idea of a University College once more reverted to the particular needs of the area.[1] Pottery and mining were still in the forefront, though Kitchener's engineering was lost sight of; a medical school re-appeared in the proposals; and there was a general assumption that the students of the College would be drawn from its immediate neighbourhood.

Thus, for over half a century there had been sporadic and conflicting proposals for a College in the Potteries. But it was only in 1946 that those who were interested in a North Staffordshire project were really faced with the task of setting down on paper with increasing precision the scope of such a College. In his first informal approach by letter to Moberly on 13 March 1946,[2] Lindsay was feeling his way cautiously with Moberly and not yet attempting to outline the exact functions of the College 'on new lines'; and his readiness to seek advice indicated that, apart from a wish to avoid the London external degree and a hope that Oxford would be interested, his mind was not set in any particular direction. Indeed until the Exploratory Committee had been constituted two months later and he had agreed to become its chairman, he was not deeply involved.

Yet it is evident that already in Stoke itself ideas were being sorted out; for Miss Malbon's memorandum[3] which was discussed with Moberly and Tawney on *27 March 1946*, only a fortnight after the receipt of Lindsay's letter, included some indications of policy which fill out the hints given by Lindsay and doubtless owe much to his advice. London degrees were not as yet wholly excluded, but the College should be concerned 'with other work besides that for external degrees'; there should

[1] See pp. 34–5.
[2] See p. 50.
[3] See p. 51.

be 'specialisation in a few selected faculties';[1] ceramics on the one hand and history, economics and sociological studies on the other, could be distinctive of the College; residence for students was considered important—a new distinctive line of policy; and the Potteries' link with Oxford should be preserved. But it is still the two themes of special local interests and the social subjects of adult education which predominate.

THE FOCUS ON SOCIAL STUDIES

These, however, were only the preliminary skirmishes. It is in a document 'prepared by a representative of Oxford University' and discussed at the next meeting with some UGC members on *25 July 1946*, that the nature and scope of a possible curriculum is first dealt with in some depth:

> The new College should have two main aims. First, it should aim to be a centre and the focus of all higher education in its region. . . . Second, it should aim to provide in at least one field of higher education a degree course of a character and quality such as is provided by no other university and which therefore from the outset would attract not merely local but national and, if possible, international interest.

Apart from providing 'a degree or diploma course directly related to a local industry or industries',

> it is suggested that the College should in the first instance be concerned mainly with Social Studies in a broad sense and not attempt to cover any considerable range of subjects outside this field. As part of this purpose there would, of course, be special departments for the training of teachers and for the training of social workers. The expanding demand for trained social workers of all kinds is a challenge. . . . In this field the new College could . . . excel.

Social studies have thus leaped into prominence; teacher-training has been revived in this newer context and is joined with provision for social workers.

[1] This is an awkward and potentially misleading phrase. The meaning is better expressed in later documents as 'concentration on a few departments of a high standard'.

The main degree structure is then outlined and already we can discern the first hints of some characteristics of the later Keele programme: a preliminary year followed by a three-year course; and the relation of honours and pass degrees.

> The College should in the first instance offer only a single[1] degree course for the B.A. examination. The general subject would be Social Studies. The normal course in Arts would be spread over three years but students would not be permitted to begin upon it until they had passed a sort of Intermediate Examination.[2] The degree examination should be conducted on the basis of awarding Honours in three Classes, and of awarding on the same examination a Pass Degree to students who satisfy the examiners without being thought worthy of Honours.[3]

The Intermediate Examination would comprise: descriptive economics, social institutions, social theory, international relations, British history from 1918, and—as a broadening touch—'science in relation to modern industry'. The main three-year course would consist of:

(a) *Economics:* economic theory; economic organisation; economic and social history from 1789.

(b) *Politics:* social and political theory; social and political institutions—national, local and international; a period in modern history either British or international, neither period to go back beyond 1789.

(c) *Philosophy:* general philosophy from Descartes; moral and political philosophy; social psychology or history of scientific method in relation to philosophy.

One language at 'a reasonable standard' would also be compulsory.

The family likeness of this degree course to the Oxford Modern Greats is unmistakable; nor is that surprising in view of the fact that the document had been prepared by 'a representative of Oxford University'.[4] What is surprising is that

[1] This is not consistent with what is said later in the document about science; but it is significant of the change in emphasis.

[2] This is the first adumbration of the Foundation Year.

[3] The relation of pass and honours degrees was eventually settled in precisely this way; but not until other alternatives had been suggested (see p. 119n.).

[4] A note made by Miss Malbon at the time indicates that G. D. H. Cole and J. S. Fulton were mainly responsible for the document. The statement of

this document, approved by a Stoke committee and submitted on its behalf, lacks any kind of precision about the 'degree or diploma course related to local industry', but what it does say has some interesting undertones of policy.

> Such a course should be based upon a study of the appropriate natural sciences but should include suitable elements of the Arts course (perhaps on lines similar to those of the old general degree course in the Scottish Universities),[1] to prevent the growth of a distorted specialisation.

In the course of the actual discussion of this document on 25 July 1946, Moberly, noting the proposal that science students should do elements of the arts course, pertinently enquired whether arts students, on that analogy, should have opportunities for studying some branch of science; and this seed of an idea did not fall on stony ground.[2]

INCREASING BREADTH

Before the Stoke delegation met the UGC group again on 19 November 1946, they had been to see the Ministry of Education to discuss their proposals for the training of teachers. A memorandum written by Miss Malbon and presented to the Ministry for this meeting on 9 September 1946, set out once again the two now familiar main aims for the College: (a) ceramics based on an advanced study of chemistry, and (b) the social sciences including economic and social history. Honours courses would at first be available only in these two disciplines; but—and this is new—'subsidiary' courses[3] would be available in biology, mathematics and physics; there would also be an attempt to link up the arts and the science courses by the inclusion of

A. E. Teale ('The Origin of the Keele Experiment', 1961) that Lindsay himself hurriedly composed the document between 23 and 25 July cannot be accepted. What he mistakenly regards as the 'original Oxford document' is an unsigned and undated 'background paper', the origin of which neither Lord Fulton, Miss Malbon, T. L. Hodgkin nor Mr Harry Taylor can now recall.

[1] Both Lindsay (Glasgow) and Fulton (St Andrews) had taken Scottish degrees. See also pp. 130–2.

[2] Moberly also referred to the possibility of a department of fine arts which would give special emphasis to design in ceramics and suggested that the college might 'exploit the appreciation of music which was so strong a characteristic of North Staffordshire people'.

[3] The memorandum does not define exactly what is meant by this term.

courses on the history of science and the history of art since the Industrial Revolution; and there would be 'subsidiary' courses also in English literature from the nineteenth century, in languages, and possibly in economic geography. So far as prospective teachers were concerned, a College department of education would be responsible for their training, for the teaching of educational psychology and teaching method, and for the supervision of teaching practice. This course for the Diploma in Education would extend over four years and include the usual three-year degree course,[1] but the final examination for the degree would not be taken until the end of the fourth year concurrently with the professional qualification. The range of the curriculum is by this time perceptibly widening by way of the 'subsidiaries', as indeed it would have to do if the subject content of the degree was to satisfy the reasonable expectation of the Ministry that holders of the Diploma in Education would be equipped with something which was actually needed in the classroom. There can be little doubt that it was the anticipated requirements of the Ministry which first focused the attention of the Stoke Committee on the need to go beyond economics, politics and philosophy.

The printed Memorandum (dated 11 November) which was discussed with members of the UGC on *19 November 1946*, was a revised and considerably expanded version of the earlier document of 25 July. It took into account the views already expressed by UGC members, and by the Ministry of Education. As before, social studies and physical science are put forward as the two things on which, in the first instance, the College should concentrate its activities. As regards social studies, North Staffordshire, as 'a diversified industrial region . . . could provide one of the most fertile fields for research in sociology'; and 'there will continue to be an expanding demand for workers in the field of public and social administration'. The functions of natural science in the College would be two: first, as a basis of research in ceramics; and, second, to provide training for scientific researchers and for teachers of natural science. Several paragraphs of the document deal with the problem of providing an adequate professional equipment for intending

[1] No mention is made in this document of an Intermediate Examination (see p. 99).

teachers, especially in the recently established 'secondary modern' schools, by means of the 'subsidiary' courses; and, as a means towards the broadening of studies—a topic now being emphasised—it is proposed that

> All students of Science should be *required* to take at least one section of their intermediate examination from those prescribed for Social Studies. Conversely, a student who intended to take Social Studies in his final examination should be *required* to take . . . a paper in the history of Science or Science in relation to Modern Industry. At a later date when more adequate laboratory accommodation became available it would be desirable that the student going on to Social Studies should be required to study, and be examined in, one of the three Sciences,[1] including laboratory work.

Two separate degree courses are now set forth, one for social studies, the other for physical sciences; and *each* has its own preliminary Intermediate course. There is as yet no 'common core'.

For the Social Studies Intermediate a student would offer two or three subjects from a list of eight which corresponds to the earlier list of six[2] with the addition of Mathematics and Economic Geography. The changes in the Final (degree) course are more radical and indeed somewhat surprising; for while the economics and politics sections are virtually unchanged, the separate philosophy section disappears and in its place a section entitled sociology makes its bow. This new section is made up by taking over appropriate elements from politics and adding social statistics; but the price paid is that general philosophy from Descartes, moral and political philosophy, and the history of scientific method are all discarded.

The scheme for the degree in physical sciences is bleak in the extreme. The Intermediate course is not tied in with the one proposed for social studies except that one of the five subjects (all presumably compulsory) is Social Theory or Social Institutions; the other four are Physical Chemistry, Physics, Biology, and the History of Science. The Final (degree) course is just the single subject Physical Chemistry.

[1] Within the context of the Memorandum, this means chemistry, physics and biology.

[2] See p. 99.

One language (which might be Latin) is to be compulsory for every degree student and could be offered at any point in his career; a second language also might be substituted for one subject in the list in the Social Studies Intermediate.

MEETING THE UGC DEMANDS

When this memorandum was discussed with some members of the UGC the narrow range of the proposed curriculum came in for severe criticism. It was doubted for example 'whether physical chemistry could be adequately taught if it was dissociated as much as the memorandum proposed from the other branches of natural science'.[1] It could not have been any great surprise, therefore, to the Stoke promoters that at its own full meeting on 3 December 1946, the UGC decided that one of the chief conditions on which its support for the proposals would depend was that the 'basis of studies in Science and Arts be adequately broadened'. The suggested schemes of studies had patently failed to win approval, even though their original scope had already been somewhat enlarged. The question now was: would simple modifications suffice or must the whole plan be recast?[2]

The next important stage in the evolution of the curriculum was the preparation of a document for discussion at a meeting on *10 June 1947*, in Stoke with the Vice-Chancellors of the three universities which had been invited to consider becoming sponsors. It was a critical occasion; for if Stoke had not satisfied the three Vice-Chancellors that they were taking the strictures of the UGC seriously, the whole project would have collapsed without hope of resuscitation. The points on which emphasis is now laid and the details of the courses of study are very different from the Memorandum of 11 November 1946, and the new document shows how much re-thinking had been taking

1 Mr Hughes, Director of Education for Staffordshire, argued in this connexion that 'if wider science subjects were admitted, the proposed University would lose its specialised character. What they had in mind was a wise start, and to widen the science side too much would bring them into line with other University Colleges.'

2 When the *Sentinel* got wind of the UGC resolution it asked Lindsay whether he thought the condition would mean that the scheme would have to be revised, and he blithely replied 'not very much' (18 December 1946)!

place in the intervening six months and how much nearer to the final Keele programme the newer proposals were.

> From the beginning the Committee has been guided by two aims. First, to provide a curriculum which would include a corrective to the prevailing departmentalism of university teaching. Second, to choose for more concentrated attention in the long run subjects particularly suited to the region served by the College (e.g. in the field of Physical Science, Physical Chemistry; in the field of Social Studies, Sociology).
>
> If the available resources of university teachers allowed, the Committee would wish to see established Professorships, Readerships and Lectureships in:
>
> *A. Social Studies:* 1. Sociology. 2. Economic Theory and Institutions. 3. Political Theory and Institutions. 4. Psychology. 5. History and Theory of Morals.
>
> *B. Arts:* 1. History. 2. English Language and Literature. 3. Modern Languages and Literature—French, German, Russian. 4. Philosophy (Methodology). 5. Mathematics.
>
> *C. Physical Sciences:* 1. Chemistry. 2. Physics. 3. Biology. 4. Geology.
>
> One of the main instruments for combating the intellectual isolation and departmentalism of university Faculties and disciplines would be the *general or intermediate course.* It would be a first year course prescribed for all undergraduates, independently of whether the remainder of their time at the College was to be taken exclusively in the Faculty of Science, Arts or Social Studies. In his first year the undergraduate would be required to take one from each of the subjects grouped under Science, Arts, and Social Studies. The treatment of the subjects would be designed to give every undergraduate an insight into the methods and an acquaintance with the main concepts of the chief fields of academic study. The responsibility for organising and integrating the course would naturally fall primarily upon the department of Philosophy.
>
> A *Pass degree* would be awarded to students who had passed the Intermediate Examination (based on the General

Course) and a subsequent Special Examination in two subjects each studied for two years to be taken normally at the end of the third year.

The Committee would wish to be satisfied that in establishing *Honours courses* the College was adding the hard discipline of intensive work to the achievement of the general course. The immediate establishment of a wide variety of Honours courses would be more likely than not to lead to a series of unrelated specialisms. It is therefore proposed that Honours courses should be confined at the start to two from each of the groups A, B and C listed above.[1]

These might be:

A. Physical Science: 1. Chemistry 2. Physics.

B. Arts: 1. History. 2. English Language and Literature.

C. Social Studies: 1. Economic Theory and Institutions. 2. Political Theory and Institutions.

Honours degree would be awarded after an examination in two subjects. It would be desirable to provide either that they might both be taken at the same level or, alternatively, that one might be taken at a higher level and the other as a subsidiary.

The change of emphasis and attitude is very striking. There is now in the forefront an attack on departmentalism; the range of subjects is enlarged; no less than six honours courses are now proposed; specific provision is made for a separate pass degree; the Intermediate course is now seen as common to all students and as a vital element in the scheme. But the issue of a single or two-subject honours was left open: the concept of breadth of study right up to the end of a student's course had not yet crystallised.

These new suggestions for the curriculum were well received by the three sponsoring Vice-Chancellors, and as a result of the discussion few major amendments were made. First it was agreed that the first professors to be appointed should, if possible, be in the following nine subjects, three from each of the main groups A, B and C: Sociology; Economic Theory and Institutions; Political Theory and Institutions; History;

[1] There seems to be no reason why, compared with the list given earlier, A and C should have changed places.

English Language and Literature; Philosophy (Methodology); Chemistry; Physics; Biology. Secondly, a sentence was added to make it clear that the pass degree need not take more than three years but that the honours degree ought to take four. Thirdly, the proposal that the organisation and integration of the Intermediate general course should be the responsibility of the department of philosophy was dropped. In its revised form[1] the paper prepared for the meeting of 10 June 1947, was forwarded by Lindsay when he wrote his formal submission to the UGC on 2 January 1948.

> We hope that the UGC will find these new proposals satisfactory and will agree that the basis of studies in Science and Arts is adequately broadened. Perhaps we may call attention to the fact that we have in the process considerably changed the emphasis of our proposals. We are more concerned with providing a curriculum for the B.A. which will include both Science and Arts and break down . . . departmentalism . . . than with concentrating on special subjects in either Science or Arts which are specially suited to the region, although we still attach great importance to the latter point.[2] We would indeed rest our claims for special consideration for the plan of being able to give our own B.A. degree if sponsored, on the importance for general University policy of this attack on departmentalism.

At the important meeting on *5 January 1948*, between a strong Stoke delegation and a large group of UGC members,[3] the proposed curriculum was not in fact a major topic of discussion: Moberly did little more than remark that the basis of studies now presented was much broader than formerly. Nor did the question of curriculum loom large at the full meeting of the UGC itself on *5 February 1948*; but it was evident that the UGC was itself conscious of the evil of departmentalism in many universities and impressed by the attempt now being made in the Stoke proposals to deal with it. The change of emphasis indicated in Lindsay's letter and in the document expounding it

[1] Now printed and dated 20 June 1947.
[2] Interestingly, the words 'although . . . point' were added only as an amendment in the draft of the letter.
[3] See pp. 63–5.

had converted the UGC and in the encouraging resolutions which that Committee passed[1] not only was there no specific reference to the curriculum at all but the Stoke proposals taken as a whole were now stated to be in the interests of university education.

THE INFLUENCE OF THE SPONSORS

What now remained was to secure the support of academic opinion within Oxford, Manchester and Birmingham; and the formulation of a curriculum which they would approve was no small part of the task. The scheme of 10 June 1947, had not been seriously amended at the meeting in Stoke with the three Vice-Chancellors and, as we have just seen, had presumably satisfied the UGC itself; but opinion within the universities themselves was more critical. The conference of university representatives which took place in Birmingham on *22 April 1948*,[2] refused to take a firm decision for or against the Stoke proposals as a whole; and in recommending the appointment of a further committee, they defined its first duty thus: 'to attempt to devise a curriculum that would . . . be acceptable to the sponsoring universities as a satisfactory university discipline.'

In the inter-university discussions which ensued an important and persuasive rôle was played by Roy Pascal, Professor of German at Birmingham. From the outset he had been sympathetically inclined towards Keele[3] and during the summer of 1948 he drafted a memorandum for his Birmingham colleagues which was subsequently discussed by all the university representatives at their private meeting on *21 October 1948*.

Starting from the revised form of the document of 10 June 1947, Pascal agreed that an academic structure of that kind would give the Stoke College an individuality of its own.

> The Pass Degree course would provide a training of the sort which is highly desirable in view of the needs of employing bodies (including Secondary Modern Schools). . . . In this respect North Staffordshire would have the advantage of providing a degree course which is different from those elsewhere. It is clear, too, that the proposed

[1] See p. 65. [2] See p. 74. [3] See p. 73n.

> Honours Degree courses in Natural Science and Social Studies, related as they are to the needs of the Stoke region, will provide a needed training.

In his comments on the first year general course, though he did not seize on the idea of a 'common core', Pascal emphasised integration as opposed to a mere spread of subjects; and he suggests social relations as the binding principle:[2]

> It is proposed in the memorandum that, for the first year, students will not be members of a particular Faculty or Department, but will all take a 'general course' in which certain combinations of subjects are possible. I would propose that students should be allowed to choose between different integrated courses[1] rather than subjects, so that whatever course they take, it will be an integrated whole. . . . I would suggest that the dominating purpose of the General Course should be the study of social relations, and that the options should provide for a bias either towards Natural Science or towards Arts.

When he comes to the proposed pass degree, Pascal is clearly influenced by the existence in a number of universities, including Birmingham, of a 'degree in general studies', in Arts or Science, which could be awarded with honours.[3]

> I would suggest that the Pass Degree course should be termed 'General Degree Course', and that Honours be awarded in this degree if the students reach a prescribed level. The Degree in a special subject would consequently be termed 'Special Degree' or 'Special Honours Degree.' If Honours may not be gained in General Subjects, this type

[1] Though not adopted as the accepted basis for the Foundation year, this idea of a choice of integrated courses may have relevance to future developments as the first year intake at Keele increases in numbers. The newer universities show the concept in operation (see p. 290).

[2] See also Pascal's article 'The universities and social purpose', *Universities Quarterly*, 1949.

[3] The aims of such arrangements were: first, to get rid of the term 'pass' which had deservedly fallen into bad repute; and second, to provide a worthy goal for students who did not want to devote themselves to a single subject in their final examination. The institution of 'general honours' degrees by some universities was already being welcomed by the Association of University Teachers in June 1930; and a whole session was devoted to this topic at the Fourth Congress of the Universities of the British Empire in July 1931 (see *Proceedings* of the Congress, pp. 134–50).

> of course inevitably falls in public esteem, and inevitably students will seek to enter Special Schools in order to get an Honours Degree. . . . The main aim of the Pass Degree Course is, however, to overcome Faculty and Departmental separatism. It might therefore be advisable to put Arts and Social Studies together in one grouping. Even more important would be the planning of the curriculum so that students taking primarily one of the groups mentioned would be encouraged to take subjects in the others—e.g. students of Natural Science or Social Studies should be encouraged or required[1] to take also English, Philosophy or a foreign language.

About honours degrees in special subjects, Pascal has little to say in general, since the number of such subjects was for some time to be limited; but this unavoidable limitation leads him to a suggestion which could have been no more pleasing to Keele then than it is now: 'It might be considered wise that at any rate for the first few years students who wish, after having done well in their first year general course, to take Honours in subjects not provided by the North Staffordshire College, should be encouraged to transfer to other universities.' The significance of his memorandum lies partly in the support Pascal gives for an integrated Intermediate course and a spread of subjects in the later years of the 'Pass degree'; but even more important is the fact that it proved to be acceptable to the representatives of the sponsoring universities and to Stoke as a basis on which further serious discussion could be built.

At the Birmingham conference on *15 February 1949*, both the Stoke members and the representatives of the three universities concerned agreed that the position had changed considerably since the North Staffordshire memorandum of 10 June 1947.

> Lord Lindsay stated that they accepted in principle Professor Pascal's Memorandum; that they regarded the academic syllabus as still not settled and capable of amendment; and that the North Staffordshire Authorities would welcome the help of the sponsoring universities in

[1] That students should be 'required' to take a subject from a group other than the one in which their main interest lay had been proposed in the Memorandum of 11 November 1946—but only in the Intermediate examination. Pascal extends the proposal to the Pass Degree course itself. That the principle should apply to Honours Degrees was a later development.

> framing a suitable academic syllabus. . . . The document had been drafted almost two years ago and that he was now himself unhappy about some of its detailed suggestions. In any case the present view of the Stoke Committee was that when the senior teaching officers of the new University College had been appointed it would be their business, relying upon the advice of the sponsors, to evolve the courses of study applicable to their own departments.

But sufficient progress had been made for the representatives to agree that their respective universities should be recommended to accept the obligations of sponsorship. As committed sponsors they could now play a still more active part.

THE ACADEMIC COUNCIL

After 15 February 1949, the Stoke promoters had grounds for optimism. But there was still very much to be done in the way of academic planning: and the first students would be arriving in October 1950. The memorandum of 10 June 1947 was admittedly out of date in several respects and Pascal's memorandum dealt mainly with principles which still had to be applied. If, for example, you were to have an 'integrated' first year course, its content had to be determined with some precision and arrangements made for its organisation by the departments of study concerned in it; the course structure of the following years had to be formulated; and since provision was to be made for the training of prospective teachers and for the practical side of social studies, these things had to be dovetailed into the broad pattern of the curriculum.

Yet until professors were appointed, there could be no Senate to make recommendations or take decisions on academic matters; and until there was a Senate there could be no properly constituted Academic Council. Fortunately the Charter was wisely drafted so that the Principal was given emergency powers for an interim period;[1] and it was therefore possible for the six representatives of the three sponsoring universities to have meetings with Lindsay, Horwood, Jenkins (the Registrar), and three Directors of Education.[2] These conferences were of

[1] See p. 83n.

[2] Pascal, no longer Dean of the Faculty of Arts, was not appointed by Birmingham as one of its members on the Academic Council.

vital importance. At the first of them on *23 July 1949*, the nature of the first year course was discussed and it was agreed that 'there should be a common course of lectures . . . supplemented by tutorial work[1] to meet the requirements of individual students'. The desirability of a further three years of study was also affirmed, though it was appreciated that this must depend on the approval of the UGC and the Ministry of Education for the financial implications of so long a course of study.

In order to cover the studies essential to the first year course a decision was taken to appoint twelve professors as soon as possible in English language and literature, modern languages (French or German), history, economics, political and moral philosophy, philosophy, public administration and local government (a designation which was later changed to political institutions), geography, mathematics, physics, chemistry, and biology. Approval was also given to the information which should be circulated to candidates for Chairs—a document of such interest for the light it throws on the concept of the College at the time, that part of it is of considerable historic importance.

> One of the main objectives which it is hoped to achieve is to give to every graduate as wide an understanding as possible of the factors which have been operative in building up our present civilisation and of the forces that are current in the world to-day. Particular attention will be given to this in the first year. It is intended that the foundation studies[2] taken before specialisation should be so presented as to give a comprehensible and integrated conception of the basic facts and principles of the main subjects to those who will not later specialise in such studies, while at the same time being a sound foundation for such specialisation. The relationship of particular studies to knowledge as a whole, the effect that the historical development of a subject had upon past civilisations and the part that it plays in present human activities, will be stressed in addition to the elucidation of its fundamental principles.
>
> It is desired to break down as far as possible any clear

[1] This is stressed here for the first time.

[2] Here seems to be the origin of Keele's specific nomenclature for its first year; Pascal had used the term 'groundwork'.

> cut divisions between different branches of study and to ensure that each student has a sympathetic understanding of the functions and importance of all the main human activities. The Professors and Heads of Departments will have the responsibility of integrating their courses of studies on these lines. . . .
>
> After a first year devoted to general studies, students will select a limited range of subjects in which they require more specialised knowledge, but it is hoped that the treatment will throughout avoid subject isolation and bring out the vital contacts of the subject with current life and thought.

At the next meeting on *7 October 1949*, a definite decision on a four-year course was taken in view of the agreement of the UGC and the willingness of Local Authorities to make their scholarships and grants tenable for that length. There was thus the elbow room needed for the planning of the degree structure; and the Ministry of Education was willing to accept 'a scheme in which teacher-training was incorporated in the four years'. Consequently a Chair of Education was forthwith added to the list of 12 professorships previously agreed. At the same time it was decided to make appointments of non-professorial heads of departments of classics and geology; the latter had been included in the paper of 10 June 1947, but classics was an entire newcomer to the teaching cadre, though obviously essential if ancient civilisations were to be properly dealt with in the Foundation Studies. Appointments in psychology, religious teaching, foreign languages other than French and German, and music were to be left till later.

The programme for the last three years of the degree course was seriously taken in hand at the meeting on *2 December 1949*, when it was tentatively agreed that the subjects of study should be divided into three groups:

A. Ancient Languages, Modern Languages, English Language and Literature, History, Philosophy.

B. Economics, Political Institutions, Psychology, Geography, History and Practice of Education, Social Science, Political and Moral Philosophy.

C. Mathematics, Physics, Chemistry, Biology, Geology.

The order of the groups differs from that proposed in the

document of 10 June 1947;[1] but so far as A and C are concerned the only two major changes are the inclusion of ancient languages and the transfer of mathematics from (A) to (C). Group B however has been considerably remodelled: geography, which had been lost sight of since September 1946, reappears and education is quite new, though the training of teachers had always been included in the functions of the College. The nomenclature of the other subjects also shows modifications.

Students were to choose at least two principal subjects (studied for three years) and not more than three; and if three, they must be taken from at least two of the groups. In addition students must take at least two and not more than four subsidiary subjects (to be studied for one or two years). Every combination of subjects must include at least one from each group.[2] In determining whether students have attained honours, the achievement in subsidiary subjects should be taken into account.

A firm hold was now being taken on the curriculum. 'Local needs' were so far in the background as to be scarcely discernible; adult education had lost its proposed place in the activities of the College. What had emerged from all the discussions was the concept of an integrated first year for all students and an element of breadth in the last three years of study.

THE FOUNDATION YEAR

Apart from affirming on 23 July 1949, that there should be a common course of lectures supplemented by tutorials in the first year, the Academic Council had very properly taken no further steps towards defining the content of the course. That was a task which the professors alone could accomplish; but we must bear in mind that though they had been appointed to Keele by the early months of 1950, they still had their normal duties to perform in the universities from which they were coming: the amount of time they had for Keele affairs was limited and the opportunities for meeting together were restricted. The surprising thing is that they got so much done in readiness for the opening of the College.

[1] See p. 104.

[2] This proposal was later modified to a requirement for some science and some non-science. See p. 163.

Despite these difficulties it is clear that by talks with Lindsay and the exchange of letters amongst themselves they grasped not only the concept of an integrated education but the nature of the practical questions which had to be put and answered. After an informal conference the preceding evening the first formal meeting of the Senate on *12 February 1950* was able to adopt some provisional plans both for the lecture course of the first year and for the 'tutorials'. Each student was to attend ten[1] lectures each week. In addition one tutorial a week would be taken in one subject from each of the three groups (arts, social studies, science), but a different tutorial subject in each group would be taken in each of the three terms, making a total of nine subjects within the year. Naturally this was only a tentative framework and countless details had still to be filled in. The professors dispersed to think over their individual contributions to the scheme; but it was Lindsay himself who soon afterwards circulated a 'Draft Proposal' on the course of lectures, which, though it differed considerably from the programme that was finally adopted, was the basis on which subsequent discussions were conducted.

In this document we first meet the idea that the lecture course should cover three broad topics or themes—the Heritage of Western Civilisation, Experimental Science, and Modern Democratic Institutions, as they were here called. But Lindsay did not envisage that these should be lectured upon in this sequence consecutively in the three terms of the session. Instead, he suggested that there should be 'two parallel courses of five lectures a week running throughout the Session'. The scheme provided that the first twenty weeks of the session should be taken up by concurrent courses in (i) the Heritage of Western Civilisation and (ii) Experimental Science; and the last nine or ten weeks of the session should be devoted to lectures on geography, political institutions, modern philosophy, moral and political philosophy, economics and psychology. In all, there would be 290 lectures arranged in rather solid blocks so that each professor gave a continuous series of lectures extending over two to four weeks. Essentially this scheme was one of juxtaposition of topics rather than integration.

Lindsay's scheme was intended as a contribution to the general pool of ideas about the first year course. The professors

[1] The average number per week turned out to be nearer eleven.

had been asked at their February meeting to send in their ideas, but by early June not all of them had done so; and on *1 July* the Senate agreed that the Principal himself should prepare detailed proposals 'in a form suitable for inclusion in the Prospectus, and that these should be circulated to members on the understanding that they would be printed as prepared unless amendments were received within a few days of circulation'.

It is evident that at this stage the need for speed was being appreciated. Yet eight weeks later Lindsay expressed his concern both about the form of the lecture course and about the relationship of the tutorials to the lectures. On *25 August 1950*, he sent a circular to the members of the Senate saying that with the help of Professor Williams he had been considering the syllabuses submitted to him by the professors and had come to the conclusion that 'we must try and reconsider the whole subject again'. He was having no easy time in bringing his team into line and it is worth quoting the later part of his letter to show the firmness he had to exercise at this juncture:

> I think most of these syllabuses are too full and try to do too much in the time. We have got to remember that every student will be doing at one and the same time *two* sets of lectures in two very different fields. What we want to give students in their first year is some understanding of these several subjects. We don't want to try and cover the ground.
>
> Secondly, I don't believe we have ever considered in any specific or definite way the relation of the tutorial work to the lectures in the first year. We have rather airily said, in considering any deficiencies in the lecture programme, that we can of course make that all right in tutorials; but we haven't ever specifically considered how we would do this.

So, only seven weeks before the first students were due to arrive, hard and fundamental rethinking was still needed in regard to the first year lectures and the function of the tutorials.

But Lindsay was not alone in planning the structure of the first year course. Stimulated presumably by Lindsay's letter of 25 August, a memorandum was put out by a small group of professors in which a new framework for the first year lectures was proposed. In place of Lindsay's parallel courses running throughout most of the session, it was now suggested that the course should be divided into three sections, each to be given in a separate term. In brief, the new scheme was to be as follows. In the first term, under the title 'Man and his Environment', lectures would 'describe briefly the content of modern knowledge, including the physical structure of the universe, the geological ages of the world, the life which exists upon it, the nature of man and human personality, and the scope and character of systematic thought'. In the second term, under the title 'Development of Western Civilisation', lectures would 'trace the growth of modern knowledge and would include a survey of the legacies of the Ancient World and the Medieval World, show the importance of the Renaissance and the Reformation, and bring out the continuity in the transmission of experience and knowledge'. In the third term, under the title 'Industrial Revolution', lectures would 'present a picture of contemporary civilization and survey the massive changes occurring in Western society during the last two centuries, stress being laid upon the political, scientific, agrarian and industrial revolutions'.

On 12 September, Lindsay sent out this scheme to members of the Senate virtually unaltered. On 27 September when the Senate met it was decided to interchange the lectures for the first and second terms so that 'The Development of Western Civilisation' took precedence of 'Man and his Environment'; but apart from that major alteration the scheme was accepted and the finer details were worked out. In all, 304 lectures were planned, two each day from Monday to Friday and one on Saturday; in the first term (Western Civilisation) there were 29 on the Ancient World, 14 on the Middle Ages, 22 on the Renaissance and Reformation, and 31 on Europe from the Reformation to the French Revolution; in the second term the 111 lectures (Man and his Environment) included physics, chemistry (with some attention to biochemistry), biology, geology, geography, climatology, scientific method, psychology, sociology, philosophy and religion; in the third term (Industrial Revolution) there were 21 lectures devoted to an Historical Introduction, 24 on the Contributions of Science to Industrial Civilizations, 17 to Social and Political Problems, 8 to the Changing Role of the

State, 7 to Modern Psychology and Philosophy, 14 to the Crisis in Civilisation and 6 to the Rise and Fall in Societies.

This programme, heavy though it may seem to be for the students, was an immense improvement on anything that had been previously constructed. From such details as have just been given, it is obvious that some topics could be dealt with under more than one major heading and to that extent there is a greater element of integration.

The structure of the first year lecture course had thus been decided upon with little time to spare; but there still remained the question of the rôle of first year tutorials and their relationship to the lecture course. At its first meeting (12 February 1950) the Senate had made more progress concerning arrangements for tutorials than for the lecture course. But little had been decided since then, and when Lindsay sent the proposed lecture course to Senate members on 12 September 1950, discussion on the arrangements for first year tutorials was evidently still at a preliminary stage. What he had to say about this matter put the major issues fairly and squarely:

> Tutorials would form an essential part of the course proposed . . . but details really cannot be settled satisfactorily until the Senate makes up its mind on certain fundamental questions . . . and I think it might help our discussion if I make a few points about it. As at present proposed the plan is that each student should go for tutorials to nine different members of staff a year, one in each group each term, but I am not sure that we should necessarily hold to this. I think these decisions were made before the general machinery was properly discussed. . . . Are we going to consider this first general year as standing by itself, and try to work out a plan by which everybody gets the best practical mixture of general lectures with more intensive discussion at tutorials, or are we going to say that this first year will be in some sense the first of a four year course specializing to some extent in the two main subjects? After giving a lot of consideration to it I think this second plan is not really practical if it is desirable. The Professors who do not deal in school subjects will have practically no students or tutorials, and popular

> school subjects like English, History, and Geography, for example, will be over-burdened. . . . We have therefore these decisions to make:—
>
> (a) Are the students to be divided for tutorial purposes into equal groups?
>
> (b) If the answer to this is yes, then are these groups to be attached to the same Professor in each division for three terms, or are they to go to three Professors in the same division, one in each term?
>
> (c) Are we going to ask one tutor to be specially responsible for one group, either for a term at a time or for three terms?

The answer which emerged to Lindsay's question of whether students should stay in the same tutorial groups for the academic year or for one term only was that they should do both: there would be both sessional and terminal 'tutorials'. This solution was proposed in a memorandum drafted by Professor Chambers which was approved by Senate on 2 October 1950. It provided for a scheme by which the student would attend 'tutorials' for the full year in two subjects with which his school experience had left him unfamiliar and in three other subjects for one term only. Thus a student who had specialised in the sixth form at school in science would take tutorials in three different sciences, one each term, but would also do tutorials in one subject each from arts and social studies for the whole session.

The scheme for lectures and 'tutorials' in the Foundation Year was thus only finally decided a fortnight before the first students arrived on 16 October 1950; lectures began on the 19 October; and the final form of the 'Prospectus' was not in fact approved until 18 October. So far as the later years of the degree course were concerned many of the details of the individual courses had still to be mapped out; but at least the main outline was clear: not less than two and not more than three principal subjects studied for three years, together with such subsidiary subjects studied for one to two years as would bring the total number of subjects up to five. Until the academic staff came into residence in the summer of 1950 progress in defining a degree structure had necessarily been slow and hesitant; but the three months immediately prior to the opening of the College had been a period of concentrated thought and discussion. The broad aim of the College was well established in the minds of the Senate: their task had been to translate it into practical terms and this they had accomplished.[1]

[1] The one important thing which had not been decided was the question of the pass degree. The Prospectus stated that candidates who satisfied the requirements in the examination in principal subjects at the end of the three principal years would be awarded the B.A. degree and went on to indicate that: 'the degree will be awarded with Honours to those who attain the prescribed standard. In determining whether the requirements have been satisfied for both the ordinary degree and for the degree with Honours, the standard attained in the Subsidiary Subjects will be taken into account'. The memorandum to the UGC in July 1946 had seen the pass degree as the consolation prize for those who did not achieve honours; the document of 10 July 1947 contemplated a separate course for a pass degree; the view taken in October 1950, seems to be that while there will be no separate provision for the two categories of degrees, honours will be awarded only to students of some distinction. See pp. 99, 104–6, 162.

Five

Lindsay and Keele in Context

THE PLEA FOR BREADTH

No account of the formulation of the Keele curriculum would be complete without some consideration of two closely related themes: the context of educational ideas which had currency at the time when the College was being founded; and Lindsay's own ideas and the influences which stimulated his thought or confirmed his own intuitions. Keele was experimental, but not revolutionary; indeed the importance and value of the experiment lay precisely in the fact that it set out to put into practice ideas on university education which had been gaining ground for some considerable time. The exact form taken by the Foundation Year and the later stages of the degree course was a pragmatic answer to practical problems and not the expression of a recklessly new or iconoclastic educational philosophy.

Excessive specialisation in university studies and the attendant evil of departmentalism, against which Keele was intended to be an effective protest, had a long history. As Lindsay once remarked,[1] specialism can be traced back as far as the introduction of the Tripos examinations at Cambridge and the Honours Schools at Oxford in the early nineteenth century which were devised in order to raise the intellectual standards of those two universities. The danger was not at once apparent. In 1870 the throwing open of posts in the higher Civil Service to open competitive examinations gave an impetus to specialising since mediocre marks were scaled downwards to penalise any relative superficiality of knowledge. The demands of the new grammar schools (founded as a result of the 1902 Education Act) for teachers of particular subjects in place of the more general form master encouraged students, especially in the civic universities, to aim at a single-subject honours degree. As the technological revolution had got under way, the increasing

[1] 'A dual task in higher education', *Listener*, 16 March 1950.

importance and complexity of the particular sciences and the need for people who had received an intensive training in them did more than anything else to accelerate the process. The growth of research schools in all the universities, to which the introduction of the Ph.D. degree in 1919 largely contributed, also played its part. Nor was it only in the sciences that specialisation grew rampant: many subjects in Faculties of Arts narrowed their scope and their contacts. Specialisation was identified with 'study in depth'; its opposite was not encouraged as 'study in breadth' but was labelled as 'smatterings' or 'dilettantism'. What was most serious of all was that the concept of the university as a place where young people were not merely trained to earn a livelihood in the learned professions but were educated for living in a wider sense, was implicitly abandoned.

From the early 1920s an increasing number of serious writers both here and abroad drew attention to the situation and advocated a variety of remedies or palliatives. Thus, for example, the American writer Abraham Flexner in his *Universities: American, English and German* (1930) ruthlessly pilloried the excessive and often trivial vocationalism of many courses in the universities and colleges of his own country and drew attention to examples of the same kind of thing in some English institutions.[1] A. N. Whitehead, writing from Harvard, protested in his *Aims of Education* (1932) against the isolation of studies from each other: 'A man who knows only his own science, as a routine peculiar to that science, does not even know that. He has no fertility of thought, no power of quickly seizing the bearing of alien ideas. He will discover nothing, and be stupid in practical application.' Another writer, Walter M. Kotschnig, in his introduction to an international symposium (*The University in a Changing World*) remarked:

> The oneness of learning which once united all the universities, irrespective of their differences, has broken down. . . . Let there be no mistake—the agglomerate of facts which is the common possession of all institutions of learning, scientific inventions which become universal

[1] Flexner regarded research achievements as the main criterion for the standing of a university. A broad 'education for citizenship' did not particularly attract him as a function of a university.

property as soon as they are made, are not an equivalent for that lost unity of truth and learning.

In England perhaps the most striking contribution in the inter-war years was the thinking of M. Alderton Pink, who, it is interesting to note, was a headmaster and not a university teacher. In his book *If the Blind Lead* (1932) he advocated a first degree course in 'Modern Humanities' consisting of the social and natural sciences and philosophy—an idea which has a clear affinity with the Keele programme; and in his article 'Suggestions for a reformed university curriculum' which appeared in the *Universities Review* of 1933 he penned something which could almost have been incorporated in a Keele manifesto:

> If the university curriculum is to be justified, it must be based on an educational principle, and one which is adequate to the needs of this age. . . . Whatever other function the university may have, it is primarily a place in which the most intelligent young people may be trained to become intellectual and social leaders. . . . Actually the only kind of selection now in operation in the university is that which is involved in specialization. And specialization has no philosophical basis; it is rooted solely in expediency and practical convenience. . . . The university makes no provision for the co-ordinating type of mind . . . I assume that the aim of university education is to further human welfare by equipping the best minds for effective intervention in the philosophical and practical problems of today. The acquisition of knowledge and skill in a single department will not be adequate for this purpose. . . All studies should be related to social purpose.[1] The practical inference from these general principles is that single subject courses should be replaced by carefully-planned courses in grouped subjects.

The stimulus of war time, however, and the incentive to plan for the future sharpened academic perceptions and consciences in British universities and brought forth between 1940 and 1950 a number of books and articles in which basic

[1] This pregnant phrase anticipates similar words of Lindsay and Roy Pascal.

questions were raised about universities and their functions. In this country the chief books were *Redbrick University* by 'Bruce Truscot' (E. A. Peers), *Education and the University* by F. R. Leavis, *Redbrick and these Vital Days* by 'Bruce Truscot', *Some Thoughts on University Education* by Sir Richard Livingstone, and *The Crisis in the University* by Sir Walter Moberly; and though not by English authors, three other books of this period were of special significance for Keele because of their influence on Lindsay: Adolf Löwe's *The Universities in Transformation*, The English translation of José Ortega y Gasset's *Mission of the University* (1944), and the report of a Harvard Committee on *General Education in a Free Society*. The Association of University Teachers circulated a draft *Report on University Developments* in April 1943[1] which formed the basis for many fruitful discussions within the individual universities; in the autumn of 1944 the *Political Quarterly* devoted a whole issue to articles on university matters;[2] and in the autumn of 1946 a new periodical, the *Universities Quarterly*, was launched to provide a forum for opinions on university affairs of every kind.[3] There was a new crispness in the academic air.

It is not possible here to analyse in detail or even to summarise the views and proposals contained in all the writings and periodicals just mentioned; but it will be pertinent to our main purpose to quote, by way of illustration, some few of the opinions which have a bearing on the educational thinking of the founders of Keele. Adolf Löwe, Ortega y Gasset, and the Harvard Report, are however deferred to the later paragraphs which deal with Lindsay himself.

> The idea of liberal culture has been defeated and dissipated by advancing specialization. . . . There seems little hope of improvement, unless in some kind of formal academic

1 The final form of the Report was published in May 1944 in the *Universities Review*.

2 Among these articles were: 'The functions of a university' by the philosopher John Macmurray; 'The university and its region' by Bruce Truscot; 'Arts faculties in modern universities' by Professor Bonamy Dobrée of Leeds; and 'The social studies in the universities' by G. D. H. Cole. An article on 'The integral university' by C. H. Waddington, Professor of Animal Genetics at Edinburgh, appeared in the *Political Quarterly* for 1946.

3 In early issues there were published: 'The modern universities' by G. Templeman (later Vice-Chancellor of Kent); 'The teaching of social studies in British universities' by G. D. H. Cole; and 'The relation of teaching and research in social studies' by Lord Lindsay.

provision designed to bring specialisms into communication. (F. R. Leavis, 1943).[1]

The university must be a place where knowledge is *unified*, and not merely a common house for disjointed specialisms. Culture is synthetic and total . . . The crux of the cultural problem for the universities lies in the unification of Arts and Science. In a proper university education two things must be combined which correspond to its two functions as a focus of culture and as a place of research. It must combine a balanced general education with specialized training in some particular department of study. It is not enough to provide a general education for some students while offering specialized training for others. It must provide both for all its students. (J. Macmurray, 1944)

The view is sometimes expressed that the knowledge and interests of students, on completing their university course, are often narrow and confined. We believe that the degree courses in their present form do not correct this narrowness, and that reform of the courses of study is urgently needed. . . . For the first year of university study, or for the first two years, all students should pursue courses which provide instruction in a group of correlated subjects. . . . The normal First Degree course should be four years from entrance. (AUT Report, 1943–4)

There is a great deal to be said for making the first year at the university . . . a period not of study for any specific, or even mixed, degree course, but rather a general introduction to the problems of the modern world. Rightly planned and executed, it could be the university's greatest safeguard against the dangers of premature specialization. (G. D. H. Cole, 1948)[2]

Undergraduate education has never been thought out as a whole. It has simply grown, and its development has been determined by a combination of *vis inertiae*, the pressure

1 Leavis advocated 'making a scheme of liberal education centre in the study of English literature'.

2 Cole disappointingly added: 'There should, however, always be provision for students who can prove their capacity to go on at once to honours work to be allowed to do so if they prefer to skip the preliminary general year'!

> of circumstances and a struggle of individual subjects for a place in the sun. . . . The weakness (of our undergraduate education) is an exclusive specialism which there is no attempt to counteract. (Livingstone, 1948)

> The student is being trained with some success for competence in his special occupation. But that part of his education which looks to his life as a responsible human being and a citizen has fallen behind. . . . We need, but do not get, a 'humane' education, that is an education of the whole man (which must include both Humane Studies and the study of the Natural World). . . . There is room for much experiment in method. (Moberly, 1949)[1]

LINDSAY'S APPROACH

These few quotations indicate some trends of thought which undoubtedly had their influence on those who were responsible for the form the Keele curriculum eventually took: an attack on narrowness and specialisation, an insistence on the coherence of knowledge and a plan for a wide and liberal culture. We can now turn our attention to Lindsay himself. He was generous in acknowledging what he owed to others in building up the Keele programme and, as we have seen, his associates on the Academic Council and in the embryonic Senate did in fact contribute valuable help. But he was the key figure: he was not only the most senior of the group but he was outstanding among them in the range of his interests, in the width of his reading, in his contacts with educational thought and practice at home and abroad, and above all in his intellectual power and in the force of his personality.

Lindsay, unfortunately, did not expound his views on education in any formal and comprehensive treatise; but it is not difficult to piece together from his other books and articles a reasonably coherent picture of his opinions. The essential thing to realise in this connexion is that the mainspring of his life and work was his belief in the value and the rightness from a Christian standpoint of democracy; and it was that belief which

[1] The method Moberly preferred was 'widened professional courses'. Bruce Truscot somewhat similarly argued that desirable breadth of outlook could be secured by regarding a special Honours course not simply as an end in itself but as a focus to bring perspective to other areas of knowledge.

coloured all his views on education and on the function of the universities. The liberal Oxford tradition of concern for public service was particularly congenial to him and in this he was the lineal successor of other outstanding Balliol men: Benjamin Jowett, T. H. Green, and his immediate predecessor as Master, A. L. Smith. It was from this belief in democracy and the ideal of service to the community that there stemmed first his devotion to adult education and ultimately his dedication to Keele. This sequence of interests is important. So far as universities were concerned, he held that their social function was primarily in their service to the democratic state: to this, research and the training of experts should take second place.

Democracy in Lindsay's view was based on a fundamental belief in human equality and he was fond of quoting the saying of an officer in Cromwell's army: 'the poorest he that is in England hath a life to live as the richest he'. This human equality, Lindsay said, could not be proved and was ultimately a question of religious faith; and so: 'If our Christianity becomes dead or conventional, our churches formal and unreal, our democracy will soon be the same'[1] If equality was the basis of democracy, the aim of a democratic government followed from this. It was 'that free men should live their own lives', an ideal which was exemplified by the activities of voluntary groups or associations in society. In the past the universities had served the community by preparing men for the professions. They had given doctors, priests and lawyers an understanding of men and life as well as a technical training. But the functions of the university had been altered by the democratic revolution:

> A democratic nation today has to be a well-educated nation. . . . We cannot become an educated democracy, able to use all our latent ability for the wise and democratic conduct of politics, without a great extension of adult education.[2]

Lindsay's work for the Oxford Extra-Mural Delegacy was thus the natural outcome of his belief in the duties owed by the university to the community and the democratic state. Education had to be as widespread as possible if democracy was to thrive.

But Lindsay identified another revolution taking place

[1] *I Believe in Democracy*, p. 35.

[2] *I Believe in Democracy*, p. 36.

concurrently with and endangering the democratic revolution—the technological revolution. Already in 1929 he was pointing out the difficulty of reconciling expert knowledge with democracy. We need an expert legislator, but

> What is needed, and what is most difficult, is to combine the technical knowledge of the expert with the practical experience and understanding of the common life of the ordinary public. The expert has to be sensitive to public opinion; the ordinary man has somehow to discuss, with some understanding of what the expert's proposals amount to.[1]

He went on to counter the charge that democracy was open to the criticism of being able to raise public interest only by 'forms of collective excitement such as nationalism or party enthusiasm' by arguing that: 'These artificial and irrational forms of uniting men are necessary just so far as they are not naturally united in sharing a wide common culture and participating in a common life where there are no cultural enclaves, where there is real spiritual communication among groups.' These early concerns both with the rôle of the expert in a democracy and with the need for a common culture and a common life if democracy was not to be open to attack, are the basis upon which his later educational ideas developed.

It was natural that the coming of war should have reinforced these ideas in Lindsay's mind. In a series of talks given at the time of the fall of France in 1940, he showed himself interested in the fact that democracy took longer than the totalitarian regimes to adapt itself to new conditions. Planning was essential if democracy was to survive; but, he asked, was this compatible with the maintenance of democratic leadership (which, in contrast to totalitarian leadership, was thrown up by society and not separated from it).

> Planning has come to stay and, indeed, to increase. It needs skill and knowledge and rare qualities. Can we have expert knowledge and keep democratic? . . . With the enormous growth of specialized knowledge, the gap between the ordinary man and the specialist has widened. Till something is done to fill this gap, democratic

[1] *The Essentials of Democracy*, pp. 79–80.

> leadership will not be nearly as effective or decisive as it might be. Specialization . . . is so exacting that it may produce an isolated life. That is a real tragedy for the specialist and for the community. The challenge must and can be met.[1]

This problem of the expert and the specialist continued to exercise him more and more.[2]

> The difficulty is that, as the complexity of modern knowledge increases, departmentalism and specialization seem more and more necessary. But the inter-relation of the different departments of human knowledge is also growing every day. The man who only 'knows more and more about less and less' is becoming a public danger. We must give our minds to getting the right balance between specialization and expert knowledge on the one hand and a wide outlook and general understanding on the other. The curriculum of our universities needs to be overhauled to see that this balance is achieved.

Again in an article on 'The universities of England and Wales' in *The Educational Year Book* for 1943, he wrote: 'The demands that our complex modern civilization has created . . . have made it difficult for the student to get that general outlook on life, that wide and informed understanding of civilization which a university ought to give.' When the opportunity came to take the lead in the planning of the new College he saw to it that part of its purpose should be to 'break down the specialisation and departmentalism which are the curse of the modern universities'; and the Foundation Year and the spread of subjects in the three later years were the instruments of that determination.

Nor did Lindsay ever lose sight of his basic tenets:[3]

> Karl Mannheim used to say that the condition of democratic planning was 'social awareness'. He meant that democracy could not plan as a democracy unless there was in it a widely spread understanding of the purposes and possibilities of society. . . . To produce such social awareness

[1] *I Believe in Democracy*, pp. 30–6.

[2] 'A plan for education', *Picture Post*, Vol. 10, No. 1, 1941.

[3] *Universities Quarterly*, II, 3, May 1948 ('The relation of teaching and research in social studies').

> all over the country seems to me the primary duty of university faculties of social studies, both in their internal and their extra-mural teaching.

That is why social studies occupied so overwhelmingly predominant a position in the earlier proposals sent to the UGC in July 1946 and why it continued to rank as one of the three major sections in the structure of the curriculum. It also explains why Lindsay emphasised the primacy of teaching: 'I hold the perhaps heretical opinion that teaching is a university's first function and research is important to it because the teacher who is himself adding to knowledge is a better teacher.'[1]

From early 1948 when the UGC accepted the broad proposal for a new College and more so from the middle of 1949 when the sponsoring universities agreed to help, Lindsay's attention became increasingly concentrated on the actual programme of studies. His interest in adult education and the part the College might play in it had not diminished; but the immediate task to be faced was to fashion the kind of undergraduate university education on which his heart was now set. In articles and addresses he took opportunities to bring before a wider public the educational philosophy which impelled him. His main themes became more insistent: the need for a wide and informed understanding of civilisation, the importance of social values, the dangerous cleavage between arts and science, the incubus of departmentalism, the broadening of the outlook of the expert. And after the College had been opened, with missionary zeal he continued to expound what was being done and what it was hoped to do.[2] He was not the enemy of the expert or of specialised studies, the need for which he fully realised; his concern was that they should be related to a wider spiritual and cultural life and be consciously put in a social setting.

There is one final point to be made. We saw in chapter 4 the vast amount of hard work Lindsay put into the final stages of the planning of the Keele curriculum. By nature his mind

[1] Ibid. In this opinion, he aligned himself with Jowett who held that the chief duty of the tutorial fellows was to teach undergraduates, only incidentally to undertake research.

[2] In addition to articles cited in previous footnotes, see also: 'An experiment in university education' in *Journal of Education*, November 1949; 'The function of the universities' in *Nature*, 16 December 1950; 'The University College of North Staffordshire' in *The Highway*, February 1951, and an article with the same title in *Universities Review*, vol. 24, October 1951.

dealt with broad principles from which he did not depart; and without an examination of the voluminous correspondence he had with colleagues—much of which has probably not been preserved—to say nothing of his unrecorded conversations, it would be impossible to assign this, that or the other detail of the programme definitely to him. As H. J. Perkin has aptly remarked: 'As long as the framework met his demand for "seeing things together" and yet providing the "lessons for hard disciplined thought" . . . he was infinitely flexible about the details of the syllabus.'[1] Yet however much others may have contributed to the various ramifications of the Keele curriculum, one clear fact is beyond dispute: had it not been for Lindsay's vision of what was needed and his persistence, no comparable experiment in university education would have been brought about at that stage in our history.

SOME INFLUENCES ON LINDSAY

From time to time Lindsay mentioned those influences on his educational thinking of which he was particularly conscious: the old Scottish M.A. degree, his observation of American university and college education, his involvement in the reorganisation of German universities, and a number of writers whose views he found valuable and congenial. Writing about Keele in a Glasgow University magazine in 1950, he said: 'Three of our Professors besides our Principal and our Librarian are graduates of Glasgow and in some ways our experiment is inspired by memories of the old Glasgow M.A. as it still existed at the end of the last century.' The 'traditional' Scottish M.A., which was a first degree, not preceded by a B.A., covered seven subjects: Humanity (Latin), Greek, Mathematics, Logic with Metaphysics, Moral Philosophy, Natural Philosophy (Physics) and English.[2] The academic year ran only from October to March, thus making it possible for students, the great majority of whom were poor, to earn a livelihood during the long summer vacation; and four such years were needed before a student could present himself for the examination for the degree. The order in which the subjects were studied was

[1] *New Universities in the United Kingdom*, p. 58.

[2] See e.g. J. Kerr, *Scottish Education*, 1910, and J. D. MacKie, *The University of Glasgow*, 1954.

also part of the tradition: e.g., the classics and mathematics alone were studied for the whole of the first two sessions. It was this rigid curriculum, a severe test of ability and industry but the doorway also to advancement in later life, which has remained embedded in folk memory. The university Commissioners of 1858, however, introduced some important modifications applicable to all four Scottish universities: students who showed that they had a satisfactory knowledge of Latin, Greek and mathematics when they entered the university might graduate in three years; the subjects were now divided into three groups in each of which an examination could be taken as soon as a student had attended the necessary courses and so achieve his degree piecemeal;[1] and a student who had satisfied the examiners in each of the three groups could subsequently present himself for a further examination for honours—an innovation in Scotland—in Classical Literature, Mental Philosophy, Pure Mathematics with Natural Philosophy, or Natural Sciences. Again in 1892 the Commissioners introduced other changes which further alleviated the rigidity of the old curriculum by permitting alternatives. But seven subjects were still required. Of these, four had to be: (i) either Latin or Greek; (ii) either English or a modern language or History; (iii) either Logic with Metaphysics or Moral Philosophy; (iv) either Mathematics or Natural Philosophy. The fifth subject was restricted so as to secure that at least one of the four groups just indicated into which the curriculum was now divided must be taken as a whole, though for this purpose English could be substituted for a subject in group (iii) and Chemistry was admitted as an alternative in group (iv). The remaining two subjects of the seven were free options within the range of subjects in which the university provided instruction—and that might not give much elbow room.[2] The practical effect of these changes was that three, and in the majority of cases four, subjects of the old curriculum had still to be included.

[1] The three groups were: (i) Latin and Greek; (ii) Logic with Metaphysics, Moral Philosophy, and English Literature; (iii) Mathematics and Natural Philosophy. The Commissioners believed that examinations in the separate groups would lead to a 'more accurate knowledge' of each subject with a consequent raising of standards than 'if the whole subjects of the course were embraced in one examination'.

[2] It was at this time also that a summer term was instituted as part of the normal academic year.

This then was the ordinary degree course available when Lindsay went to Glasgow in the 1890s. As he recalled it when he was occupied with the Keele programme, it had a very definite attraction. There was so wide a spread of subjects that the question of specialisation could not arise: in addition to a classical language, every student had to do some philosophy and either mathematics or a science; and it was this breadth that he had in mind when he referred to the Scottish degree. There was of course no conscious attempt to bring out the relationship between one subject and another; but a good student who did more than 'scrape through' received a sound education which could put his mind at full stretch in several important areas of human knowledge.[1] By 1950 the number of subjects which had achieved a place in all university curricula had expanded far beyond what was dreamt of in 1892 and it would have been unrealistic to try and mould Keele closely on the old Scottish pattern; but at least Keele could aim at producing men of the sort of quality with which Lindsay had been familiar in his young student days.

Lindsay's knowledge of American universities and colleges was wider than is generally realised; and from them he gathered a wealth of ideas as well as an admiration for their variety and freedom to experiment. In the winter of 1928–9 he lectured at Harvard; and at Swarthmore he gave the William J. Cooper Foundation lectures which were published under the title of *The Essentials of Democracy*. From this time he became the close friend of Frank Aydelotte, President of Swarthmore, who was himself a creative force in American university education.[2] In the spring of 1932 he lectured on 'Christianity and Economics' at the Union Theological Seminary in New York. As Vice-Chancellor he attended the Harvard Tercentenary Celebrations in 1936. There was a three-month visit in the autumn of 1942 when he gave the Terry lectures at Yale on 'Religion,

[1] By the time some of Lindsay's younger colleagues at Keele had gone to Glasgow as students, the curriculum had been further modified by additional options; and their admiration for the 'Scottish M.A.' would be in part nostalgia for something they had not themselves experienced in its full rigour.

[2] Aydelotte (1880–1956) was a Rhodes Scholar at Brasenose from 1905 to 1907 and President of Swarthmore from 1921 to 1940. An English scholar by training, his important works on education included *Honors Courses in American Colleges*, 1927, and *Breaking the Academic Lock Step*, 1944.

Science and Society in the Modern World'; he met, not for the first time, Adolf Löwe, whose book, *The Universities in Transformation*,[1] he greatly admired; and, sponsored by the British government, he toured universities to talk about Britain in war time, including in his travels Columbia, Ann Arbor, Chicago, Madison, Berkeley, Los Angeles, Leland Stanford, Pasadena and Claremont. His last visit was in 1946 when he lectured at Indiana and received an LL.D. from Princeton.[2]

In his speech on university education in the House of Lords on 14 May 1947, he drew attention to two types of American institution which had interested him. First, there were the Massachusetts and California Institutes of Technology where experiments had for many years been made in broadening the scientific curriculum by courses in the humanities and social studies.[3] But it was the 'liberal arts colleges' which had the greater influence on his thinking. Historically, the colleges of liberal arts were the first institutions of university standing founded in the American colonies. The earliest was Harvard College (1636) and by the end of the eighteenth century eight others (including Yale, Princeton, Columbia and Dartmouth) had been established. There are now well over one thousand such colleges; some are separate and independent, others are part of universities; the majority deliberately restrict their total student enrolment to something less than 1000. Many were founded by religious denominations with a view to educating the future clergy and some still retain strong religious affiliations. Their common hallmark is that they provide for the bachelor's degree a four-year broadly-based curriculum which is not primarily vocational in character. A considerable number of them now award a Master's degree as well; and a few like Bryn Mawr and Radcliffe also have a doctoral programme. It was, of course the undergraduate studies which attracted Lindsay.[4]

[1] See p. 138.

[2] These details were kindly given by Lindsay's daughter, Lady (Drusilla) Scott.

[3] In these experiments Frank Aydelotte had played an important part while he was Professor of English at M.I.T. (1915–21).

[4] The *American College*, a series of articles edited by N. Sanford, contains an important article 'Higher education in a changing society' (pp. 894–939) by Professor W. A. Campbell Stewart which is of particular use for British readers.

The earlier colleges had only a restricted curriculum, though some 'natural philosophy' was generally included. But with the proliferation, both in the humanities and in the sciences, of subjects of university status, the problem arose for the colleges of ensuring that students had some common background of knowledge and values which could be expected of an educated person. Scarcely any two colleges handled this problem in precisely the same way and the experiments in dealing with it have been, and still are, manifold. But there are four major solutions which it is appropriate to mention here in connexion with Keele.

The first is to regulate both positively and negatively the way in which a student spreads his studies amongst the various departments and disciplines and the extent to which in the later years of his course he may concentrate his attention on more specialised fields.[1] These 'distribution requirements' set out to harmonise the student's freedom of choice with the need for a reasonably coherent and inter-related pattern of studies; basically this is the same kind of concept as that which underlies the British degrees in 'general studies'.

The second broad solution which has found much favour is to provide survey or 'orientation' courses in the humanities, social studies and the physical and biological sciences. These are spread over the first two college years and occupy from one-half to almost the whole of a student's time, depending on the particular college he is attending. At their best such courses, when wisely selected and consciously related to each other at appropriate points, can and do achieve a conspectus of human knowledge of great educative value and at the same time can provide a sound basis for later concentration on particular areas. There is inevitably a danger that an over-enthusiastic or possessive teacher might try to use such a course to attract

[1] In part this solution was a reaction against the 'free elective' system introduced at Harvard in 1862 by President Charles W. Eliot and widely imitated elsewhere. At its worst it permitted any combination of subjects however bizarre (Greek, Entomology and 'Public Speaking'—an actual example) and demanded little or no study in depth in any of them. The bad effects were accentuated by the normal American practice of awarding a degree on the basis of a certain number of 'credits' accumulated by attendance at, and examination in, single-semester courses. The 'elective' system was, however, drastically modified from 1910 onwards by the requirement that a student should 'major' in some area of study and by the later introduction in many institutions of 'Honor programmes'.

students to his own department without due regard to the student's best interests; and there is the more general comment to be made that diversification is in itself no guarantee of an educative integration, and certainly no substitute for it. But the underlying principle that specialisation should be deferred until horizons have been widened is one that is closely related to the Keele ideology; and Lindsay's observation of the principle as it worked out in practice at American colleges may well have strengthened his own convictions.

The third solution to their problem with which the liberal arts colleges experimented, is the so-called 'great-books curriculum'.[1] The core of this programme is the reading and study of approximately one hundred carefully selected great books of the Western tradition; and to this central concern, the study of modern languages, mathematics and science is subordinated. A curriculum of this kind became available (but was not imposed on everyone) at Columbia in 1919; it was a prominent feature of the reforms introduced at Chicago when R. M. Hutchins was President (1929 to 1945); and the small St John's College at Annapolis startled America in 1937 by basing on it the whole four years for all its students. Other colleges too have been influenced by the experiment and incorporated some part of the programme in their schemes of study. To many British readers, though perhaps not wholly so to Lindsay,[2] the idea may seem to reach the limit of triviality; but experience shows that when the books are well chosen and the course is well conducted, a scheme of this kind (even if, and perhaps

[1] The idea was first tried out at the end of World War I by John Erskine with American soldiers in France who were awaiting transport back to the United States. In 1919 Erskine set up an honours course on this principle for third and fourth year students at Columbia. It was one of Erskine's pupils, Mortimer Adler, who was invited to Chicago by Hutchins. In the 1950s a Great Books Foundation was set up, with its base in Chicago, to train lay people to lead discussions on specific parts of 'great books'. These discussion groups have become a regular part of adult education programmes all over the United States.

[2] In his article 'The place of English studies in the British universities' (*English Studies Today*, 1951), Lindsay relates how he helped to devise a course of lectures for people from tutorial classes: 'We did it by taking a period of English history and doing the literature along with the history and the economics and the philosophy, and so on. . . . Those organizations were a very great success, and I think it is worth developing something like this at university level.' The point need not be laboured, but one suspects Lindsay would not reject the 'great books' scheme out of hand; and the wide reading list of the Foundation Year may in part be related to his idea.

especially when, adopted only in part) can be an effective instrument of general education at college level.[1]

A fourth solution is the method known as 'individual guidance' which a number of colleges have tried. The first year or two of a student's course is devoted to elective courses chosen by the student solely for exploratory purposes so that he can discover which interests him enough to serve as a basis for later concentration. This exploratory idea has some similarities to the terminal and sessional courses in the first year at Keele; but there is nothing corresponding to Keele's Foundation Year lectures. Unlike the survey and orientation courses elsewhere, these exploratory courses, however, are kept small so that there is intimate contact between student and teacher and an advisory system ensures that every student is guided by a member of the faculty in planning his future programme of studies.

From the variety and experimentations of the New World, we now turn to the re-organisation of universities in a country of the Old World. In 1948 the Military Governor for the British Zone in Germany appointed a University Commission to enquire into the need and possibility of university reform. Of the twelve members of this body, ten were German representatives of the universities, technical universities, churches, trades unions and economic life; with them as colleagues they had a professor of the Federal Technical University of Zurich and Lord Lindsay. His participation in this Commission came at a period when Keele was uppermost in his thoughts and the interchange of ideas between him and his German colleagues on the Commission came at a particularly opportune time. Though he did not himself write the Report, it is known that it was he who made it possible for an agreed document to be produced by such a varied group of people.[2]

The Report dealt with virtually every aspect of German

[1] A common approach is to ask students to concentrate their attention on: (i) what the author actually said; (ii) what he meant by what he said and how this is related to what others have said on the topic, before or since; and (iii) its relevance to their own times and to the world of today. Under these headings a good student could range far afield.

[2] See the appreciation of Lindsay in *The Times* of 29 March 1952 by Sir Robert Birley who at the time was Educational Adviser to the Military Governor. An English version of the Report, *University Reform in Germany*, was published by the Foreign Office late in 1949.

universities. Much of the detail is, of course, applicable only within a German setting; but two topics which were prominently discussed are relevant to Keele: the place of the university in society and the proposal to institute a 'studium generale' to be taken by students in their first two terms.

> In refusing to be complacent about the state of the universities the Commission was impressed by two things: (a) they have not kept step with the social changes of the times; (b) they train the specialist intellect and not the whole man and are tending to break up into aggregates of specialist institutes. . . . The training of the student must not be restricted to giving him theoretical information needed for his future profession. He must be made as far as possible not only a useful specialist but also a useful human being. To understand our world, a general education is needed. Everybody must be socially conscious. Everybody must possess civic and political awareness. Failing this, the different scientific and professional groups will be senselessly isolated; the cultural heritage of the West will disintegrate. The problem is how to make the student aware of the moral, and in the last resort religious, foundations of community life. . . . To reach these goals and to prevent the university splitting up into highly specialised schools, the Commission recommends the increased cultivation of the 'studium generale'. The teaching staffs of the universities should work out a comprehensive programme of general education and basic sciences. This would be for students of all the faculties.

Even though this Report did not have an immediate or dramatic impact on German universities—that could scarcely have been expected—it is a document of considerable historic interest in that it shows how close some German thinking was to trends of opinion elsewhere. Especially noteworthy is the stress laid on the importance of the Western cultural heritage, the need for social conscience and awareness, the function of the university in the service of society, the dangers of specialisation, the narrowness of the expert and the necessity to provide a broader general education for every student. In reading some parts of the Report one has an odd feeling that they are almost 'pure Lindsay'. How far he himself had injected his ideas into the Commission it is now impossible to say; what is certain is that his contacts with his German colleagues did nothing to weaken but much to strengthen his own convictions about what Keele should do and in some measure how it should do it.

Finally in this survey of the background to Lindsay's ideas, reference must be made to three books to which he himself acknowledged his indebtedness. The first is Adolf Löwe's *The Universities in Transformation*, a slim volume published in 1940. Educated in Germany, Löwe had joined the staff of the Arts Faculty at Manchester and viewed the English educational scene with a critical but sympathetic detachment. The universities, he observed, were no longer educating a leisured class, but were primarily regarded as agencies for social ascent and as training schools for remunerative professions. Under the pressure of such changes the traditional form of cultural education had more and more lost its meaning, and this at a time when, because of general social conditions, cultural and moral education was much more necessary than it had ever been before. The universities' true concern must be with 'a new cultural education which is both to balance and underpin vocational education', and 'to interpret the structure and dynamics of the modern world both in its natural and social aspects'. For the cure of the ills which he diagnosed one of his proposals was that every student should spend two years out of four on an introductory course embracing: (1) History, new humanities (including sociology and psychology) and the study of civilisations; (2) philosophy and literature to which mathematics and certain subjects of the natural sciences might be added; but, as a rule, not more than three subjects should be chosen by a student, though various syllabuses would have to be offered for different talents and interests. Clearly there are some parts of this 1940 plan which could have set Lindsay's mind working on the lines which led to the Foundation Year.

It is related that in his address in October 1950 to the assembled students the morning after their arrival Lindsay told them in some detail how much he owed to the Spanish philosopher José Ortega y Gasset. Described by one writer as 'the most European mind in Spain', Ortega (1883–1955) was Professor of Metaphysics at Madrid from 1911 until the outbreak of the Spanish Civil War in 1936; but he was much more besides: a prolific and influential essayist and pamphleteer, editor-publisher concerned with the issuing of works of Spengler, Marcel Proust and James Joyce, and a political leader among Spanish intellectuals. His *Mission of the University* was written in 1930; but it was the translation into English in 1944 which gave it prominence.[1] It is a strange, disturbing, untidy, repetitive sort of book of sixty-five pages, in parts closely reasoned, in other parts oracular and rhetorical, sometimes concerned with purely Spanish problems, at others dealing with the widest educational issues. His main concern was with his own concept of culture:

> Life is a chaos, a tangled and confused jungle in which man is lost. But his mind reacts against the sensation of bewilderment: he labours to find 'roads', 'ways' through the woods, in the form of clear firm ideas concerning the universe. The ensemble of these ideas is culture in the true sense of the term. Culture is what saves human life from being a mere disaster. Man lives, perforce, at *the level of his time*, and more particularly, at *the level of the ideas of his time*. Culture is the *vital* system of ideas of a period. . . . The convulsive situation in Europe at the present moment (1930) is due to the fact that the average Englishman, the average Frenchman, the average German are *uncultured*: they are ignorant of the essential system of ideas concerning the world and man, which belong to our time. This average person is the new barbarian, a laggard behind the contemporary civilization, archaic and primitive in contrast with his problems, which are grimly, relentlessly modern. This new barbarian is above all the professional man, more learned than ever before, but at the same time more uncultured—the engineer, the physician, the lawyer, the scientist. The blame for this unpredicted barbarity, this radical and tragic anachronism, rests primarily with the pretentious nineteenth-century university of all countries. . . . Hence it is imperative to set up once more, in the university, the teaching of the culture, the system of vital ideas, which the age has attained. This is the basic function of the university.

[1] Translated, with an introduction by Howard Lee Nostrand, Princeton University Press, 1944.

Towards the end of his book Ortega sets out the pattern of cultural studies with which universities should be concerned, whatever other professional training they may provide; here he is much more definite and concrete. The primary function of the university is to teach the great cultural disciplines, namely: (1) The physical scheme of the world (physics); (2) The fundamental themes of organic life (biology); (3) The historical process of the human species (history); (4) The structure and functioning of social life (sociology); (5) The plan of the universe (philosophy). 'Personally, I should make a Faculty of Culture the nucleus of the university and of the whole higher learning.... From all quarters the need presses upon us for a new integration of knowledge, which today lies in pieces scattered over the world.' It was doubtless Ortega's insistence on the need for a broad and integrated culture within the body politic and particularly as a function of the universities which, together with his concern about democracy,[1] attracted and inspired Lindsay and led him to speak to those first students of Ortega's ideas; but how much his Keele colleagues gained from Ortega when working out the details of the Foundation Year is quite another matter.

The third of the books which Lindsay valued highly was the Harvard Report, *General Education in a Free Society.* This Report, initiated by President J. B. Conant, was drawn up by a distinguished committee of Harvard professors and immediately on its publication in 1945 was everywhere acclaimed as a major contribution to educational thinking. Though inevitably conditioned by the American high school and college background and directed towards particular policy proposals for Harvard College, the Report is wide in its scope and pregnant with ideas.[2] First, a few quotations will illustrate the points of view from which the Committee surveyed its task.

> It seems that a common ground between some, though not all, of the ideas underlying our educational practice is the sense of heritage. The word heritage is not here taken to

[1] Ortega's rather earlier analysis of the problem of democracy *La Rebelión de las Masas*, 1929 (trans. *Revolt of the Masses*, 1932), was one of his most influential works.

[2] Professor W. A. C. Stewart writes to the author: 'The Report was required reading for young professors at Keele—but not all of them did their homework thoroughly.'

> mean mere retrospection. The purpose of all education is to help students live their own lives. The appeal to heritage is partly to the authority, partly to the clarification of the past about what is important in the present.
>
> Specialism is the means for advancement in our mobile social structure; yet we must envisage the fact that a society controlled wholly by specialists is not a wisely ordered society. . . . The problem is how to save general education and its values within a system where specialism is necessary.
>
> General education is especially required in a democracy where the public elects its leaders and officials; the ordinary citizen must be discerning enough so that he will not be deceived by appearances.

At the time the Report was written the Harvard undergraduate curriculum offered a wide catholicity of choice: one prescribed course in English composition for freshmen who had not demonstrated their proficiency; a reading knowledge in one of ten languages; a freshman programme which gave a choice of forty-six courses; a choice of 'concentration' among thirty-two fields, many of them subdivided; and a prescription regarding distribution of courses which was so liberally framed as to make a very high degree of specialisation possible. On this the committee commented:

> The present system . . . is weak indeed in the opportunities it provides for the development of a common body of information and ideas which would be in some measure the possession of all students. There has been, in other words, no very substantial intellectual experience common to all Harvard students. It would seem clear that communication on an advanced level is impossible unless those who are seeking to communicate with each other have some common body of knowledge and ideas. . . . The undergraduate, whether he be a concentrator in the sciences, the humanities, or the social sciences, should be able to talk with his fellows in other fields above the level of casual conversation. He should share in a common understanding of the heritage which is the possession of his generation.

This ideal at which the committee was aiming is closely consonant with the underlying spirit of the Keele programme. So far the parallel is important. But the methods suggested by the Harvard group for bringing their ideal into effect differ in important respects from those which prevailed at Keele; and if we devote some space to describing them in outline, it is not simply as an exercise in comparative education but as a set of solutions of which Lindsay and his colleagues were well aware but which they did not adopt. The key to the Harvard scheme is to be found in their views on the relation of special to general education:

> General and special education are not, and must not be placed in competition with each other. General education should provide not only an adequate groundwork for the choice of a speciality but a milieu in which the speciality can develop its fullest potentialities. . . Special education instructs in what things can be done and how to do them; general education is the appreciation of the organic complex of relationships which gives meaning and point to the speciality. To some degree it should suffuse all special education. . . . We wish to avoid a system in which general education is carefully segregated from special education as though the two had nothing in common. . . . It would be a mistake to set off a certain period for general education, leaving the remainder for non-general education, as though general education ceased at a certain point and had no relevance to subsequent study. . . . General education should be a pervasive and lasting influence as well as a set of course requirements.

At Keele general education is, of course, not wholly 'segregated' in the Foundation Year, though concentrated there; for its 'suffusion' in the later years of the degree course Keele has relied on the spread of subjects between subsidiaries and principals and on the two-subject Final.

The Harvard approach to the problem determined the degree structure which they advocated. Of the sixteen courses required for the Bachelor's degree, six were to be in general education and three of these were to be designated and compulsory: one in the humanities, one in the social sciences and one in the sciences.

> The prescribed courses in the humanities and the social sciences would be expected to furnish the common core, the body of learning and of ideas which would be a common experience of all Harvard students, as well as introductions to the study of the traditions of Western culture and to the consideration of general relationships. In the area of the sciences it is proposed that there be established alternative courses to meet the needs of those students who come to college with marked divergencies in their preparation and plans for special study.

The three designated courses would be taken during the first two years; the other three less restricted 'second-group' courses in general education would be taken in the third and fourth years and would be selected from a considerable range of 'approved' courses. As compared with Keele, it would perhaps be fair comment first, that even in the earlier years the idea of 'integration of disciplines' is not advanced as a primary consideration; and secondly that the effect of options in 'general education' in the last two years of study is that a common core of knowledge and ideas depends almost entirely on the two designated courses in the humanities and social studies taken in the first two years.

It would take us too far afield to examine the general education courses in any detail but there are a few points of interest which should be mentioned. (1) The compulsory course in the humanities which the Committee proposed was 'Great Texts of Literature', an idea already familiar to us from the programmes of some liberal arts colleges.[1] (2) For the compulsory course in the social sciences, the title suggested was 'Western Thought and Institutions', which for all Keele students will have a familiar sound. (3) The two alternative compulsory courses in science were to be: one in the principles of physical science, the other in the principles of biological science; but no specific provision was made for consideration of the links between them. (4) The Harvard Committee were of the opinion that, so far as general education courses were concerned, tutorial discussion, particularly when combined with the writing and critical analysis of essays, could help to give a greatly increased breadth of view and maturity of

[1] See p. 135.

judgment; but it was not assumed that this method of instruction would be used by all departments.

The importance for Keele of the Harvard Report is to be found not in the details of the arrangements which the Committee recommended for Harvard, but in the stimulus it provided to the thinking of those who were engaged in planning the curriculum for a new college. Its carefully reasoned exposition of the broad principles on which its recommendations were based, its discussions of the place which the various disciplines should occupy within the scheme, and its suggestions for the content of individual courses—all these, emanating as they did from a group of the most experienced members of the faculty of a university of great standing, demanded the most careful consideration. It is no wonder that a copy of the Report which belonged to Lindsay and is now in the University Library is copiously marked with marginal lines.

Six

College and University I: Academic

A CHEQUERED PAGE OF HISTORY

The history of Keele's first twenty-one years can most effectively be presented not by recording events as they occurred year by year but by concentrating attention on a number of topics which have special significance in the development of the College and the University. First and foremost Keele must be considered in relation to the educational ideas on which it was founded—how the implementation of these ideas worked out in practice, how and why they were modified, the kinds of courses the students actually chose, and the growth of research. Of secondary importance, but far from negligible, are the solutions which were found for other problems of various kinds which were associated with the rise of a new institution and in various ways affected its educational policies: expansion in numbers, the physical development of the site, and finance. Even the granting in 1962 of a Charter which conferred full university status cannot be regarded as a sufficiently decisive point in the history of Keele for a formal division to be made there. So far as the real essentials of the development of Keele are concerned, the College and the University are one. The Charter, though it was of great importance in marking the end of sponsorship and in enabling Keele to confer its own higher degrees, did not have the same significance as the granting of a University Charter had had for the earlier university colleges. In their cases a University Charter was the first accolade of independence they received and the granting of it was a sharply defined watershed in their destiny; but for Keele the Charter was not so much a new framework of existence demanding new orientations and responsibilities as a readily foreseeable widening of the kind of liberty which in large measure the College had already been privileged to enjoy.

Nevertheless, in the annals of Keele there were some events

whose very timing was critical for the welfare of the College: we refer particularly to the fact that within a period of less than nine years, death deprived the College of the leadership of three holders of the office of Principal.

At the time he agreed to assume the Principalship, *Lord Lindsay* and his colleagues were aware that his health was precarious and he had no expectation that he would be able or willing to hold the office for more than a very few years; his great hope was to see the new College set as firmly as possible on its feet. In the summer of 1950 his health caused much anxiety, but he recovered sufficiently to welcome the first students in October. He had already marshalled his young professorial colleagues as best he could and worked out with them a scheme of studies for the first year at least. During the 1950–1 session and for much of the one that followed his resolute hand was almost always at the helm; but after a short illness he died on 18 March 1952. What that meant for the College can easily be judged from our earlier chapters where the dominant part he had played in the foundation of the College has been recounted. It was his knowledge, experience and vision which had brought disparate aspirations into focus; it was his drive, energy, advocacy and even flexibility which had surmounted obstacles and won over objectors. Others before him had thought of a College in North Staffordshire; but without him, the aim would not have been achieved; and without the decisive influence of his ideas, Keele would not have been a College where a vitalising experiment in university education was undertaken.

It was a full twelve months before a new Principal was appointed and free to assume his office on 1 April 1953; in the intervening period the Vice-Principal, Professor F. A. Vick (Physics) served as Acting Principal.[1] The new Principal, *Sir John Lennard-Jones*, was in many ways as great a contrast to his predecessor as could have been imagined. A graduate of Manchester and Cambridge, he had been Professor of Theoretical

[1] The College Statutes regulated the procedure for the selection of a Principal who 'shall, subject to the approval of the Academic Council, be appointed by the Council after consideration of a Report from a special Committee of the Council and Senate'. The joint Committee set up in 1952 consisted of: (i) the Chairman of the Council, Ald. the Rev. T. Horwood, (ii) the Acting Principal, (iii) seven members of the Council, (iv) three representatives of the Academic Council, (v) seven members of the Senate appointed by the Senate. Bcademic opinion thus predominated.

Physics and Dean of the Faculty of Science at Bristol (1925–32) and Plummer Professor of Theoretical Chemistry at Cambridge (1932–53); elected a Fellow of the Royal Society in 1933, he was awarded the Davy Medal in 1953 for his work in the field of the application of quantum mechanics to the theory of valency; during World War II he was in charge of a section of armament research at the Ministry of Supply and later (1947–53) was Chairman of that Ministry's Scientific Advisory Council. Distinguished as a scientist and experienced in administration, Lennard-Jones came to Keele at the age of fifty-eight, in sympathy with the aims of the College and eager to promote its development. It could have been anticipated that during his tenure of office he would have complemented the qualities and interests of his predecessor in ways which would have strengthened the fibre of the College and firmly established its reputation for teaching and research. He did indeed have time to make his influence felt in important ways: he reorganised the financial administration of the College, overhauled its committee system, set in motion a review of the Foundation Year and sought ways to reduce the teaching load of his colleagues; but even before he could write his first Annual Report he was stricken by illness and died on 1 November 1954.

Again the Vice-Principal, now Professor J. W. Blake (History), was appointed as Acting Principal until a successor was found. This time the interregnum lasted for almost two whole sessions and it was only on 1 September 1956 that a new Principal took up his duties. In *Sir George Barnes* Keele was again fortunate in being able to appoint as its academic head a person of quite unusual distinction whose interests and previous career, markedly different from those of Lord Lindsay and Sir John Lennard-Jones, would bring another dimension to the life of the College. Intended for a naval career, George Barnes was educated at the Royal Naval Colleges of Osborne and Dartmouth; but when a defect of eyesight thwarted his ambition he went to King's College, Cambridge. After three years of teaching at Dartmouth and five as assistant secretary to the Cambridge University Press, he joined the Talks Department of the BBC in 1935. It was here that his qualities of charm, persuasiveness, imagination and firmness had full play. As Head of the Third Programme from 1946 and then as Director of Television from 1950 to 1956, he exercised a wise and wholesome influence in two of the most important areas of the Corporation's activities which was widely recognised and acclaimed. His acceptance of the Principalship at Keele was not surprising to those who knew how deep was his interest in education and how strong was his social conscience; and thanks to his extensive acquaintance with every facet of cultural and artistic life, and his particular devotion to music, he brought with him an experience and an attitude to life which was invigorating for staff and students alike. Sir George found Keele with its tiresome committees and its individualistic professors very different from the BBC; yet he interested himself with great energy in every aspect of College affairs; if a student society needed encouragement he gave it unsparingly; if a part of the estate needed clearing of brushwood, he joined with a willing band of students to see that it was done; and with the local communities he established or fostered a new and easy pattern of relationships. Everything was of good augury for the future; yet after his first two sessions he too had to struggle against ill-health, and on 22 September 1960, he died, a few days after his fifty-sixth birthday.

For a third time a Vice-Principal, Professor W. A. C. Stewart (Education), became Acting Principal for the 1960–1 session. Thus for four sessions out of the eleven during which it had been in existence the College had been without a Principal. All three professors who successively took on the burden of the Acting Principalship were convinced adherents of the Keele ideals in education; they not only carried on the work of the College but planned, as far as they could, for the future. But for a university institution an interregnum is inhibiting. The temporary holder of so important an office as a principalship must refrain from initiatives and policy decisions which might embarrass the next permanent incumbent and some loss of momentum is inevitable. Furthermore, the ethos of an academic institution depends a great deal on the personality and educational insight of its head. At Keele until 1961 there was no sufficiently continuous influence of that kind apart from the memories Lord Lindsay had bequeathed to it; and though individual members of the Senate and the Academic Council could not always agree among themselves about what it was precisely that Lindsay had said or implied,[1] a hard core of opinion prevailed which

[1] In September 1958 Professor A. E. Teale presented to the Senate at their

tended to look to what the College 'had been intended to do' rather than to what it might do in the future.

The fourth Principal was *Harold M. Taylor*, a New Zealander by birth (1907) who graduated first at the University of Otago and later at Cambridge where he was Smith's Prizeman (1932) and became a Fellow of Clare College (1933–61). A mathematician by training and a lecturer in that subject at Cambridge (1934–45), he became the Treasurer of the University (1945–53) and subsequently Secretary General of the Faculties (1953–61). Distinguished academically and no less experienced than his two immediate predecessors in the complexities of administration, his interests were wide and in the field of Anglo-Saxon art and architecture in particular he could speak and write with the authority of an acknowledged expert. During his six years' tenure of office until September 1967, his quiet efficiency not only consolidated what had already been achieved but organised all that was involved in doubling the number both of students and of staff.

On the retirement of Harold Taylor, who in 1962 had become the first Vice-Chancellor of the University, there was fortunately no interregnum and *Professor W. A. Campbell Stewart*, head of the department of education, was appointed to succeed him. A Scot by birth (1915), Professor Stewart had graduated at University College, London, and after a period as teacher of English in schools he held posts as lecturer in education at the University Colleges of Nottingham and Cardiff prior to his appointment in 1950 to the Chair at Keele. As one of the founding groups of professors and a judicious admirer of Lindsay, he knew the whole history and ideology of Keele; he had served as Acting Principal; he was well known as a writer on educational topics;[1] and he had been Visiting Professor in Education in the Universities of McGill (1957), California (1959) and Manchester (1962–3). It is only rarely that a member of a Senate enjoys the confidence of his colleagues to the extent that

request a 'Memorandum on the aims of the founders of the College'. The comments made on this document by his fellow members show how different were the emphases placed by them on the various points advanced by Teale. Nevertheless a revised memorandum was eventually circulated to all members of staff to help them to get or recover their bearings.

[1] His books include: *Quakers and Education* (1953); *An Introduction to the Sociology of Education* (1962 with Karl Mannheim); *The Educational Innovators* (2 vols, 1967–8, with W. P. McCann).

his appointment as their leader is acceptable: Keele was fortunate in having such a man at hand.

In contrast to the sad events which clouded the earlier years of Keele, it is with pride and satisfaction that the College can recall other occasions of a very different kind. On 17 April 1951, Her Majesty Queen Elizabeth, Consort of H.M. King George VI, officially opened the College, a signal mark of Royal interest and favour which brought great encouragement to the youthful institution. Later, as the Queen Mother, Her Majesty paid two other visits to the College; on 2 May 1961, at the celebration of the tenth anniversary of the opening of the College; and on 1 December 1965, to receive the Honorary Degree of D. Litt. on the occasion of the dedication of the Chapel.

Early in 1956, after the Earl of Harrowby had resigned the office of President of the College on grounds of health, H.R.H. The Princess Margaret accepted an invitation to succeed him; and when the Charter was granted in 1962 she became the first Chancellor of the University. When extending its invitation the College had expressed the opinion that 'as a young institution engaged on an exciting educational venture, it would be fitting to have the gracious encouragement of a young member of the Royal Family holding the highest office in the College'. The invitation was cordially accepted and the happy and close relationship which thus began has brought great joy to Keele, particularly to the students who have deeply appreciated the informal contacts which their Chancellor so evidently delights in making with them.

CHANGES IN THE FOUNDATION YEAR

The Foundation Year involved a number of assumptions. The ideal of the educated and civilised man as one who had an acquaintance with Greek and Latin literature and the poets of his own country, was appreciative of the plastic arts and music, and had perhaps an amateur's knowledge of the science of his own day, was valid for the seventeenth and eighteenth centuries. If not by birth, he was by culture a 'gentleman'. But the founder of Keele was aiming at something other than this. Lindsay wanted not merely to give his students a wide range of interests and to bridge the gap between the arts and the sciences, though both these motives were acceptable to him. He was primarily interested in the sociological significance of education; and for him the criterion of an educational system or of a university curriculum was the extent to which it fostered the harmony and well-being of society as a whole. Basically he had a moral and indeed a religious purpose which the new College was ultimately to serve. He went deeper than those who just aimed at relating subjects to one another on an intellectual plane. It is a misconception to think of Lindsay's idea as *simply* one of 'general education'.

Yet what he wanted to achieve could be accomplished only within the framework of a more general education than was at that time usual at university level. His early colleagues might easily mistake the surface of his ideas for their deeper significance; there is more than a suspicion that some of them did. The first assumption made at least by Lindsay was that a broad course would prove to be an avenue to a view from the hilltops, not a desultory meandering in the plain. It would be a purposeful integration, not a chaos of miscellaneous information. The second assumption, for which there was great justification, was that it is the university which is the place where this process can be attempted most effectively. At the time Keele was being planned, the schools, because of their specialised sixth form curricula, were failing to ensure a breadth of knowledge and outlook in their pupils; it is arguable that, neither then nor now, could there be many schools which, under the pressure of external examinations and with the staff at their command, would be able at best to give more than a meagre foretaste of what Keele proposed to do on a larger scale; and it is indisputable that the age of students at the university and their growing maturity are vital factors in the success of any such educational programme. A third assumption was that a broad curriculum, with whatever end in view, was good for everybody and suitable for all. This ignores the existence of quite gifted individuals whose intellectual and temperamental constitution is such that they can find virtually no interest in the humanities on the one hand or the natural sciences on the other; but this assumption had little or no practical effect for Keele since people of that kind would be unlikely to be attracted by the novel curriculum. The fourth assumption, which goes back to the early plans for an 'Intermediate Year',[1] was that an

[1] See p. 99.

immediate and inescapable impact must be made on students in their very first year in preference to possible alternatives; and (as part of the same assumption) that while some breadth of interest was to be demanded also in the later years, the effect of a concentrated first year course would permeate all subsequent study in the College. The fifth and most important assumption was that such a first year course could be satisfactorily planned and, what was even more problematical, that it could be handled with a common purpose by a group of teachers not all of whom might themselves evince that breadth of outlook which the course was intended to inculcate.

The first programme of studies for the Foundation Year was agreed upon only a short time before the College opened.[1] Even if the circumstances had been the best possible, it could scarcely have been expected that a perfect solution, if such there be, would have been reached at the first attempt. What had been achieved was a list of titles for some 300 lectures grouped under three broad headings, and a plan for sessional and terminal 'tutorials' spread over the humanities, social studies and the natural sciences. The purpose of the Foundation Year, on which the success of the Keele 'experiment' so largely depended, had been defined as an integrated study of man in his environment and of the heritage of Western civilisation. But the lectures had still to be prepared and delivered and it was only when the first group of students had been exposed to them that any assessment could be made of their effectiveness either in regard to the suitability of their content or to their relationship to one another. The 'tutorials', too, involved a new and untried concept. During the first session also, in addition to all the administrative, siting, financial and other problems, the curriculum for the last three years of the degree course had to be discussed and organised. It was a time of stress and strain probably without parallel in the history of any young institution of university standing: there were so many new things to be done.

Whatever were the deficiencies of the first series of lectures and 'tutorials' no one was more aware of them than the Senate at Keele; they realised that from this first tentative encyclopaedic jumble no clear unifying idea was emerging and that students were being subjected to a succession of lectures

[1] See pp. 113–18.

between which there was often only a nominal connexion. What is not generally appreciated is that continuously from the end of the first session the Foundation Year has been critically scrutinised and on three occasions, in 1957, 1963 and 1966 very considerably modified. The minutes of the Senate, of its Academic Planning Committee, of the Boards of Studies, and above all of the Foundation Year Committee which became a permanent body from 1954, abound in resolutions and memoranda focused on the dynamic improvement of the Foundation Year. At the risk of over-generalisation, we can say that the main concerns have been: first, to make the lengthy course of lectures as coherent as possible; second, to ensure the conscious and active participation of the students themselves in all parts of the first year course; and third, to relate the lectures themselves to other aspects of the course.

The process of revision started very early when, at the end of the first session, the Senate asked the Boards of Studies to submit their proposals; and some re-arrangement of the lectures scheduled for the Spring Term was adopted for 1952–1953. A more fundamental attempt to solve some of the problems was made when the Senate decided in 1953 that for each term a head of department should be placed in charge of lecture arrangements with power to revise the lecture list 'drastically' and reconsider the list of books recommended for reading; these three heads of departments—Professors Blake, Gemmell and Gallie—would also have charge of the lecture course over the entire academic year and would be responsible for its unity. Such an assignment demanded tact and forbearance in dealing with colleagues; but the triumvirate not only avoided or resolved disharmony but secured the assent of the Senate and the Academic Council to two important innovations. The first of these was the introduction for session 1953–4 of 'lectures of an introductory and review type so that students could appreciate more clearly the general plan of the course', a device which with its later refinements has done much to bind the course of lectures into a significant whole. The other new feature, strongly advocated by the Principal, Sir John Lennard-Jones, was the institution of seminars, later called 'discussion groups', which would meet once a week under a continuing chairman and would 'bear directly on the content of the Foundation Year lecture course'. In this way students would have a less passive attitude to the course and be stimulated to think critically about the content of the lectures; and each student was to present to his discussion group at least one essay or paper during the session—surely not a heavy requirement. At this stage the chairman of each discussion group of six to ten students could 'invite a member of staff to attend any session of his seminar' and it was hoped somewhat optimistically that each lecturer in the Foundation Year course would 'provide short summaries of the major points of each lecture for circulation to each chairman a week before the relevant session of his seminar'. This was the first step towards the current practice of having a member of staff from each of the three Boards of Studies participating at each meeting of a discussion group and so ensuring that, whatever the subject for discussion might be, there would be someone present who had some acquaintance, however marginal, with it.

The further reforms which came fully into effect at the beginning of the 1957–8 session were the result of nearly three years of consideration by the Foundation Year Committee during which comments, criticisms and suggestions had been collected not only from members of staff but from the students as well. There was a wide consensus of opinion that the number of lectures should be reduced. It was proving impossible for a student to keep up with the background reading 'because of the immense variety of topics and the rapidity with which space and time are surmounted in the course of the lectures'; and the history department was finding that the chronological framework of the course was imposing an undue burden on them. A proposal however that only eight lectures each week and a total of 200 should be given was felt to be impracticable; and the only reduction which was effected was to a number around 260. But the number of lectures was only part of the problem: coherence and balance was of still more importance. Here the task of the Committee was 'rendered all the more difficult by the intransigence of some participants', as, for example, when 'one Head of Department declined either to reduce the number of lectures which he gave or to alter the presentation of his material'. In the event the aim of the lecture course was still once more defined, on this occasion as being 'to introduce the student to some of the methods and information necessary to an estimate of the inheritance, the problems and the achievements of Modern Western Man'. The broad scheme of the original course of lectures which had already been modified from time to time, was radically altered. The first section, 'Background and Heritage of Modern Western Society', now dealt with the natural environment, the evolution of life and 'some of the achievements of Western man, from the Greeks to the Industrial Revolution, emphasising particular elements such as classical literature and philosophy, or Christianity, which form part of an enduring tradition'—still a forbidding diet. The second section, 'Western Society in the Industrial Age', laid stress on the rise and effects of industrialisation, while the third section, 'Creative Man', attempted 'to survey the achievements of the human mind, particularly in modern times, analytically rather than historically'. It might be doubted whether the burden on the students or the demands on the staff had been lightened and whether an apprehensible coherence had yet been achieved. Within this framework, the intricate mosaic of the separate lectures was necessarily rearranged. Each department was to make its contribution to the general themes in the form of groups or blocks of lectures but would have a free hand in determining what should go into its own block of lectures—a potentially dangerous compromise. This at least relieved the Foundation Year Committee of the invidious task of deciding the subject matter of an individual lecture; and it would now be seductively possible for a department to adjust its own contribution according to the different interests of staff members over the years. Two great advantages which were foreseen were first that students could now settle down to the serious study of one thing at a time and secondly that a closer relationship could be established between the lectures and the discussion groups.

During this same period, 1955–7, when the basis of the lecture course was being remodelled, attention was also given to the terminal and sessional courses which at first had been called 'tutorials'. The three different terminal courses taken in successive terms were intended in the main to enable a student to keep in touch with subjects he had already studied at school and some of which he might wish to pursue in his later degree course. The two sessionals, however, were an introduction to subjects which had not been studied seriously, if at all, in school; they were regarded as an excellent way of achieving 'disciplined scholarship and experience of working hard under direct supervision'. There was, of course, the important proviso that the terminals and sessionals should be distributed over the three major areas into which the Keele curriculum was divided: (a) humanities, (b) social studies and (c) natural sciences. Unlike the discussion groups, these two types of course were never intended to be mere appendages to the Foundation Year lectures. They served quite a different purpose and have been much more important than the lectures in influencing students in their eventual choice of principal and subsidiary subjects in the degree course. It was in the sessional courses in particular that professors could stimulate an interest in their own subjects; and in the discussions about these courses in 1955–7 more than a glimpse was seen of the cloven hoof of departmentalism. A proposal was made in 1956 by the Foundation Year Committee actually to increase the number of weekly classes in sessional courses in all subjects from one to two, and the number of hours of permissible laboratory work from two to four. The reasons advanced were an odd mixture: the sessionals, since they involved opportunities for continuous study of a subject, were a better test of a student's ability; they were more easily examinable than the lecture course; if more time were available for them, arts students might be induced to change over to science. The effect of this proposal would be that, unless the lecture course itself was curtailed from ten to eight hours a week, the formal weekly teaching load for students would rise from sixteen to twenty hours. Only the Board of Natural Sciences was in favour of the proposal; but two results did ensue: formal examinations for sessional courses were introduced; and from 1958 special transfer courses, with a compensating lightening of other requirements, were made available in some of the science subjects for arts students who wished to change over.[1]

The second major revision of the Foundation Year lecture course was carried out in the early 1960s. Student numbers were increasing and over 200 freshmen had been admitted in

[1] Such courses are still offered in mathematics, chemistry and physics for students who come to the University inadequately prepared but wish to take one of the subjects at principal level.

October 1960; the Nuffield Foundation had just made a gift of £20,000 to provide a Foundation Year Library and a further £5,000 to enable a study of the structure, significance and effect of the Foundation Year to be undertaken.[1] As an exercise in self-criticism, the Report of the Foundation Year Committee which came to the Senate in November 1961, could not be faulted:

> To summarize our conclusions in one sentence—as at present organized the Foundation Year affords neither a coherent pattern of instruction nor a systematic discipline in learning . . . The student either attempts too much or too little. If he attempts to follow up the lectures by individual reading he finds they are too various and far too numerous for him. If he does not attempt to do this he becomes merely passive. In neither case is he required to do systematic reading and systematic writing on the topics lectured about. In these circumstances it is difficult for him to see the intention of the course. As experience has shown too, it is very difficult both to set an examination on these lectures and to mark such an examination . . . Many students abandon the search for coherence in the Foundation Year and set themselves a more limited but very utilitarian task of making sure they pass the end of year examination. To this end they will concentrate on topics which they have already covered in the VIth Form or for the rest on those topics which past examination papers show are likely to be examined at the end of the year.

The first and most important part of this process of reorganisation was completed in time for October 1963. It had taken three whole sessions for agreement to be reached. Among the proposals which were unacceptable, two had their interest. The first was that the number of Foundation Year lectures should be halved: a drastic device which would have undermined the generality of the course and caused heart-burnings in departments whose contributions would need to be curtailed. The second was that the sessional courses should be closely related to, and indeed based upon, the topics dealt with in the lecture

[1] This study, by the senior tutor, A. H. Iliffe, was published in 1968 as *The Foundation Year in the University of Keele* (Sociological Review Monograph 12, 1968). For details see chapter 7, pp. 258–65.

course: a complication which could easily have stereotyped the lecture course itself and eviscerated the sessionals. But the alterations which were eventually approved for October 1963 marked a distinct improvement. First of all, the lectures were still to be organised in blocks but each block was to illustrate or elaborate a particular and clearly defined 'theme'; secondly the discussion groups were to be more closely associated with the 'themes' of the lectures and with prescribed readings; thirdly—and it is remarkable that, apart from a minor requirement for written work in connexion with the discussion groups, so little attention had been previously given to the point—students were to present fortnightly essays;[1] fourthly, the Foundation Year Library was to make material supplementary to the prescribed reading available so that students who wished to pursue a particular 'theme' could do some advanced reading. Finally, the end of session examination was to consist not of rather general essays but of three question papers on the Foundation Year 'themes'.

It was not in the nature of the Senate at Keele to leave well alone if there was a hope that something better could be done. The reforms of 1963 were only the first part of a continuing process of revision. The occasional lectures of 'an introductory or review type' which had been introduced ten years earlier seemed to have had no great effect in improving the coherence of the lecture course as a whole; and there was a growing demand for interdepartmental themes which might foster a better integration. In the course of the discussions perhaps the most extraordinary proposal to which an airing was given was that there should be a group of staff specially concerned with the Foundation Year. There could have been no quicker way of ruining the Foundation Year itself and destroying the collective responsibility of the staff for the curriculum as a whole. Much wiser counsels prevailed and by October 1965 a new scheme had been agreed and was put into operation in 1966. Based on the idea of 'themes' which was a critical part of the 1963 reforms, the newer 1966 programme of Foundation Year lectures has so far stood the test of time and experience. In the committee report which came up for the approval of the Senate it was described as[2]

[1] The number of essays was reduced from fifteen to nine from October 1964.

[2] The Committee was also 'concerned to ensure that all departments should

> a mainly genetic survey of the 'development and achievements of modern man' . . . In the first two terms a 'theme' structure is retained, but has been amplified in three important ways: first, so far as possible the themes have been reconstructed so as to appear in single-week units (Main Thread); second, after the first two weeks, Friday lectures are devoted to regular forward and backward link-surveys, the same topic recurring at three-weekly intervals (Recurrent Topics); and third, where appropriate, . . . auxiliary themes have been inserted into the main stream in order to treat in greater depth certain events or ideas (Discursive Treatment). In the third term the genetic treatment leads into a series of lectures on the current growing points of knowledge.

In these general terms the scheme may not be easy to grasp;[1] but the reader who wishes to see how it works out in practice will find in Appendix III the complete 1970–1 lecture list. There have been some minor modifications in the lecture list since October 1966; but the only important innovation since then has been the introduction of 'objective tests' on the lecture course. These have played an increasingly important part in the assessment of Foundation Year students. One such test is set each term, is based solely on the content of the lectures and consists of fifty multiple-choice questions to be answered in a one-hour paper. Students who score an average of 60 per cent or more in the three tests are excused from all three papers in the end of year examination on the lecture course.[2]

---

play some part in the Foundation Year lectures programme, but not that these parts should be equal, nor even that all departments should have some guaranteed minimum share'. The abandonment of the previous pattern of 'departmental equality' was partly justified on the ground that the lecture course as such was not significant in determining a student's choice of principal subjects in his later years. Needless to say, those professors whose allocations of lectures were reduced were not very pleased about it.

[1] In recent years students have been provided with an admirable ninety page guide to the Foundation Year programme. This sets out week by week the lecture list and alternative topics for the discussion groups, together with the relevant essay subjects. The second half of the booklet redistributes this same material under departmental headings with the addition of reading lists. No student could fairly complain that he was adrift in a chartless sea.

[2] The Foundation Year examinations are entirely internal and there is no outside assessment of any kind. Apart from withdrawals due to personal or health reasons, the mean failure rate in the Foundation Year examinations

The process of revising the original Foundation Year programme thus occupied sixteen years. Whether this means that the Foundation Year is now regarded as being as satisfactory as it is ever likely to be, is another matter; in dealing with so wide-ranging a survey of knowledge as is attempted at Keele, the perfectionist will always see points where improvements may be made. What it is of importance to reiterate is that all the elements of the Foundation Year as it now exists are parts of a functional strategy. The lectures are not the whole story. The discussion groups not only function as an extension of the lectures for the further exploration of particular themes, but serve as a group anchorage, as an administrative staging point for the collection of essays, as a pastoral basis through the 'general tutor' system, as a means of involving all the academic staff in the Foundation Year and providing inevitable cross-discipline participation with colleagues. The terminals maintain continuity between a student's sixth form work and later degree studies and at the same time provide new perspectives on familiar subjects. The sessionals are planned to provide worthwhile one-year courses complete in themselves where students can apply their minds seriously to a subject within an unfamiliar group of disciplines. It is the interweaving of these different functional strands which gives strength to the fabric of the Foundation Year.[1]

---

for the 1950–63 intakes was 5·5 per cent and there has been little variation since then. Failure in the internal examinations on the first year sessional courses at one time reached a mean of 6·8 per cent but has fallen to under 2 per cent (see A. H. Iliffe, *The Foundation Year in the University of Keele*). The Senate has on a number of occasions considered whether the burden on the students in the Foundation Year is excessive and has repeatedly come to the conclusion that it is not.

[1] In March 1959 the Director of the London School of Economics made a proposal to Keele that for a minimum period of three years ten students a year who had been accepted for the LSE and were also acceptable to Keele should be invited to spend a preliminary year at Keele to take the Foundation Year. In principle the Senate and the Academic Council were in favour of such a scheme, though it was realised that the financing of such students for an additional year would be one problem and residential accommodation at Keele would be another. Hoped-for help from a national Foundation was not forthcoming; and before the scheme could be tried, the LSE abandoned it because of changes in its own curriculum. This episode, however, is disquieting in so far as it suggests that the Foundation Year is a detachable entity, a pre-degree substructure on which any other institution could build. The full meaning and importance of the Foundation Year, however, depends also on its interaction with the later years of Keele's own curriculum.

THE STRUCTURE OF DEGREE STUDIES

When the College opened in October 1950 a broad outline of the curriculum for the three years following the Foundation Year had been agreed. The first Prospectus indicated that students would study two or three principal subjects throughout the three years together with such number of one year subsidiary subjects as would bring the total number up to five; and there was the proviso that at least one subject, either principal or subsidiary, must be chosen from each of the three main groups: (A) humanities, (B) social studies, (C) natural sciences. By October 1951 a start had to be made on implementing this scheme and two difficulties immediately presented themselves: first, accommodation for classes and laboratories was still very limited; and secondly, though the staff had been increased mainly by the appointment of assistant lecturers, it was not yet sufficient to cope with a full range of principal and subsidiary courses in addition to the Foundation Year lectures, terminals and sessionals. Consequently the introduction of subsidiaries in German, philosophy, physics and chemistry for non-scientists, and geology for scientists had to be postponed; even the practical work for science students in subsidiary chemistry had to be done in the summer vacation of 1952 because the necessary laboratories were only then in readiness. Biology indeed was the only science department which was able to offer separate subsidiary courses for both scientists and non-scientists—a pattern which was important for the Keele plan in that it gave opportunities for arts students to do serious work outside their own group of subjects.

But these were only temporary obstacles. There was also a handful of questions to be settled about the possible combinations of subjects. Greek and Latin were at first each separately acceptable as principal subjects—but both together could not be offered, a rigid but unrealistic application of the doctrine of breadth which was wisely rescinded in December 1954; until constitutional arrangements affecting the two philosophy departments were finally settled in 1965, philosophy and moral and political philosophy were regarded as forming a single principal subject, though they could be offered separately as subsidiaries; and the combinations of subjects at both levels which were thought appropriate for the B.A. degree with the

Diploma in Education or the Diploma in Social Studies took several years to sort out satisfactorily.

Decisions had also to be taken about the kind and classification of the B.A. degrees which the College would award. It was only in February 1953 that agreement was reached after the Senate, its own Academic Planning Committee, the Boards of Studies and the Academic Council had exchanged reams of paper with each other; and the Academic Council had to show some firmness before matters were settled. Interesting items among the rejected proposals were: that 'students who do not appear to be capable of taking the full Honours Course, but who are otherwise reasonably satisfactory may be required to take a modified course leading to a Pass Degree'; that the second class in honours should not be subdivided, or alternatively, that there should be no third class; and that there should be part I and part II examinations for the degree.[1] The division of the second class, which otherwise would have embraced too wide a spread of achievement, kept Keele in line with most other universities. It was the decision not in any way to provide a separate course for a pass degree which was of permanent significance for the Keele curriculum;[2] and when the matter was again raised in December 1963, the Senate saw no reason to change its opinion.

None of the decisions so far outlined radically altered the structure of degree studies which had been decided upon before the first students arrived. As with the Foundation Year, it was experience of the practical application of these initial arrangements which led to changes in them. The initiative for what was to be the most important change, the reduction in the number of required subsidiary subjects from three to two,[3] has been attributed to the College's second Principal, Sir John Lennard-Jones, who was concerned about the work-load on the students. Satisfied though the Senate might be that the work for the Foundation Year was not excessive,[4] they had qualms

[1] It was the (C) Board of Studies (natural sciences) which advocated this arrangement.

[2] See pp. 99, 104–6, 119n.

[3] Or from two to one if three principal subjects were offered. Only 8 per cent of students have so far offered three principals and then only in combinations of history, philosophy, economics and politics.

[4] See p. 160n.

about the later years. The evidence of the subsidiary examinations in 1951–2 and 1952–3, the comments of the students themselves and some headmasters' protests all pointed in the same direction; and discussion of the problem began in the autumn of 1953. The Senate's Academic Planning Committee felt that:

> a distinction can be drawn between a Subsidiary subject taught primarily as a support to a Principal subject or subjects and a Subsidiary subject taught solely as a contribution to a student's general education—a 'general course': two full Subsidiaries should be taken in the second year, the 'general course' in the third year and for two terms only.

Attractive though this suggestion might be in so far as it seemed to provide a broadening element in the penultimate year of the curriculum and so reinforce the benefits of the Foundation Year, it did not stand up to the criticisms of the Senate.[1] In February 1954 the Senate recommended that the number of subsidiary subjects should be reduced from three to two. It went still further by agreeing that the spread of subjects over all three main subject groups should be modified so that students in future would be specifically required to offer one principal or one subsidiary subject from groups (A) and (B) combined and one from group (C). This new scheme came into effect for students completing their Foundation Year in 1954 and has not since been changed. Not only has the total load been lightened[2] but the concept of including a science and a non-science subject in the degree course has replaced the insistence

1 A number of other suggestions of interest were considered: (i) a scheme in which three subsidiaries would be examined, but passes only required in two —a glaring temptation to the lazy student; (ii) a scheme under which one of the subsidiaries would be taken in the Foundation Year, possibly in substitution for one of the sessionals; (iii) a '2½ subsidiary' scheme: a student would convert one of his sessionals into the 'half-subsidiary' by taking an additional examination in the September following the Foundation Year; thereafter he would have only two subsidiaries to do; (iv) a scheme by which one of the subsidiaries, taken in the second year, would be based on one of the three main topics of the Foundation Year course then current i.e., Man and his Environment, The Development of Western Civilisation or The Industrial Revolution—an idea akin to the other rejected proposal for a 'general course' subsidiary.

2 From 1953–4 onwards the Senate has toyed with the idea that reductions in formal teaching hours would be possible in most subjects at both subsidiary and principal levels. But at Keele, as elsewhere, individual heads of departments always have good reasons why the principle should not apply to them.

on the broader requirement of one subject from each of groups A, B and C.

Before the new regulations could come into effect they had to be approved by the Academic Council; and the attitudes expressed by some members of this body cast further light on the controversial nature of the decision to drop the third subsidiary. The Academic Council was certainly appreciative of the problems posed by the curriculum and as early as October 1953 had put forward the view that:

> a distinction must be made between 'tool' Subsidiary subjects (e.g. Mathematics taken by a student reading Principal Physics and Chemistry) and 'broadening' subjects (e.g. the course 'Physics for Arts Students'). There should be a place in the course for Subsidiary subjects taken, not to provide a certificate of proficiency in the subject, but to give an understanding of the subject in relation to the whole scheme of knowledge. This might be attained by converting at least one of the present Subsidiary subject requirements into a broadening Subsidiary subject, covering the range of a whole group of studies, and providing a link with the Foundation Year.

Clearly the thinking of the Academic Council at this stage was along lines similar to some of the suggestions which the Senate was soon to be mulling over. But when the Senate's recommendations to reduce the number of Subsidiaries first came officially to the Academic Council in April 1954 three members abstained from voting approval. The spearhead of the opposition was a Manchester representative, Professor Graham Cannon: 'a suggestion more contrary to the aims and ideals of the founders of the University College it is hard to conceive.' The feeling of uneasiness was such that in the Annual Report for 1953–4, Professor F. A. Vick who was in charge during the illness of Sir John Lennard-Jones felt it necessary to allay anxiety: 'Some people have been heard to say that this is tantamount to acknowledging the failure of the Keele experiment. I do not believe that anyone need worry himself unduly because we ask for two Subsidiaries instead of three.'

There was another bone of contention, too. In May 1956 the Senate with the approval of the Academic Council resolved that candidates gaining over 70 per cent in a subsidiary subject should be awarded a Distinction:[1] This would be an incentive to serious work. But Graham Cannon was still not satisfied that sufficient stress was being laid on the subsidiaries. He wrote to the Principal, Sir George Barnes, in October 1956: 'What shocked me most was that the marks of the Subsidiary subjects were not added in to the final total to settle the final class. They were only referred to in borderline cases! What it means is that N. Staffs is awarding a General Honours Degree on two subjects alone'.

A scheme which Graham Cannon evolved to remedy what he regarded as a serious defect in assessment procedure did not however find much favour either with the Senate or the Academic Council and as Professor Finer pointed out:

> It takes no account of maturation. It influences Finals by taking into account standards reached one or two years before Finals have been sat. It would encourage students to choose their Subsidiaries from subjects they had already done at school, instead of being influenced by us to select Subsidiaries which, in combination with their Principals, can broaden their education.

Indeed in March 1957 the Senate reaffirmed the line it had always taken that marks gained in subsidiaries should be taken into account only in borderline cases and then only with the effect of raising a student from one class to another. And there the matter was allowed to rest.

The most serious temptation, however, to make a fundamental change in the degree structure arose from the problem of securing a larger intake and out-flow of students on the science side. There was dissatisfaction with the proportion and with the general quality of students whose applications indicated that they hoped to offer two sciences at principal level; the records showed that almost half of such students who were admitted dropped one science subject and one-fifth of the total dropped both; and the ratio of graduates with two science subjects was about 1 in 8. The matter was rather brought to a head in 1960 when the College undertook to adopt, in response to the UGC's call for more scientists, a policy for admissions which would

[1] The distinctions awarded have never exceeded 10 per cent and in some years have been as low as 5 per cent.

lead to two-thirds of the increase in student numbers from 800 to 1,200 being students who would read at least one science principal subject.

In May 1961 the Senate accepted a proposal that those taking two science subjects would be awarded an oddly entitled degree of B.A.(Sc.), but rescinded its resolution at the very next meeting. Two and a half years later, in December 1963, the Senate discussed the introduction of honours degrees in a single subject which might have attracted more science applicants, but could not be persuaded to accept so radical a change in policy. The problem however persisted and a special committee set up in 1965 produced a revolutionary proposal in February 1967. According to this scheme, students who proposed to read two principal science subjects would be offered direct entry, without a Foundation Year course, to a three-year course leading not to a B.A. but to a B.Sc. Honours degree.[1] They would in addition have to offer two subsidiary subjects, one from the humanities, the other from social studies; and they would have the option of taking a one year postgraduate Certificate in Education. As the committee was aware, this proposal would create a category of Keele graduates who had not done the Foundation Year; and apart from other difficulties which need not be detailed, this feature of the recommendation was more than the Senate was able to swallow.

So the basic structure of the degree course still remains in 1971 that which was decided upon in 1954. What has changed has been the range of principal and subsidiary subjects from which a student can choose, and this is the topic of the next section of this chapter.

NEW COURSES AND NEW SUBJECTS

After the initial decisions had been taken in 1950–1 regarding the subjects which were to be available for study in the degree course, the next few years were not marked by the introduction of many new courses or the establishment of new departments. This was not due to any lack of progressive ideas but to the financial and economic conditions affecting all university development in the early 1950s. It was not only that the flow of finance from central sources was restricted as one economic

[1] This has significance for Keele's current discussions; see pp. 294–6.

crisis followed another, but many building materials were in short supply so that licences to commence new constructional work had to be severely rationed. The introduction of new courses of study at Keele would have required both additional staff and further building; and as we have seen,[1] even the plans for offering subsidiary courses in all subjects were hindered precisely by this lack of staff and of teaching accommodation. These shortages could only be remedied by a larger infusion of money and a more generous allocation of building licences than the UGC was prepared to provide. After all, the UGC could not fail to recall that even when the College opened in 1950, the scope of its teaching was already much wider than that which had been originally suggested.[2]

The College indeed was not shy in asking the UGC for what it judged to be its needs; but the answers it received were chilly; and when Lindsay and the Vice-Principal visited the UGC[3] in July 1951 they were told that: '(*a*) the number of Honours Schools was greater than formerly anticipated, and that some reduction might be made; (*b*) the suggested student-staff ratio was too low and it was improbable that a ratio of less than one to 7½ would be acceptable.' This was a policy of retrenchment not of development; and over four years later it was still clear that the UGC would not view new developments at Keele in a very favourable light. The UGC[4] visited the College in November 1955 and at its meeting with the Senate 'questions were asked about the possibility of decreasing the number of subject-combinations offered, about further integration between the teaching of Principal subjects and about the fitness of our graduates to proceed immediately to research'. At its meeting with Council, however, the UGC had some complimentary things to say:

> They were impressed with the spirit of the College and were convinced that the experiment was worth pressing on

1 See p. 161. 2 See chapter 4.

3 By this time Moberly had retired and the new Chairman was Sir Arthur Trueman, successively Professor of Geology at Swansea, Bristol and Glasgow, Deputy Chairman of the UGC from 1946 and Chairman from 1949 to his death in 1953. His attitude to Keele was critical and his relationship with Lindsay none too easy.

4 The Chairman was now Sir Keith Murray (later Lord Murray of Newhaven), formerly Fellow and Bursar (1937–53) and Rector (1944–53) of Lincoln College, Oxford; Chairman of the UGC, 1953–63; Hon.D.Litt., Keele, 1966.

> with—any initial scepticism was now gone. They were particularly interested to find that more than one school of thought existed within the College on academic matters, and they regarded it as a healthy sign that the courses offered by the College should be kept constantly under discussion and review.

Yet the opinions they expressed about the future were a clear warning to exercise restraint in further developments:

> The Chairman said that in making plans for the next quinquennium the UGC's advice to the College would be to aim at consolidation, and not to endanger the success of the experiment by too great a diffusion of effort, either in particular specialisms, in research programmes or in an Institute of Education. He suggested that any increase in staff should be applied in the first place to the main existing work of the College rather than to extending the range of subjects or activities.

Comparisons are sometimes made between the growth and rapid proliferation of new subjects in the newer universities of the 1960s and the slow rate at which Keele expanded its academic programme; in this matter the UGC's pronouncement is an important factor to be taken into account.

The effect of the UGC's attitude is only too evident. When consideration began to be given from the mid-1950s to the introduction of new courses, the emphasis was on courses to be taught by existing departments rather than on the establishment of new departments. In 1956 and 1957 the scheme was evolved for Foundation Year *transfer courses* in science subjects, which were started in October 1958.[1] Another scheme which was considered at this time, but which was never put into practice, was one for new subsidiary courses, the teaching of which would be shared between different departments—a suggested example was a course to be called 'Language' and taught by the English, modern languages and philosophy departments. In 1957 the Senate approved the introduction of honours courses in *International Relations*[2] and in *Social*

[1] See p. 156.

[2] A later Senate document of May 1966 recalls the origin of this course: 'the Professors of Economics, Politics and History were persuaded by the Suez

Analysis, both of which were new only in a limited sense; for both were joint courses taught by existing departments: International Relations by history, economics and politics, and Social Analysis by politics, philosophy and economics. The student taking these courses undertook to do what he had in fact always been able to do, to study the three principal subjects of the contributing departments: what the new courses did do was to select from the instruction offered by the contributing departments those elements which would together provide an integrated programme and a common focus.

These were innovations very much within the framework of what already existed. For more fundamental developments the College was, in the late 1950s, indebted not to the UGC but to the generosity of outside individuals and institutions. *Music* was the first of these. In 1958 an appeal was made by the Reverend Arthur Perry, Lord Mayor of Stoke-on-Trent, and raised £4,600 for a Directorship in the subject.[1] The Senate was jealously cautious and laid it down that none of the cost of such an appointment should fall on general College income. The post was filled on a part-time basis from November 1958; and from January 1964, when the Perry Fund and the Sir George Barnes Memorial Fund were merged, Mr G. M. Pratt was appointed as full-time Director of Music. The subject was included in the curriculum at subsidiary level in October 1965, as a group A option; and with a grant from the Leverhulme Trust Fund a string quartet, now known as the Lindsay Quartet, was established. No small part of the Director's work has been the co-ordination of musical activities on the campus, including the University Orchestra and the Choral Society.

Next in order came the College's first research Chair, in *Communication*, which from 1959 was financed for an initial seven-year period by the Granada TV Network Ltd. The initiative for the foundation of this chair came from Granada, not from the College; and the precise nature of the work to be undertaken naturally depended very much on the interests of the holder of the post. D. M. MacKay, reader in physics in the

crisis of 1956 that their existing facilities were inadequate to enable undergraduates to acquire the material and the techniques necessary for critical analyses of such affairs.'

[1] It seems likely that Sir George Barnes played an important part in encouraging the idea.

University of London, was appointed to the Chair in 1960 and the progressively expanded department now directs its research to four related areas: (i) the information-processing functions of the brain and nervous system; (ii) the principles of organisation of mechanisms with 'brain-like' functions; (iii) special problems of the blind and the deaf; (iv) electrophysiological methods applied to clinical problems.

For the institution of a separately organised course in *American Studies* the College was indebted to the United States Government. In his 1958–9 Report, Sir George Barnes mentioned a visit made to Keele by the cultural attaché at the American Embassy: 'he was struck by the attention already being paid to American studies in the Departments of English, History and Politics; and his apprehension of our need for a new post before the next quinquennium led to this gift.' Thanks to an initial grant of £1,800 a year for three years,[1] a lecturer was appointed early in 1960; and a course in American Studies at principal level became available for students from October 1961. This involved a study of the history, politics, geography and literature of the USA, together with a 'special subject' which 'would be to some extent interdisciplinary', and in the examination of the course 'it is intended that the artificial distinction between subjects be broken down as far as possible by the framing of interdisciplinary questions'. The growing importance of the subject at Keele was further recognised in 1965 when a non-professorial department of American studies was formally established with Dr D. K. Adams in charge. The David Bruce Centre for American Studies is named after a former US Ambassador (Hon.D.Litt., Keele, 1966).

In the 1960s as the College grew in numbers and its income increased there was more elbow-room for academic developments and this decade saw the introduction of further new principal subjects, the setting up of new departments and the creation of new Chairs. The claims of *psychology* had been recognised by Lindsay in his 1950–1 Report because of its importance for education and social studies. For the first three years instruction in the subject had to be provided in the

[1] The outside aid, which had enabled the course to be commenced, was continued when, in 1964, the American Council of Learned Societies provided funds for a lectureship in American literature for four years, together with a capital grant for the Library.

Foundation Year by the Professor of Education and it was not until 1953 that a separate lecturer, Mr A. H. Iliffe, could be appointed and a course at subsidiary level arranged. For several years modest expansions were made and finally in 1962, as a first priority for the 1962–7 quinquennium, Dr I. M. L. Hunter, lecturer in psychology at Edinburgh, was appointed as Professor and head of department and the subject could be studied at principal level. Another need which had been felt increasingly was remedied in 1964 when Dr D. Thompson, Director of Research at the International Commission of Jurists at Geneva, was appointed as Professor of *Law*; and from October 1965 the subject has been taught as a principal subject in group B, and as a sessional or terminal in the Foundation Year.[1]

Developments also took place in the arrangements for modern languages. *Russian studies* were included by the Academic Council as the last item in a short list of possible appointments for session 1956–7 but it was October 1958 before funds permitted an assistant lecturer to start work with a subsidiary language course for scientists, such as was already being conducted in French and German. The scope of the department steadily expanded and, with Dr E. Lampert in charge as senior lecturer from 1965 and as Professor from 1968, a principal level course was established to embrace Russian literature, history and institutions as well as the language; and special Foundation Year arrangements were made for students without 'A' level Russian to progress towards full degree work. As part of the reorganisation in modern languages the original single department which covered *French* and *German* was divided into its two constituent elements in October 1969, each with its professorial head.[2] About the same time changes affecting philosophy and politics took place. In 1950 there had been three related departments: philosophy (in group A), moral and political

[1] The Law Society has agreed that in approved cases a number of exemptions may be claimed by Keele students from the Society's examinations for qualification as a solicitor.

[2] So far as modern languages are concerned the range at Keele is confined to French, German and Russian. In 1963 the University submitted to the UGC (Parry) Committee on Latin-American Studies a proposal for an Institute 'to give post-graduate instruction, provide courses for the personnel of British firms trading in the area and act as a national centre for documentation'. Nothing came of this proposal and no steps have been taken to include Spanish (or Italian) in the normal curriculum.

philosophy (in group B), and political institutions (in group B). As was mentioned above,[1] the overlap between the first two had created a problem at principal level; and in 1965 it was agreed that these two should be merged under the title of *philosophy* (in group A) when Professor Teale retired in 1968 and the name of the third was changed to politics.

In group B a still more significant modification was introduced. Although social studies had loomed large in the early plans for the College, no Chair in the subject was included in the first list of appointments. In 1951 Miss Mary R. Glover had been appointed as a lecturer in the department of political institutions and as Director of Practical Training[2] for candidates for the Diploma in Social Studies, an arrangement which held until her retirement in 1965. The potentialities of Keele as a centre for such studies were recognised as early as 1953 when the Institute of Sociology vested the management of the *Sociological Review* in the College and finally handed over all its assets to the College in November 1956. An editorial committee which includes among its members several distinguished sociologists from outside Keele publishes under Keele auspices three issues of the Review each year together with occasional monographs. In 1957 a lectureship in *social statistics* was instituted and a generous gift of £50,000 was later made by the Nuffield Foundation as an endowment[3] for a *Statistical Research Unit in Sociology* which commenced its operations in January 1964 with a Director at its head.[4] But there was still no Chair of Social Studies as such, and the serious study of the subject was available only to candidates for the Diploma in Social Studies. In planning for the 1967–72 quinquennium, however, the Senate agreed that social studies should, under the name of *sociology*, become an option at principal level whether or not a student proposed to take the Diploma,[5] and that a separate

[1] See p. 161.

[2] Director of Social Service Training from 1952.

[3] It was agreed that the whole sum should be paid at once and invested in the building of staff houses, the income from which would finance the Unit.

[4] The unit is independent and not included in any of the Boards of Studies. A proposal was made in 1964 that a number of research activities that had been going on in different departments of the University should be linked rather more formally together in an Institute of Applied Social Science which would undertake projects of value to the University and to trades unions, Local Authorities and business interests; but the necessary funds have not been forthcoming.

[5] More recently called the Diploma in Applied Social Studies.

Chair in Sociology should be created. As the first holder of this post the University appointed, as from 1 January 1969, Dr R. Frankenberg, reader in sociology at Manchester who had been seconded as Dean of Social Sciences in the University of Zambia.

Apart from the Chair in Communication, the developments just detailed concerned groups A and B alone;[1] and it is convenient to round off the list with a reference to one casualty and one temporary addition. It will be recalled that a lecturer in religious knowledge had been among the earliest appointments.[2] The title of the post was altered to *historical theology* in 1952; the subject was included as an option at subsidiary level; and when plans were being discussed for the 1962–7 quinquennium a Chair was envisaged for session 1965–6. The lecturer,[3] however, resigned in 1961 and the whole future of the subject was re-considered. There was some hope that outside financial support might be raised and there were plans afoot for the removal of the Lichfield Theological College to Keele; neither hope was fulfilled but after some delay a temporary appointment was made to the lectureship. Nevertheless the Senate was uneasy; money for the period 1962–7 was after all not going to permit all desirable developments; the subject had not shown any tendency to increase in numbers and 'the existence over a long period of Subsidiary subjects which were not developed into Principal subjects led to unsatisfactory consequences, particularly for members of staff involved'. So despite the protests of the Humanities Board of Studies, it was decided that, though some teaching in the subject must be maintained in the Foundation Year, it should otherwise be discontinued from the end of the 1966–7 session. Lord Lindsay would have been deeply pained.

A promising new feature of life at Keele was inaugurated in 1962 when the Gulbenkian Foundation, with which Sir George

[1] This is a convenient place to mention two other matters of academic interest. (i) In 1952, thanks to arrangements made between the Meteorological Office and the department of geography, a well-equipped meteorological station was erected on a site not far from Keele Hall. It is now called the Climatological Station and its observations are regularly sent to the relevant scientific organisations. (ii) In 1960, in co-operation with the North Staffordshire Field Club, the College undertook publication of an annual periodical, the *North Staffordshire Journal of Field Studies*, which contains articles on local history, geography and archaeology.

[2] See p. 89n.

[3] R. B. Henderson had retired in 1954 and was succeeded by T. A. Roberts. The post was later held by A. W. Heathcote (1962–7).

Barnes was closely connected, made a grant of £1,500 a year for three years to enable the College to offer an annual *Fellowship in the Creative Arts*, to be held by a dramatist, poet, painter or sculptor who would live on the campus pursuing his own activities and stimulating the interest of students in his work. The Foundation generously renewed their grant for a further two years and the College provided funds for an additional year; but for 1968–9 money was too scarce to continue the Fellowship and the Annual Report briefly noted 'we must as soon as possible find money from somewhere to start this up again'.[1]

The developments in the subjects of group C have in the main been within the initial patterns of instruction planned by the individual departments and mostly consist of the additional options at subsidiary and principal levels made possible by increases in staff. In *biology* as a principal subject, alongside his basic course a student must now take an advanced course either in the physiological or in the evolutionary and ecological aspects. In *chemistry* the physical, inorganic and organic fields are all covered in the courses at principal level and the subsidiary option for non-scientists has been more closely integrated with the lectures and sessionals of the Foundation Year. In *geology* a special alternative subsidiary in geochemistry has been evolved as a 'bridging' subject for students interested in one or other of the facets of earth sciences.[2] *Mathematics* is now able to offer three subsidiary courses, one for students who have taken the subject to an appropriate stage in the sixth Form and will be taking a physical science as a principal subject, another for students less well qualified on entry who will be taking principal subjects in the social sciences, and a third for other students who may be interested. In *physics* a student is offered in his third principal year a choice of selected topics which include solid state physics, modern mechanics, quantum mechanics and quantum physics; and the two subsidiary courses now available are designed to meet the needs of two different groups of non-specialist students.

[1] The holders of this post have been: 1962–3, J. Hall, playwright; 1963–4, L. Leeson, painter; 1964–5, B. M. Macdonald, sculptor; 1965–6, R. Dean, sculptor; 1966–7, Ian Henderson, painter; 1967–8, N. Jackson, poet.

[2] A proposal made in January 1964 for a research group in earth sciences to carry out research across departmental boundaries in geophysics, geochemistry and soil science, has not been effected.

In addition to these quite normal increases in the number of courses of instruction, there have been three other developments which merit mention. The first of these is in *computer science.* The need for an electronic computer had been brought to the notice in the UGC in 1961, but without avail. The lack of such a piece of equipment was proving to be a major obstacle to the development of research not only in the natural sciences but in other fields; and it was fortunate that in 1963 the Research Committee of NATO provided an IBM 1620 computer for work under Dr R. McWeeney's direction on quantum theory and allowed it to be used for other purposes as well. When Dr McWeeney, who had been elevated to a personal Chair in 1964, moved with his machine to a Chair in Sheffield in 1966, things could have been difficult had not the UGC just previously agreed to the installation at Keele of a more advanced type of machine (an Elliott 4130) which was in operation by July 1967. Already in 1963 a Computation Director (Dr. H. H. Greenwood) had been appointed and an independent Computing Centre was established in 1967 and two alternative subsidiary courses were organised, one for students in groups A and B, the other for scientists. The second development was in *astronomy.* In 1962 a twelve-inch refracting telescope was obtained from the University of Oxford for use in some branches of the research programme of the department of physics; it also enabled practical demonstrations to be given in connexion with the Foundation Year lectures on astronomy; and from 1967 it became possible for students without any previous knowledge of science or mathematics to offer the subject at subsidiary level. Thirdly, in 1967 a research *Unit of Cardiology* was established in the department of biology with the help of a gift of £20,000 made by Mr W. E. Dunn; and a programme of research is now being carried out on problems arising in heart surgery, the design of pumps for extra-corporeal flow, the clotting of blood and the effects of hypothermia and anoxia on brain and nervous tissue.

Before we pass from the topic of courses and departments we must make particular reference to the changes which have taken place since 1950 in the headships of the original fifteen departments. The first holders of the posts knew Lindsay and came under his personal influence; most of their successors did not and if the changes had occurred more rapidly than they did there is no knowing how the Keele ideology might have been modified or whittled away. As things have turned out, the newcomers have contributed their varied ranges of experience to the maintenance and evolution of what is basic in the Keele pattern of education. Let us take the departments in the order in which they were mentioned in chapter 3.[1] W. B. Gallie was succeeded in 1954 by A. G. N. Flew, lecturer in philosophy at Aberdeen; A. E. Teale's Chair in Moral and Political Philosophy was discontinued after his retirement in 1968; J. W. Blake was succeeded in 1964 by W. M. Simon, a graduate of Wesleyan University (Connecticut) and Yale, who held a Chair in History at Cornell University, USA; W. W. Chambers was succeeded in 1954 in the Chair of Modern Languages by K. Brooke, lecturer in German at Belfast: his title was altered to Professor of German in 1969; a personal Chair in French (within the department of modern languages) created in 1962 for R. J. North became an established Chair in 1966 to which J. H. Broome was appointed in 1968 when North left Keele for Birmingham, and in 1969 French became a separate department;[2] B. R. Williams in Economics was followed in 1959 by E. M. Hugh-Jones, fellow and tutor of Keble College, Oxford, who on his retirement through ill-health in 1968 was succeeded by L. Fishman, a graduate of California and Professor of Economics in the University of Colorado, USA. When S. E. Finer left for Manchester in 1966, his successor was M. Harrison, senior lecturer in government at Manchester. When W. A. C. Stewart became Vice-Chancellor in 1967, S. J. Eggleston, senior lecturer in education at the University of Leicester, succeeded him as head of the department of education and G. N. Brown, recently Professor of Education at Ibadan, succeeded Stewart as Director of the Institute of Education with professorial status. Mathematics like economics has seen two changes in the headship. I. N. Sneddon was followed in 1956 by D. S. Jones, senior lecturer in Manchester who left for St Andrews in 1964 and was succeeded by A. P. Robertson, senior lecturer at Glasgow. The vacancy in physics created when F. A. Vick left in 1959 was filled by D. J. E. Ingram, reader in electronics at Southampton. Finally, to complete the list of professorships, a personal chair

[1] See pp. 88–9.

[2] Both North and Broome had joined the staff of Keele in 1951.

in Organic Chemistry was created in 1966 for I. T. Millar; the Directorship in Adult Education held by Roy Shaw became a Chair in 1968; a personal Chair in Social Geography was created for H. B. Rodgers in 1970; and in 1971 A. J. Smith, senior lecturer at Swansea, was appointed to a newly-established second Chair in English.

COMBINATIONS OF SUBJECTS; DEGREES AWARDED

What then do all these academic developments amount to in terms of students' preferences and achievements? This is a topic where even the least numerate of readers must be prepared to face some figures; for much of what has to be said is quantitative. From October 1950 to October 1966 inclusive, 3,609 students entered Keele and the 1966 entry would be expected to graduate in 1970, apart from those few modern language students who were intercalating a whole year abroad between their second and third principal years. Of these 3,609 entrants, 3,028 (almost 84 per cent) have taken B.A. degrees, the classification of which we shall consider later. The remaining 581 who did not complete their courses of study consist of 380 (10·5 per cent of the entrants) who withdrew because of academic failure and 201 (5·5 per cent) to whom other reasons apply. Half of the academic failures occurred at the end of the Foundation Year and very few in the Final year. It is well known that the over-all 'wastage' rate differs from university to university, from faculty to faculty and from year to year; it rises in some circumstances to almost 20 per cent but can fall as low as 10 per cent. The figures just given for Keele, which show an average over-all wastage of 16 per cent, refer to the entire period of sixteen relevant years. During this time the purely academic failure ratio has fallen from a high level of 15 per cent among the entrants in the first three or four years to 9 per cent for those who entered in 1963–6. This fall would seem to be due to two main causes: the pressures on the students have been reduced by the modifications in the degree structure we have indicated above, and the wider range of choice of courses has the effect of not forcing students to offer subjects, particularly at subsidiary level, for which they have little enthusiasm and no particular aptitude.

Before we look in detail at the combinations of subjects

presented at principal level, it is worth while to set out in the following table the relative popularity of subjects as shown by the number of students taking them. Even when allowance is made for the fact that some subjects, such as American Studies, Psychology, Sociology, Law and Russian, have not been available as principals throughout the period, Table 2 gives a fair indication of the balance of studies in the College and the University:[1]

Table 2 Number of students taking each subject—1954–70

Subject	*Students*	%	*Subject*	*Students*	%
History	837	13·6	Geology	195	3·2
English	780	12·7	Maths	193	3·1
Politics	737	12·1	Amer. St.	151	2·4
Econ.	578	9·4	Sociol.	130	2·2
Geog.	485	7·9	German	121	1·9
Philos.	364	5·9	Soc. St.	120	1·9
French	290	4·7	Latin	92	1·5
Biology	259	4·2	Law	58	0·9
Physics	258	4·2	Greek	41	0·7
Chem.	238	3·8	Russian	11	0·1
Psychol.	220	3·6			

How then did students combine these subjects? Out of the 3,028 degrees awarded up to July 1970, 837 (27·6 per cent) have been entirely in group A subjects, 471 (15·5 per cent) in group B, 347 (11·5 per cent) in group C, and 1,373 (45·4 per cent) in combinations of subjects from different groups. Of the 1,373 last mentioned, 924 (30·5 per cent) combined groups A and B, 359 (11·9 per cent) groups B and C, and 90 (3·0 per cent) groups A and C.

Table 3 classifies, in descending order of frequency, the 837 degrees awarded entirely in group A.

Table 4 shows the distribution of the 471 degrees awarded on two principal subjects taken from group B.

The distribution of the 347 degrees awarded in group C on two principals, both taken in the natural sciences, are shown in Table 5.

[1] The numbers take account of the 106 students who offered three principals.

Table 3 Degrees awarded in group A—1954–70

Subjects	Degrees	%	Subjects	Degrees	%
Eng./Hist.	237	28·3	Fr./Hist.	25	3·0
Eng./Philos.	147	17·6	Eng./Lat.	21	2·5
Eng./Fr.	112	13·4	Fr./Lat.	16	1·9
Fr./Germ.	63	7·5	Eng./Germ.	15	1·8
Amer. Stud./Eng.	40	4·8	Hist./Lat.	14	1·7
Amer. Stud./Hist.	38	4·5	Germ./Philos.	10	1·2
Hist./Philos.	32	3·8			
Greek/Lat.	26	3·1	17 others[a]	41	4·9

[a] These forty-one include unusual combinations of Greek with English (5), French (3), Philosophy (3), German (2), or American Studies (1).

Table 4 Degrees awarded in group B—1954–70

Subjects	Degrees	%	Subjects	Degrees	%
Soc. Stud./Sociol.[a]	120	25·5	Psychol./Sociol.	13	2·7
Econ./Geogr.	106	22·5	Politics/Sociol.	12	2·6
Econ./Politics	95	20·1	Econ./Sociol.	12	2·6
Geogr./Politics	32	6·8	Politics/Psychol.	10	2·1
Econ./Psychol.	25	5·3			
Geogr./Sociol.	16	3·4	Law/5 others[b]	30	6·4

[a] All but four of these students also took the Diploma in (Applied) Social Studies.

[b] These consist of Law with Politics (9), Sociology (7), Economics (7), Psychology (6), or Geography (1). The last combination is no longer permitted.

Table 5 Degrees awarded in group C—1954–70

Subjects	Degrees	%	Subjects	Degrees	%
Maths./Physics	105	30·2	Chem./Geol.	24	6·9
Chem./Physics	75	21·6	Geol./Physics	18	5·2
Biol./Chem.	58	16·7	Chem./Maths.	13	3·8
Biol./Geol.	51	14·7	Others	3	0·9

One's first impression from the three tables of distribution just given is that they show very much the same pattern of combinations of subjects as one might expect to find in other universities if regard is had only to the evidence they provide of the interests of the students; but it needs to be borne in mind that in other universities, except where 'combined honours' courses are available or a change of subject between a part I and a part II is possible, one or other of the two subjects would be taken only at an ancillary or subsidiary level. Furthermore—and the point bears repetition—at Keele not only are two subjects taken as principals, but they are backed up by one-year subsidiary subjects in two other disciplines in the first or second years of the degree course.

We turn now (Table 6) to the content of the degrees for which the principal subjects were taken from more than a single Board.

Table 6 Subject combinations in group A with B

Subjects	*Degrees*	%	*Subjects*	*Degrees*	%
Hist./Politics	228	24·7	Amer. St./Geog.	29	3·1
Hist./Geogr.	90	9·7	Philos./Econ. Politics[b]	23	2·5
Econ./Hist./Politics[a]	83	9·0	Amer. St./Politics	22	2·4
Eng./Politics	68	7·4	Fr./Econ.	20	2·2
Eng./Geogr.	54	5·8	Fr./Politics	18	1·9
Eng./Psychol.	44	4·8	Eng./Sociol.	15	1·6
Hist./Econ.	43	4·8	Hist./Psychol.	15	1·6
Philos./Politics	36	3·9	Hist./Sociol.	12	1·3
Philos./Psychol.	30	3·2	Others	94	10·1

[a] This is the joint honours course in International Relations; see p. 169.
[b] This is the joint honours course in Social Analysis; see p. 169.

Again these combinations of subjects which link groups A and B could easily be paralleled, apart from the level at which they are offered, in other universities when the distribution of subjects amongst the faculties or the inter-faculty arrangements have the necessary flexibility.

Of greater interest are the combinations of a subject from

group A or B with a subject from group C; for it is here that the gap between the natural sciences and other subjects should most effectively be bridged. Among the 449 students who offered a science and non-science combination, 359 took a subject from group B and 90 a subject from group A. The most frequent resulting linkages are shown in Table 7.

Table 7 Combinations of subjects from group A or B and group C

Subjects	*Degrees*	%	*Subjects*	*Degrees*	%
Geogr./Geology	88	19·6	Phil./Maths.	17	3·9
Econ./Chem.	57	12·7	Econ./Physics	16	3·6
Geogr./Biol.	53	11·4	Psychol./Physics	12	2·7
Psychol./Biol.	40	8·9	Psychol./Maths.	11	2·5
Econ./Maths.	35	7·8	Phil./Biol.	11	2·5
Econ./Biol.	29	6·5	Eng./Biol.	8	1·8
Phil./Physics	23	5·1	Others	49	**11·0**

As in the case of combinations of subjects from groups A and B, so here, there are some pairings of subjects, such as Geography with Geology, which would be possible in other universities, though it might not be possible to offer them as at Keele at the same level; but there are others, such as the rather surprisingly popular association of Economics with Chemistry, which it would have been virtually impossible to achieve at least prior to Keele's foundation. Amongst the forty-nine combinations which have not been detailed in Table 7, there is none which has been offered by more than four students, and some of these are no longer allowable, partly because the timetables render them impracticable, partly because they are thought to be too bizarre. But by and large it can be claimed that the Keele curriculum does present opportunities for interesting juxtapositions of subjects and that—in so far as these opportunities are being used—Keele is educating a number of people whose unusual qualifications fit them for positions where a knowledge of two apparently distant subjects could become a growth-point for interdisciplinary advances in knowledge or techniques.

What has been attempted in the preceding paragraphs is a general picture of the combinations of principal subjects. A complete statistical survey of the Keele curriculum would take account also of the subsidiary subjects offered in conjunction with the various combinations of principals, though it might be doubted how much of real value such a survey would contribute apart from reinforcing the point that the range of disciplines with which a student becomes acquainted in his degree course at one level or another is wide and varied.

In this context there is another distinctive feature of the curriculum still to be mentioned, that is to say, the combination of a degree with a concurrent qualification in education or in applied social studies. For the degree with the *Certificate in Education*, a student must, in addition to practical work in teaching, read two principals and take one subsidiary in addition to the education course.[1] Up to 1970 a total of 515 students (17·0 per cent of all graduates) had succeeded in achieving this arduous task. They have been included in the tables given above of subject combinations; but it is worth mention that of this category, 192 (37·3 per cent) offered subjects entirely from group A, 40 (7·8 per cent) from group B, 33 (6·4 per cent) from group C and 250 (48·5 per cent) from a combination of groups. *The Diploma in Applied Social Studies*, designed for people who will seek posts in such fields as probation, child care and medical social work, involves the academic study of sociology at principal level together with other social sciences (including law) and supervised practical work. In all, 116 (3·8 per cent of all graduates) have passed the courses necessary for the degree and 112 have been awarded the Diploma.

The two noteworthy features in Table 8 are the low percentage of class I degrees obtained in group B and the high figure for the combination of group A with C. The pattern of awards fluctuated notably in the earlier years: in the 1954 examinations, out of 109 candidates 10 (9·0 per cent) were awarded class I degrees, but 12 (11·0 per cent) obtained only a pass; in

[1] From October 1968, Education became allowable as a principal subject in combination with principal Chemistry, Physics or Mathematics. Two subsidiaries have also to be taken, one of them being a second science. If practical teaching work is undertaken in addition, the Certificate in Education also is awarded. This scheme is designed for students who 'wish to become specialists in Science or Mathematical education, working in schools, colleges, industry, broadcasting or publishing'. No such students have yet had time to graduate.

Table 8 Classification of degrees awarded from 1954 to 1970

Group	*I*	*%*	*II(i)*	*II(ii)*	*III*	*Pass*	*Total*
A	38	4·5	255	419	107	18	837
B	11	2·3	149	219	78	14	471
C	30	8·6	77	108	81	51	347
A with B	33	3·6	304	468	105	14	924
B with C	13	3·6	86	135	107	18	359
A with C	10	11·1	25	28	23	4	90
Total		135	896	1,377	501	119	3,028
%		4·5	29·6	45·5	16·5	3·9	100

the next year, out of 111 candidates none obtained a class I but 13 (11·7 per cent) were given a pass. Subsequently a more stable distribution began to appear with an occasional exception as in 1967, when the highest ratio of class I degrees was awarded (22 out of 226, 9·7 per cent). A precise comparison with national averages is not easy to make, first because such figures have only been published since 1966,[1] secondly because Keele is basically an 'honours only' university; but what evidence is available is sufficiently significant to justify Table 9.

Table 9 Degrees awarded by Keele and national average

Degrees	*All universities 1966–9* *Nos*	*%*	*Keele 1954–70* *Nos*	*%*
Honours	118,930	75·0	2,909	96·1
Pass	39,664	25·0	119	3·9
Total	158,594	100·0	3,028	100·0
Class I	10,769	9·0	135	4·6
II(i)	33,546	28·2	896	30·8
II(ii)	44,904	37·7	1,377	47·3
II (not divided)	9,715	8·1	—	—
III	19,996	17·0	501	17·3
Total hons	118,930	100·0	2,909	100·0

[1] In *Statistics of Education*, Vol. 6, University Grants Committee, for 1966, 1967, 1968, 1969 (HMSO).

It is evident that a class I at Keele has not been easy to gain; and if we can assume that some of the undivided class II in other universities would be of II(i) quality, then the Keele II(i) is not more generously awarded than elsewhere. There is no kind of evidence to suggest that the comparative paucity of class I degrees is related to the quality of students applying to and accepted by Keele. The class of degree of which a student is thought worthy, and especially where class I is concerned, seems to have depended on two factors. The first is that the standard set by the external examiners in consultation with the departments could have been, and probably was, influenced to some extent by what would be expected in range and depth of knowledge from a single-subject Final candidate. The second—and more important—reason is that a crude summation of the marks gained in the two principals has never been regarded as a valid criterion; and for the higher classes of degree neither subject is permitted to fall below what is regarded as the appropriate minimum for the particular award. The application of such rules tends to exclude from classes I and II(i) students whose performance in one of their principals is weak, however brilliant they may be in the other. Of the 515 students who combined a degree with the Certificate or Diploma[1] in Education, only 11 (2·1 per cent) achieved a class I,[2] 144 (28·0 per cent) a II(i). In the degree course associated with the Diploma in Applied Social Studies, only 1 student (0·8 per cent) out of 116 was awarded a first, but 42 (35 per cent) gained a II(i).

HIGHER DEGREES; RESEARCH; THE LIBRARY

For the first few years anyone who joined the academic staff at Keele must have realised that there was one sacrifice he could not avoid making; for a time he would have to abate, though perhaps not wholly discontinue, his scholarly investigations or his scientific research. Laboratory space and equipment were as yet woefully inadequate and the resources of the library could barely meet the needs of the undergraduates; and the hours that could be spared from teaching, tutoring and

[1] The term Diploma was not used after 1969.

[2] The most successful of these students were those who took two principals in group C: 3 (9·1 per cent) out of 33.

committees were all too few. Nor were the impediments to personal research the whole story; for there was no immediate prospect of having the stimulus of postgraduate students and so building up a research side to one's department. In the case of the earlier university colleges the connexion with London had meant that their graduates could stay on and work for a higher London degree. It was here that Keele seemed likely to pay quite a stiff price for its independence unless the sponsoring universities gave a helping hand. Already in January 1950 before the College opened, the Academic Council had the foresight to survey the situation and recommended: first, that negotiations should be undertaken for a scheme whereby the sponsoring universities would allow their own graduates to pursue research work for their own research degrees under approved conditions in the College; secondly, that, though the matter was not yet urgent, consideration should also be given to the position of graduates of the College itself; and thirdly, that professors might make arrangements with the universities from which they came to continue their research there by making periodic visits. At that time universities were more chary than they are now of awarding a Master's degree or a Ph.D. on work which was not done inside their own institution and under the supervision of their own staff. As Lindsay remarked in his 1951 Report, though Birmingham and Manchester[1] had been ready to do all they could, 'their Statutes created certain difficulties. . . . It would be much more simple if we could get authority to give our own research degrees and we hope for an alteration to the Charter to that effect.' Both universities—Birmingham sooner than Manchester—found it possible between 1951 and 1953 to agree to arrangements with Keele and in 1956 formally renewed them for the 1957–62 quinquennium. The first higher degrees under these schemes were conferred in 1957: two Ph.D. degrees and two M.Sc. degrees at each of these two sponsoring universities. All told, up to 1963 Birmingham awarded 33 M.Sc. degrees and 18 Ph.D.s to students working at Keele, most of them Keele graduates; Manchester awarded 9 M.Sc. degrees and 12 Ph.D.s; and, by an extension of the arrangements, Southampton awarded 4 Ph.D.s and Sheffield 1. The first four of Keele's own degree of Ph.D. were conferred in July 1964 and the first Master's degrees,

[1] Oxford seems not to have been approached.

one M.A. and one M.Sc., in 1965. As an alternative to a Master's degree awarded on a research thesis, from 1965 it became possible in a number of departments to obtain a Master's degree by examination after pursuing a full-time postgraduate course of formal instruction; and within this scheme some interesting combinations are offered: Mediaeval Studies (English, history and French or German), Victorian Studies (English and history), Criminology (law and sociology), Ceramic Technology (chemistry and physics, in association with the North Staffordshire College of Technology); and in the department of physics a special feature is made of the M.Sc. course in quantum electronics. Up to June 1970 there have been 66 Ph.D. degrees awarded, 7 in the humanities or social sciences and 59 in the natural sciences, mostly in chemistry or physics. The degrees of M.A. by thesis number 43 and by examination 32; and there have been 23 M.Sc.s by thesis and 30 by examination. In the 1970–1 session, there were 252 full-time postgraduate students.

By its very nature personal and departmental *research* cannot be the subject of statistical analysis and only the broadest picture can here be sketched of the increasingly significant part which it has played in the development of Keele. Mention has already been made[1] of the special provisions for research in communication in 1960, computer science in 1963, statistics in 1964 and cardiology in 1967; but important as these are, they do not reflect the wider research activities of the staff as a whole. Lord Lindsay's 1951 Report gave a list of publications by members of the small staff during the first year of the College; but most of the work had clearly been done beforehand and it was four or five years before the list grew appreciably longer. Then two factors began to make themselves felt: the staff increased and the heavy burdens of teaching and departmental administration were eased; and outside donors, particularly large local and national industrial firms as well as governmental agencies began to give materials and equipment and financed research projects, studentships and assistantships. Amongst these organisations Mullard, ICI, Shell, Esso, the Nuffield and Leverhulme Foundations, the Department of Scientific and Industrial Research, and the Medical Research Council were prominent benefactors. One of the disadvantages of the early years was that there was so much to do at Keele that there were

[1] See pp. 169–75.

few opportunities for the staff to get away and see what was being done in their subjects elsewhere. From the later 1950s as the Annual Reports show, it became more and more possible to release members of staff for the stimulus of holding visiting posts in other universities at home and overseas and to grant straight study leave. For the first time the Principal's Report for 1959–60 devoted a special section to research in addition to the usual list of publications. For example, within the humanities the Keele collection of manuscripts and documents was being classified and analysed and archaeological sites in the area were being studied preparatory to later excavations; in the social sciences there were enquiries into voting behaviour in local and national elections, into the economics of the National Health Service, and a comparative study, embracing several universities, of the attitudes of students to their courses; in physics there was research in the detailed structure of organometallic compounds and the mechanism of irradiation damage, in the problems of gas discharges, and in the factors affecting the strength of glass fibres; in chemistry workers were engaged in studies of natural products, polypeptides, organometallic and other compounds, together with research into molecular structure and cationic polymerisation. These are but a selection of the projects which were being undertaken within ten years of the foundation of the College; and it is evident that once the initial difficulties had been surmounted there has been no lack of research drive and fruitful activity. One problem, however, remains, especially for the science departments. Much modern equipment is highly sophisticated and expensive and an item which at Manchester or Birmingham, say, would represent only a small fraction of the money available for equipment looms very large in an institution the size of Keele. Research projects have therefore to be carefully selected in relation to the resources likely to be available. It is true that the importance or excellence of research is not directly related to its cost; but the limitation of the range of possible projects necessarily has some repercussions on the recruitment and retention of staff in an age when devotion to scientific machinery can be in conflict with dedication to an institution. Nevertheless in a number of departments, both scientific and non-scientific, strong research teams have been built up and in 1970–1 in addition to members of staff and postgraduate students there were over fifty research fellows and assistants engaged full-time in investigations.[1]

'The very heart and lungs of the body corporate' is a phrase which aptly describes the function of a *University Library*, without which both teaching and research would wither and die; and at Keele a Librarian (Mr S. O. Stewart) was the first member of staff to be appointed after the Principal and the Registrar. When he took up his duties in October 1949, the Librarian faced the triple problem of acquiring books, periodicals and other appropriate material, of housing what he obtained, and of cataloguing it so that it was accessible for users. The initial capital grants made by the UGC provided funds for purchases and a number of universities and public libraries as well as private donors generously supplemented these resources. When Keele Hall was ready for occupation, the old library there was fitted with new shelving and Lady Lindsay formally put the first book in its place in August 1950. By April 1951, £20,000 had been spent and more of Keele Hall was taken over. By the summer of 1952 there were 40,000 volumes and most of the administrative staff were ejected from the Hall into a building outside to make room for the Library. Acquisitions still accumulated; Lord Lindsay's personal library was donated to the College and the Institute of Sociology transferred 10,000 volumes and masses of pamphlets from Le Play House. The Report of 1953 recorded the possession of 60,000 volumes of which 25,000 only had yet been catalogued; a year later there were 70,000 volumes of which 31,500 had been catalogued. Yet all this was only the curtain-raiser to the drama staged by the Librarian.

There lived in Edinburgh a certain Dr Charles Sarolea, the first holder of the Chair of French in the University there, a *littérateur* and publicist, and a compulsive acquirer of books. His library of 200,000 volumes was chaotic; the books were

[1] The *Keele Andean Expedition* calls for mention as a co-operative enterprise. After some eighteen months of intensive preparation this expedition spent nine weeks during the 1965 summer vacation encamped in a remote valley in the south-east Peruvian Andes. The members were Dr Peter Floyd (geology), Mr Peter Webster (biology), a Keele graduate, two Keele undergraduates and a Cambridge student. Two major first ascents of mountains over 18,400 ft were made and nine first ascents of peaks between 17,000 and 17,500 ft. An extensive geological survey was made of the area and a representative collection of the plant life was brought back and lodged in the Herbarium at Kew.

scattered all over two large houses in Royal Terrace, stacked three and four deep in all sorts of places including both sides of the staircases. When he died in 1953 the Trustees of his estate tried to dispose of this collection but no one would face what G. K. Chesterton had called 'one of the monstrosities of the world'. The learned libraries of Edinburgh and members of the University staff were allowed to go in and select what they wanted and pay on the valuation of a well-known local bookseller. A friend suggested to Mr Stewart that he too should go and have a look; and three days of selecting resulted in the purchase for £150 of five tons of books, enough to fill a whole railway container. The Keele Librarian, however, was conscious that there was a great deal more worth having; the Trustees, for their part, were anxious to dispose not only of the books but of the two houses; a bargain was struck at a very advantageous price which was never disclosed; and in a hectic fortnight in the summer of 1954 about 100 tons of books came by road and with the help of students were unloaded and deposited in a disused Methodist Church school in Newcastle-under-Lyme. There they languished for three years; but when the school storehouse had to be relinquished in 1957 another home had to be found. This time it was a disused brickworks at Madeley, three miles to the west of Keele, which had more recently been used for growing mushrooms. A grant for the purchase of shelving and for additional staff was received from the UGC; further funds were later provided by the Leverhulme Trust, and year after year the academic staff, wives and many other friends of the College volunteered to share in the sorting and listing. When the operation was completed 'at least the spines of the books were visible, perhaps for the first time since they were purchased in the second-hand bookshops of Edinburgh and the continent, and on the *quais* of Paris and Lyons'. By 1960 most of the index cards had been filed in the main Library and it became possible for specially requested books to be made available to readers. All told, after the rubbish had been weeded out, there were 125,000 volumes most of which will eventually find their true home in the new library building.

The Sarolea collection was not the only important acquisition. In 1956 Mr Raymond Richards placed on loan at Keele a first selection of the Sneyd papers and in the following year sold to the College on generous terms the whole of his collection of manuscripts, manorial and court rolls, charters and other documents. These included the contents of the Muniment Room of the Sneyd family at Keele Hall: there was a wealth of family correspondence going back to the Reformation, a miscellany of estate records, a fine set of manorial rolls of Tunstall and Keele, the latter dating back to 1328 when the manor was held by the Order of St John of Jerusalem. Much of the material had for a time been at the John Rylands Library in Manchester where, to the great advantage of Keele, it had been sorted and listed.[1] In 1959 when the Stoke-on-Trent Public Library system was being re-organised, the City donated two large consignments of books to the College. The year 1961 was especially notable for additions: the Nuffield Foundation gave £20,000 for the Foundation Year Library; Josiah Wedgwood and Sons transferred the Wedgwood Papers for deposit in the Library in a specially equipped archives room; an opportunity arose to purchase a large collection of Arnold Bennett's letters and other literary items, including a missing manuscript volume of his Journal, hitherto unpublished; and Sir George Barnes had bequeathed his valuable collection of books on naval history and Lady Barnes presented to the Library the major part of his music. The latest major gift was the presentation in 1968 of the unique and valuable collection of Charles W. Turner of London containing 1,400 volumes illustrating the history and development of mathematics and related subjects from the late fifteenth century onwards; with its rare first editions it is one of Keele's most treasured possessions.[2]

From the outset the Librarian's cry had been for space and more space. By 1955 the College owned 205,000 volumes and uncounted pamphlets; 80,000 books had been squeezed into Keele Hall itself and 42,000 of these had been catalogued. Though need for new buildings of their own was uppermost in the thoughts of most heads of departments, the claims of the Library could not be denied. An architect, Sir Howard Robertson, was appointed in 1956 in the hope that building could commence in 1959. The first stage was in fact completed and in use in 1961 and this with the second stage was formally opened

1 In all there were 242 boxes of Sneyd papers and 265 of miscellaneous historical material.

2 In 1955 the Earl of Harrowby placed a collection of pictures, furniture and books, including much of the library of Lady Mary Wortley Montagu, on temporary loan to the College.

in October 1962 by Sir Sydney Roberts, lately Master of Pembroke College, Cambridge and for many years Secretary of the Cambridge University Press. An addition even to this new Library was begun in 1964 and brought into use two years later with the result that there is now accommodation for 600,000 volumes and places for 750 readers together with informal reading areas. Such was the happy ending—for a time—to fifteen years of makeshifts.

Already in 1955 it was evident that the initial capital grant was running low and during the 1956–7 session it was exhausted; the salaries for staff, including cataloguers, were a first charge on the annual Library budget and money for new acquisitions became so scarce that for the last three months of the 1957–8 session virtually no purchases could be made. Since then the Council has provided an allocation for the Library which varies between 5·5 per cent and 6·0 per cent of the annual budget of the University[1] and the number of new volumes added annually to the Library has risen from 3,500 to 7,000 so that by the end of the 1969–70 session the number of catalogued books had reached the very useful figure of 260,000.

ADULT EDUCATION; INSTITUTE OF EDUCATION; MEDICAL SCHOOL

Before passing on to the next chapter and the more general questions of the expansion of numbers and other developments, there are still three matters of educational importance which remain to be dealt with, all of them involving relationships with outside bodies. The first is *extra-mural studies*, an activity which at Keele as elsewhere has come to be known as *adult education*. It was natural that the University College, whose foundation owed so much to the adult education movement, should wish to play its part in that work. Indeed at an informal meeting at the Master's Lodgings in April 1949, Lindsay made it clear that he thought the College should see extra-mural teaching as an essential part of its work; he planned to have an extra-mural department from the outset and, after the field

[1] In the UGC (Parry) Report on Libraries, 1967, the figure of 6 per cent was recommended as 'a standard below which British university libraries should not be allowed to fall'. In 1967–8 (the latest evidence), the figure for Great Britain as a whole was 3·9 per cent and only eight institutions reached 6 per cent.

had been surveyed, the College could take over responsibility from Oxford in its second year. The representatives of the Oxford Delegacy had some misgivings about this plan: its own fifteen full-time tutors in the area would have to be consulted; work in the Potteries gave Oxford a valuable insight into industrial and trade union problems; and would extra-mural students be allowed to study for degrees at the College, as at Birkbeck College in London, by means of evening classes? No, the Delegacy thought Oxford should continue to have the responsibility, with the College gradually assuming an increasing share of the actual work. As might have been expected, however, sensible collaboration was established almost as soon as the College opened: three of the Oxford Delegacy tutors were appointed to give part-time help in the College itself, Miss M. R. Glover in social studies, T. P. Roberts in English and R. B. Cant in economics; and several members of the College staff lectured in the area for the Delegacy and the WEA, an important aspect of these informal arrangements in that it brought the staff of the College into closer contact with the area and established those personal relations and mutual confidence on which any satisfactory division or transfer of responsibility had ultimately to depend.

The difficulties which attended the negotiations[1] over the next ten years were not just storms in teacups. In North Staffordshire there was quite a network of committees, sub-committees and joint committees all concerned with adult education. The Oxford Delegacy was involved, so was the WEA, so were the Local Authorities who gave financial support. If the College wished to participate, how would it fit in; how would existing arrangements and organisations be accommodated to a new structure without doing harm to adult education itself; how would spheres of activities be demarcated; if the College had its own department of extra-mural studies what would be the functions of its head and how would his work impinge on what had for so long been the accepted pattern; and, above all, would the highly valued link with Oxford be broken? These were prickly issues and at times one or other of the organisations involved found it hard to see things from any other point of view than its own.

There was also the financial aspect of the matter. In the sub-

[1] These are expounded in some detail in R. A. Lowe's M.A. thesis, 1966.

mission of estimates to the UGC for the 1952–7 quinquennium the College broached the idea that the College should have responsibility for extra-mural teaching in its area, that Oxford would transfer part of its Delegacy funds in support of it, and that any additional expense would be borne by a supplement from the UGC. The Chairman of the UGC (A. E. Trueman) thought the accountancy complications could be surmounted with Oxford's consent; but the UGC as a whole thought the College might be trying to do too much during the early years of its existence. Some years later another difficulty arose from the fact that the Ministry of Education which made financial contributions to support adult education activities, needed to deal with a single properly constituted 'responsible body': there was no permanently acceptable half-way house between the old arrangements in North Staffordshire and a full department at Keele. It took some time for the point to be fully appreciated—but we must return to the early 1950s.

When the College opened Lindsay redoubled his efforts. His aim was still the one he had made clear in the spring of 1949: the College would take over the work of the Oxford Delegacy not later than the beginning of the 1952–7 quinquennium and a Director would be appointed. He wrote what he hoped were persuasive letters, he composed memoranda himself and commented on those of others, he attended meetings however inconveniently arranged. Eric Tams, the Secretary of the WEA District, was worried about the part the WEA would have in the various schemes which were proposed, especially since in the country as a whole there was a school of thought which would have relegated the WEA to making provision for the 'educationally underprivileged', regardless of the fact that WEA classes led on in many instances to attendance at tutorial classes. There was talk too about 'university imperialism'. The inherent delicacy of the situation was minimised by the fact that on the Oxford side there were three people who could see all aspects of the question: Lucy Sutherland, Principal of Lady Margaret Hall, who was on the Academic Council of the College, T. L. Hodgkin, who had been organising tutor for the Delegacy in the Potteries, and F. V. Pickstock, who was a product of the Longton tutorial class[1] and was now Deputy Secretary of the Delegacy. Lindsay himself came to see the

[1] See p. 21.

difficulties more clearly and by the end of 1951 was prepared to agree to a scheme whereby responsibility for adult education would be transferred from Oxford with certain safeguards: there would be a Director of Extra-Mural Studies; he would work through a committee which though formally a College committee would be one in which the WEA, the Local Authorities and the College would have 'equal shares'; and the Secretary of the WEA and the Director would be joint secretaries of such a committee. It was on this basis that on 4 March 1952, a new sub-committee of the important North Staffordshire Committee for Adult Education[1] resolved that 'the University College should take over responsibility for extra-mural work in North Staffordshire in October 1953, or as soon as should be found practicable'. The principle was agreed; but many constitutional and financial details still needed to be worked out. A fortnight later Lord Lindsay died.

The driving force which could have brought events to a head was no longer there; other pressing tasks at Keele claimed time and attention; and so the proposals for extra-mural studies were not immediately pursued. Yet Lindsay's efforts were far from fruitless; several of the professors had been appointed to outside committees concerned with adult education; and what was vital was that some hard spadework had been accomplished and all interested parties knew the nature of the ground. Sir John Lennard-Jones had intended to reopen negotiations but illness prevented him from taking any effective steps. It was not until 1954 that Professor Stewart (Education) took the initiative and asked that the matter should again be considered. A group of Oxford representatives visited Keele in April 1955 for discussions and it was 'generally agreed' that, although complete responsibility would undoubtedly be transferred in due course, a transitional period (if possible, of determined length) of shared responsibility was desirable.

Talks and correspondence proceeded at a leisurely pace through the later months of 1955 and the spring of 1956 and at the end all the parties were in accord that a new University Extra-mural Committee for North Staffordshire should be set up to represent Oxford, the College and the WEA, and be collectively responsible for adult education in the Potteries. The Committee met for the first time in February 1957 with

[1] See p. 37.

Professor Lawlor as one of the joint secretaries. This scheme did not go as far towards a transfer as the one for which Lindsay won abortive acceptance in 1951; there was no department or Director of Extra-Mural Studies envisaged for the immediate future but an active committee had now come into existence through which it might be possible to prepare for a final transfer of responsibility. Keele took the precaution, however, of including in its estimates to the UGC for new developments within the 1957–62 quinquennium an extra-mural department as its second priority: if events proved to be propitious for a transfer it did not want to be short of the necessary funds.

The new arrangements proved to be reasonably satisfactory, though it was always understood that they were transitional. The first move towards a further review of the situation came in fact from Oxford when F. W. Jessup, the Secretary to the Delegacy, suggested to Sir George Barnes in 1959 that the question of responsibility should be settled well in advance of the next (1962–7) quinquennium. Since neither a Senate Committee on Adult Education nor a Joint Advisory Committee could technically be the body which employed tutors, the idea was advanced that there should be a Senate-Council Committee whose Chairman would be the professor, at that time Lawlor, who was charged by Senate with the supervision of extra-mural work. This proposal was indeed embodied in a paper written by Barnes in May 1959; and so far from staking a claim for a department, he commented that: 'it would seem unnecessary to set up forthwith a Board or Department along the lines familiar elsewhere.' Eric Tams of the WEA, however, urged that the WEA 'would wish to see a Department which would have the standing within the College and the machinery to carry out the programme of extra-mural work effectively'; and Pickstock at Oxford reported that the tutors 'felt very strongly that adult education in the College should be organized in a Department with its Head having professional status: without this, adult education would be a poor relation.' Barnes was not convinced; and after receiving these comments wrote to Lawlor in July 1959: 'They fill me with gloom. They scarcely appreciate that I have a job to do in getting any tentative proposal agreed by this University. I am quite certain that it would not take an Adult Education Department in the next quinquennium.' So what had been a high priority in the estimates submitted in 1956 was to be jettisoned so far as 1962–7 was concerned: Keele had its hands sufficiently full with other problems of expansion.

Yet if one were seeking an illustration of how speedily opinions can sometimes change in matters of academic policy, no better example could be found than the events of the autumn of 1959. First the Ministry of Education was standing no nonsense about joint committees: the 'responsible body' for Keele would have to be a University department concerned with adult education. Early in November the existing Joint Advisory Committee agreed that the time had really come to discuss the transfer of responsibility and very shortly afterwards the Oxford Tutorial Classes Committee resolved that: 'In the interests of Adult Education in North Staffordshire . . . it was desirable for responsibility for extra-mural work in North Staffordshire to be transferred to the University College at the start of the new quinquennium.' It now looked as if Oxford were forcing the pace and as part of the procedure the Registrar of Oxford wrote to the Directors of Education for the Local Authorities concerned, suggesting the transfer. He pointed out, however, that Oxford would like to maintain a working connexion with the area, for instance by the exchange of staff tutors, joint summer schools, special provision for trade union education, and the continuation of some extension lecture courses. Staffordshire and Burton-on-Trent readily accepted the proposal; Stoke-on-Trent was rather more hesitant at first because, as they said, they placed a high value on the Oxford link within the city and in their view Keele would be preoccupied with its growing pains for the next five years.

During 1960 and most of 1961 the details of a scheme were elaborated and received the approval of all the bodies concerned. The basis on which the transfer should take place was: that the College should appoint a full-time Director of Extra-Mural Studies who would have the status and salary of a professor and be head of a department of extra-mural studies; that the Delegacy's staff tutors would be appointed full-time members of the College staff; that the College was to be advised on matters relating to collaboration with the WEA by a Joint Committee with the WEA; that the Senate's Adult Education Committee would continue to advise the Senate on all matters of academic policy relating to extra-mural teaching, and specifically on the College's role in extension classes; and that the College would establish and develop a library for extra-mural teaching purposes. No mention was made of any continuing activity of the Oxford Delegacy in the area.

A department of extra-mural studies was consequently put as the first priority in the estimates for the next quinquennium (1962–7) and came into existence at the beginning of the 1962–3 session with Roy Shaw, formerly Warden of the Leeds University Centre in Bradford, as the first Director. As the Principal remarked in his Report for 1961–2: 'This transfer is a most important step in making it clear to the residents of North Staffordshire that the University is a part of that district and is actively interested in its educational life.' By the end of the quinquennium it was possible to report that:

> Over a thousand adults from North Staffordshire took advantage of part-time study courses lasting through the winter. About a quarter of these came to Keele itself, the rest were served by lecturers going out to centres ranging from Leek in the north to Burton-on-Trent in the south. Over four thousand people attended public lectures, conferences and short courses.

Since 1967 the work of the department has expanded still further and the impact it makes in North Staffordshire brings the University into an ever closer and more fruitful relationship with the area.

The *Institute of Education* which came into being at Keele in 1962 stems from the post-war arrangements for teacher-training which resulted from the 1944 McNair Report on Teachers and Youth Leaders. The earliest colleges for the training of teachers in elementary schools were established by religious denominations; the first training colleges provided by Local Education Authorities date from 1904. The course of study and training extended over two years, except in colleges of domestic science and physical education where the course was three years; and most of the colleges were single-sex and residential. From 1890 universities and university colleges had begun to set up university training departments of their own which gave a one-year course for graduates who intended to become teachers and desired to have a recognised professional qualification. By 1944 there were eighty-three training colleges of which fifty-four were conducted by 'voluntary bodies' and the rest by LEAS; in addition there were twenty-two university training departments. From 1930 the Board of Education delegated much of its responsibility for the professional certification of students in training colleges to ten Joint Examination Boards[1] comprising representatives both of the colleges within an area and of a conveniently situated university institution. These Boards approved syllabuses and conducted examinations and in some instances organised short refresher courses for teachers within the area; but the Boards did not specifically foster any close relationship among the colleges, nor were the colleges in general affiliated in any way with the university institution. Subject to the over-riding control of the Board of Education, the Diploma awarded by university training departments was recognised as a professional qualification and was not within the jurisdiction of the Joint Examination Boards.

The McNair Committee was unanimous in agreeing that the teacher training colleges ought to be brought into closer contact with each other and with the university and that the scope and responsibilities of an 'Area Training Organisation' (ATO) should be wider than that of the Examination Boards. The Committee, however, divided in equal numbers and promulgated two separate statements on the question of the form the ATO should take. One group advocated university schools of education which 'would have responsibility for the general supervision of the training of teachers' and to which the training institutions would be affiliated; the other group, fearing the administrative and other burdens which the first proposal might impose on universities, presented a Joint Board Scheme which was thought to be likely to interfere less with the independence of the training colleges and the position of the LEAS, but would be empowered to undertake wider educational functions than had been entrusted to the Examination Boards. A compromise, devised by McNair himself and known as 'Scheme C', proved to be generally acceptable and by 1952 every university in England and Wales, except Cambridge, had established an Institute of Education. Under this arrangement the Institute is an integral part of the university and the col-

[1] Oxford was not involved; and only one college was associated with Cambridge.

leges are linked to the university by their membership of the Institute; it normally has an Educational Centre to provide facilities for the furtherance of its work; it has a Board of Management on which the University, the constituent training colleges (now colleges of education) and the LEAs are represented, together with assessors appointed by the Department for Education and Science; it has a Professional Committee to approve syllabuses and conduct examinations; and it has its own Director, generally of professorial status, and its own staff. Amongst its prime purposes are the promotion of the education and training of teachers, the co-ordination of the resources available for it, the organisation of further study and research in education, and the fostering of close relations between the constituent members of the Institute (including the university department of education).

During its very first session Keele began to outline proposals for its own Institute of Education. It was not simply that Keele for reasons of prestige aspired to be like other universities: an Institute would give the University College new functions in relation both to teacher-training and to research in education, and would bring the College into closer contact with its area. There were indeed three teacher training colleges within easy distance which could quite conveniently be linked with an Institute based on Keele: Alsager and Crewe which were under Cheshire auspices and at the time were members of the Institute at Liverpool and Nelson Hall which was maintained by Staffordshire and associated with Birmingham.

But before an Institute could be established negotiations had to be successfully completed with several interested parties—the governing bodies and the Principals of the three training colleges, the two universities with which they were then linked, the LEAs, the Ministry of Education which would have to approve the arrangements, and the UGC which would be providing the funds. The colleges and the universities concerned and the LEAs of Stoke-on-Trent, Staffordshire, Burton-on-Trent and Cheshire were all readily agreeable to the foundation of an Institute at Keele. That it took a dozen years to bring it into being was due to the difficulties which were encountered in persuading the Ministry of Education and, more particularly, the UGC.

In 1951 when the estimates for the 1952–7 quinquennium

were under discussion, the Council and Senate approved a proposal for an Institute and put it as the fourth item in the list of priorities; but the UGC flatly rejected it as being premature. In the next five years the College did what it could with its limited resources by providing refresher and other courses for teachers in English, history, biology and chemistry; but the need to do much more was very apparent and a more determined effort to persuade the Ministry and the UGC was mounted as the next quinquennium hove in sight. Early in 1955 discussions were initiated with the Ministry of Education in which Keele stressed three points: the proximity of the three training colleges to Keele itself; the needs of the teacher population in North Staffordshire for whom little could be done to help by ATOs as far away as Liverpool or Birmingham; and the fact that the area, consisting of an industrial centre surrounded by a rural belt, offered good scope for educational research. The Ministry's response was disquieting: two of the three colleges were in temporary buildings and their future was uncertain; the whole future of training policy was under consideration; and the value of small ATOs was doubted. At a subsequent conference early in November the Ministry agreed that on a long-term estimate there should be an ATO and an Institute, but suggested that meanwhile Keele should go steadily ahead with the work it was doing for teachers in the area. The Ministry was concerned too at the proposed expenditure of £50,000 on a building and equipment for an Institute. At the end of that same month the UGC made its usual pre-quinquennial visit to Keele and, as we have seen[1] urged on the College a policy of consolidation; and so far as an Institute was concerned, 'any expansion of work done by the Education Department with local teachers must be treated on the same basis as other academic developments'.

Thus the most that could be salvaged from the 1955 proposal for an Institute was to include among the College priorities for development during 1957–62 some provision for the expansion of existing work with serving teachers in the locality. At this point, alas, controversy arose within the College itself: to have a virtually ear-marked additional grant for an Institute was one thing; to divide up limited general income was another. A relatively modest proposal to include in the estimates the

[1] See p. 168.

appointment of three tutors who would be concerned exclusively with work with teachers outside the College, though at first accepted by the Senate, was subsequently rejected by a majority vote.

By the time plans were being made for the 1962–7 quinquennium the skies had cleared. In 1959 the College was told by the Ministry that the two training colleges whose future had previously been in doubt were now scheduled as permanent, that Nelson Hall would be moving to Madeley which was still nearer to Keele, that all three colleges were programmed for considerable expansion, and that 'the Ministry viewed with favour that there should be an Institute of Education at Keele'. The difficulty about a building had also disappeared since it was now expected that from about 1962 the Keele department of education would share a building where it would also be possible to provide facilities for an Institute. At their visit to Keele in 1960 the UGC indicated its approval of the setting up of an Institute and the College placed this project as its second priority in its estimates for 1962–7. Although the quinquennial allocation proved to be not as large as had been expected, the College, now a University, went ahead on the understanding that the Institute would develop by stages during the 1962–7 period; in 1963 a constitution for the Institute was approved; in July 1964 it was formally inaugurated with Professor Stewart as head of the University department of education and Director of the Institute. When the two posts were separated in 1967 Professor G. N. Brown was appointed as Director.

The introduction in 1960 of a three-year course in all colleges of education was a noteworthy step in the training of teachers. The wider range of academic study thus made possible led on to the institution in most universities of a B.Ed. degree for approved students of the colleges who spend a fourth year of study in the university. The regulations drawn up at Keele for the award of its B.Ed. involved, as elsewhere, an appropriate curriculum within the colleges of education and a further year of work within the Institute. The first B.Ed. degrees were awarded in 1968 and by the end of the 1969–70 session the total had reached 207, of which 12 were obtained with honours.

One hope expressed in the early proposals for a university institution in North Staffordshire, but one which unlike the

Department of Adult Education and the Institute of Education has not yet come to fruition, was that there should be a *medical school*. The Royal Infirmary at Stoke-on-Trent in particular was an important clinical centre serving a wide area; and the hope that a complete medical education for students could be provided jointly by the Infirmary and a College was a reasonable one to entertain. A proposal of this kind figured with some prominence in the 'Hanley Enquiry' of 1899;[1] and in its comments on Alderman Kemp's plea for a College in 1944, the *Sentinel* placed considerable stress on this aspect of the local needs.[2] But when negotiations between the Exploratory Committee and the UGC began in 1946, a medical school formed no part of the plan; at the meeting in March, Dr Stross as a medical man had not unnaturally mentioned to the UGC the local desire for a medical school, but in the printed submission of November 1946 no reference at all was made to the idea. Ceramics, physical chemistry, social studies and the broadening of the basis of the curriculum were the matters to which immediate attention had to be given, without embarking on even deeper waters. The *Sentinel*, however, had not forgotten and was worried lest the effect of the National Health Service Bill then before Parliament would be to sweep up the North Staffordshire hospitals and their specialist services into a region based on Birmingham;[3] a medical school was in itself desirable and an institution designated as a teaching hospital might escape the threatened 'confiscation' of endowments.

What pressures may later have been brought to bear we do not know; but in May 1951 the Senate agreed that medical teaching should be included in their long-term planning; and when Lindsay had been approached by the Stoke-on-Trent Hospital Management Committee, he had been 'very helpful';[4] even though it was now realised that it might take ten or fifteen years before the aim was achieved. When Sir John Lennard-Jones arrived as Principal the caution which was felt by both sides about the timing of a Medical Faculty was so strongly stressed by him as to kill any further proposals for several years: a Medical Faculty involved a great deal of expense on equipment, new buildings, staff and maintenance; the most that could be done would be to foster some form of co-operation

[1] See p. 27. [2] See p. 35. [3] 11 April 1946.
[4] Reported later in the *Sentinel* of 4 March 1953.

at a postgraduate level.[1] A further check to progress was the publication in 1957 of the Ministry of Health (Willink) Report which declared that 'the current output of the medical schools was more than adequate to meet the future demand for doctors'. Mistaken though this assessment proved to be, it certainly precluded the setting up of a medical school at Keele.

By 1961, however, the Ministry of Health had revised its estimates of numbers and had come to the conclusion that what was really needed was a 10 per cent increase in the entry of pre-clinical students; and the UGC recommended supplementary grants to meet the situation. A further Ministry review in 1963 showed that the prospective shortage of doctors was far more serious than had at first appeared and the UGC now recommended that 'at least one new medical school should be planned'.[2]

These events revived hopes in Stoke and in Keele. There was another factor too. New ideas about medical education were in the air:[3]

> It was suggested in some quarters that the seriousness of the medical manpower shortage justified short cuts to increase the output of doctors and that a new unorthodox pattern of medical education would produce results more quickly. Interest in proposals for a broader 'human biology' pre-clinical course led to the suggestion that existing university schools of biology could almost overnight be turned into schools of human biology and provide for the education of medical students.

The UGC itself stood firm on the need for high quality courses in anatomy and physiology, including biochemistry and biophysics, which could not be cheaply provided; but Keele had seen in the new ideas a chance to advance its claims. The Senate agreed in December 1963 that a scheme should be prepared and discussions with the local medical consultants were set on foot; and for medical students the University would even forego the Foundation Year requirement. Despite a very inconclusive and indeed somewhat discouraging interview the Vice-Chancellor had with the Chairman of the UGC in February

[1] College Council, 2 March 1954; *Sentinel*, 4 March 1954.

[2] See *University Development 1962–7* (UGC), 1968, p. 123.

[3] Ibid., p. 124. See also Dr Nicholas Malleson's *A School of Medicine and Human Biology*, 1963.

1964, Keele and its local allies forged ahead and set up something analogous to the old Exploratory Committee. Not even the announcement in July of that year that a new medical school was to be established in Nottingham stopped them in their tracks. They approached the Ministry of Health and the Secretary of State for Education, both of whom inevitably replied that they would seek the advice of the UGC.

The culmination of all these efforts was the submission to the UGC in May 1965 of an 'Outline Plan for a Medical School'. This document was more than a casual memorandum. It analysed the hospital services in North Staffordshire, the clinical material available for teaching, the size and range of the medical staff, and the medical library facilities of the existing Medical Institute. It dealt with pre-clinical courses and with clinical studies in some detail. So far as the University was concerned the basis was to be a pre-clinical degree in human biology which for medical students would occupy three years.[1] There would be: a three-year biology course on general and special biology, including anatomy and physiology sections for which some of the teaching would be undertaken by members of the clinical departments; a specially designed two-year course in physics and chemistry; a one-year course in basic calculus and statistics; and a one-year course in psychology with sociology.

Other universities[2] too were in the field for securing a medical school and the claims of Keele were in competition with them. But all hope of an early decision must have faded in September 1965 when a Royal Commission on Medical Education was appointed under the chairmanship of Lord Todd, holder of the Nobel Prize for Chemistry (1957) and Master of Christ's College, Cambridge. Forebodings increased when, in advance of the Commission's report, it was announced in August 1967 that there would be a new Medical School in Southampton. The Report itself appeared in April 1968, and what it had to say made hard reading for Keele:[3]

[1] It was intended that the degree should also be available for non-medical students who would, however, be required to do the Foundation Year. Provision was also made for students to transfer to or from the medical curriculum; and it is worth noting that students who gave up the medical course, would be expected, as a condition of graduation, to do a modified Foundation Year in a fourth year subsequent to their classified Final examinations!

[2] These included Hull, Leicester, Southampton, Swansea and Warwick.

[3] *Report of the Royal Commission on Medical Education*, HMSO, 1968, par. 386.

Plate 5 The Chancellor, H.R.H. The Princess Margaret, conferring the honorary degree of D.Litt. on H.M. Queen Elizabeth The Queen Mother (1 December 1965 on the occasion of the Dedication of the University Chapel)

Plate 6a Horwood Hall of Residence

Plate 6b The Students' Union

Plate 7a The University Library

Plate 7b The University Chapel

a Sir John Lennard-Jones (1953–4)

b Sir George Barnes (1956–60)

c Dr H. M. Taylor (1961–7)

d Professor W. A. C. Stewart (1967–)

Plate 8 Principals and Vice-Chancellors, 1953–71

> The modern medical school must be an integral part of a university which can be expected to provide in due course a full range of opportunities for instruction and research in those biological, physical and behavioural sciences which are relevant to medicine. The general scale of the university's development must be big enough to allow a medical school which is established within it to reach the desirable size without causing imbalance and distortion in the pattern of the university's activities. A university with less than 4,000 students in all would, we think, be unable to accommodate satisfactorily a medical faculty with an annual intake of 150–200 students, which in our view is the minimum required of a medical school.

The Commission dealt more specifically with Keele in the following terms:[1]

> We hope that in the period after 1975 conditions will be appropriate for the establishment of new medical schools in several other centres. The North Staffordshire conurbation offers substantial resources of population and outstandingly suitable hospital facilities in Stoke-on-Trent, which ought in the national interest to be fully used for medical education. The University of Keele is, however, relatively small and is not on present plans likely to reach a size which would permit the establishment of a medical school big enough to be, in our view, economical and educationally effective. We think that only if the University's development during the next decade is such as to open up the possibility of its accommodating eventually an annual intake of at least 150 medical students, and if the teaching in biology and other sciences is developed on an adequate scale, should a medical school be set up there; meanwhile we hope that the necessary rebuilding of some of the Stoke hospitals will be done in such a way as to facilitate the introduction of undergraduate teaching if and when the University becomes able to provide the academic setting needed for it.

Keele's initial reaction to this Report was to treat it as a challenge rather than as a defeat. After the Vice-Chancellor had

[1] Ibid., par. 392.

had an informal talk with the Chairman of the UGC, the Senate decided not to abandon the project, but to press on and develop the pre-clinical sciences during the 1972–7 quinquennium and to make senior appointments in physiology and biochemistry. In March 1969 Keele representatives met the Biology and Medical sub-committees of the UGC under the chairmanship of Sir Robert Aitken, a former Professor of Medicine in Aberdeen and recently Vice-Chancellor of Birmingham. It was made plain first, that the Human Biology approach was not acceptable because 'it would not have strong enough roots in the sciences associated with medicine', and secondly that 'the Keele academic pattern and its present programmes of Biology were not good soil in which to plant a new medical school'. It was suggested that 'Keele ought to think of the development of a medical school in terms of decades rather than quinquennia'. The realities of the situation were succinctly stated by the Vice-Chancellor in his Report for 1968–9: 'It would appear that no new Medical Schools will be founded before 1975 at the earliest. . . . Conversations with the UGC representatives during 1968–9 made it clear to us that an undergraduate medical school at Keele was not going to be on the cards for a very long time.' In one particular only was he mistaken: in October 1970 it was announced that a new medical school was to be established—at Leicester.

THE ACADEMIC COUNCIL AND A NEW CHARTER

The Academic Council whose composition and functions were detailed in Chapter 3[1] was the effective instrument of sponsorship. The six representatives of the sponsoring universities were in the majority on the Council and the fact that there were few changes over the years in the list of persons appointed meant that there was a continuity of policy and a growing commitment to the welfare of the College. The Academic Council had wide powers and in guiding an infant university whose professors were young and inexperienced it needed to combine firmness with tact and sympathetic understanding. It was an 'upper chamber' in all academic affairs and sought to advise rather than veto and coerce. For its part, the Senate saw the good sense of these constitutional arrangements and was grate-

[1] See pp. 80–1.

ful for the help of 'its Lords who agree not to be its masters'.[1] The minutes of the Academic Council show how detailed was the work it did: regular consideration and discussion of the reports of the proceedings of the Senate and of the memoranda on courses and academic developments; consideration year by year of the reports of the external examiners and suggestions on matters arising from those reports; help and advice on quinquennial estimates and other negotiations with the UGC; and involvement in all senior academic appointments. It did not, however, interfere with the content and assessment of the Foundation Year course, though it received reports on it from time to time and offered informal comment. A few examples will illustrate its activities.

There were some occasions indeed when the Academic Council rejected or referred back proposals made by the Senate. In 1950, for example, it disapproved of the inclusion of statistics as a subject in group C—a decision which postponed the proper development of the subject for several years; in 1951 it queried the nominations of external examiners in three subjects, differed from the Senate about procedures for the appointment of professors—and gained its way; and in 1953 it prevailed on the Senate to adopt its views on the classification of degrees. In 1955 it refused to support a Senate memorandum to the UGC asking for the College to be given the power to award its own higher degrees. Later on, in 1958, it referred back a scheme for sabbatical leave and rejected a proposal for a subsidiary course in archaeology, a subject which it regarded as more suitable for a postgraduate diploma; and in 1961, even at a time when it knew it would itself soon cease to exist, it had a long tussle with the Senate about the order of academic priorities for the 1962–7 quinquennium.

But for the most part the Academic Council proceeded by way of asking the Senate to consider this point or that, by requesting information to be supplied to it, and by gently indicating the views it held or might hold on a variety of topics. It proffered advice occasionally on the content of syllabuses (as in education, social studies, biology and chemistry), on the standards required in examinations (which it sometimes thought were too high), on the combinations of principal subjects available, on the way in which new subjects, such as Russian, were

[1] W. A. C. Stewart in a memorandum of August 1954.

being developed in the College, on the future financial implications involved in the acceptance of tempting offers of help from outside to embark on Communication and American Studies, and repeatedly on the urgency of Library needs. It concerned itself too with such diverse topics as the 'wastage' rate in the second and third years, the salaries of professors and the tenure of assistant lecturers, the alleviation of the teaching load on members of staff, and all the complicated issues arising from proposals for expansion. Perhaps its most delicate task was its consideration of external examiners' reports. It had itself devised a form which these reports should take and sometimes an examiner unfamiliar with Keele, albeit unwittingly, penned remarks which would have caused embarrassment all round had not the Academic Council handled the situation with discretion.

Apart from the business it conducted at its meetings, held two or three times each term, there were two other ways in which the Academic Council was of benefit to Keele. The first arises from the fact that whereas the sponsor members rarely changed, the representatives of the Senate generally served only for three years; consequently within the twelve or so years of the Council's existence many members of the Senate had the benefit of sensing how outstanding people in old and established universities handled academic affairs. The second point is still more important. The Academic Council nominated three of the sponsor members to sit on the College Council where they personally carried great weight, reinforced the College's own academic representation, and guided the lay members, few of whom had sat on a university body before, in university procedures and helped them to appreciate academic purposes, values and needs.

The first session of the College had barely ended when Lindsay in his Annual Report for 1951 somewhat precipitately raised the questions of higher degrees: 'it would be much more simple if we could get authority to give our own research degrees and we hope to apply for an alteration to the Charter to that effect.' The idea simmered; and in 1955 the Senate wanted to present to the UGC when it visited the College in November a memorandum on postgraduate degrees.[1] The Academic Council,

1 Among the reasons which the Senate advanced for wishing to organise its own postgraduate work and award higher degrees, was one which has a

however, as we have previously mentioned, did not think the time was yet ripe for such a development. At this stage there was no definite intention to do away with sponsorship and seek the status of a fully independent university: after all, Hull had received its Charter only in 1954 and Exeter in 1955, while Leicester was still waiting in the wings; and Keele was little more than five years old. But after 1955 events moved rapidly; the UGC began to contemplate the foundation of new universities to cope with the pre-Robbins expansion; and from 1957 encouragement was being given to Brighton, York, Norwich and other places to establish universities with a Charter and full degree-granting powers. It is not surprising therefore that in February 1959 when Sir George Barnes was still Principal, the Senate at Keele on his initiative set up a Charter Committee which would grapple for many months with the constitutional and legal issues involved in the preparation of a petition and draft Charter to be submitted to the Privy Council. By October 1960 sufficient progress had been made for the College Council itself to appoint a Joint Charter Committee on which the Senate and the Academic Council were represented.

While all the hard work on the Charter and Statutes was proceeding, negotiations were taking place with the UGC and the sponsoring universities.[1] In May and again in July 1960, the Chairman of the UGC had long talks with Keele representatives; he was in general sympathy with the desire for a Charter, though a final decision would depend on the support given by the sponsors and on the UGC's own visit to Keele in November; but it was his own opinion that there was now no need for sponsors: the Keele experiment must stand on its own feet, the pattern was set, and no sponsors could change it now even if it were desirable. The UGC was at this time considering the draft Charters of some of the newer universities and was an

bearing on one aspect of the Keele B.A. degree. 'Our graduates need further specialized teaching in those parts of their chosen field which could not be adequately covered in their undergraduate course, and also some extra training in experimental techniques to enable them to tackle research problems.' What was true for 1955 is presumably still valid in 1971. Keele's own solution has been to institute Master's degrees by examination (see p. 186) alongside those awarded on a thesis.

[1] Because of the illness of Sir George Barnes, the Vice-Principal, Professor W. A. C. Stewart, conducted most of these negotiations on behalf of Keele.

influential clearing house for the exchange of ideas. The informal advice it gave to Keele on many points was consequently of great help and even after the draft had gone to the Privy Council the UGC suggested a number of acceptable modifications.

There was some trouble, however, in securing the unanimous support of the sponsors. By the middle of June 1960 Oxford felt there was no need for further discussion on the question of full university status: Keele had established a considerable position in a comparatively short time and there was no reason to think they would not now be capable of managing their own affairs. The Manchester Senate, though somewhat worried about the division of functions between the academics and the lay Council, also accepted without much delay the strong recommendation of its representatives on the Academic Council to support Keele. It was Birmingham which was the stumbling block. There it was felt that Keele still had administrative difficulties; that the relation between the Senate and the lay Council still needed to be worked out satisfactorily; that instead of imaginative proposals for development in the next quinquennium it had nothing to offer but plans for extra assistants and 'mere trivialities'; and that, although there were no grounds for worry about academic standards, some sort of an advisory body was still required. It is ironical that the University which had turned the tide of opinion in favour of Keele when the foundation of the College was under discussion[1] should now be so unsympathetic. Oxford and Manchester were not swayed by Birmingham's objections; it was rather their influence coupled with the arguments Keele advanced in its own defence which eventually prevailed on Birmingham in December 1960 to support the grant of a Charter and concur in the demise of sponsorship.

The rest can be briefly told. By May 1961 Keele's petition and draft were ready for submission to the Privy Council and after some final amendments the Charter received the signature of the Queen in Council on 6 December 1961, and was finally sealed on 26 January 1962.[2] On 5 July 1962, Princess Margaret

[1] See p. 74.

[2] The University of Keele Act, dissolving the University College and transferring all the property and liabilities of the College to the University, was passed on 24 May 1962.

was formally installed as the first Chancellor: the College had become a University.[1]

The two fundamental changes introduced by the new Charter were, of course, the omission of provisions for sponsorship and the lifting of the restriction on the granting of degrees to the B.A.; but there are other matters of interest too. In place of the Vice-Presidents of the College we have a Pro-Chancellor who is also Chairman of the Council and three Deputy Pro-Chancellors—a number which could satisfy the *amour propre* of each of the Local Authorities; a Deputy Vice-Chancellor, Boards of Studies, the Chairmen of such Boards and the Students' Union all now receive Charter status. Furthermore, a new body, called the *Assembly*, is established; it consists of all members of the Boards of Studies; it must meet once a year and by custom now meets each term; and, though it has only the right to discuss university matters and has no direct representation on other bodies, it is a kind of academic Parliament—a device which is to be found also in the Charters of some of the newer universities. The Association of Past Students, though it has no mention in the Charter, has by Statute a seat on the Council and several on the Court. In place of a statement about the eligibility of women as students or as members of the Court and Council—which would have read very oddly when already the Chancellor was a woman—we find the much more modern and pertinent proviso that 'no religious, racial or political test shall be imposed'. Finally, the Foundation Year is expressly excluded from the obligation on the University to appoint external examiners.

It is the Statutes which deal with the composition and detailed functions of the university bodies. The *Court* remains a large representative body.[2] The composition of the *Council*, however, is significantly modified. On the lay side, the representatives of the three Local Authorities are reduced from ten to seven but

[1] Surprise has sometimes been expressed that 'Keele' rather than 'North Staffordshire' was the name decided upon for the University; some critics even see in the choice a deliberate slight on the County of Staffordshire and the City of Stoke-on-Trent, to both of which authorities the College was indebted in so many ways. 'Keele', however, rather than 'University College of North Staffordshire', had long been the name by which the College was generally known at home and abroad and it would probably have persisted whatever other official title had been chosen.

[2] In 1949 a donation of £1,000 entitled the donor to life membership of the Court; the new Charter prescribes £10,000.

the Council itself can appoint by co-option seven additional members. On the academic side, in addition to the Vice-Chancellor, *ex officio* membership is given to the Deputy Vice-Chancellor and the Chairmen of Boards of Studies; the number of other members of the Senate is raised from five to six with the proviso that at least two (not one, as formerly) shall be non-professorial members of the Senate; and in place of the Academic Council members, each of the three former sponsoring universities appoints a representative and so retains an important link with Keele. In addition, the past students elect one member; the WEA continues to have one member, but the Oxford Extra-Mural Delegacy is no longer represented. All told, the size of the Council has risen from thirty-three to forty-two and the number of strictly academic members from ten to fourteen. Yet, though the 'balance of power' is thus virtually unaltered, the degree of control which the Council may exert over the academic affairs of the University is much more carefully and specifically defined and limited. In the composition of the *Senate* there is a sweeping change which reflects the increasing democratisation of academic government. Whereas the 1949 Statutes provide only for 'at least two representatives of the permanent teaching staff other than the Professors and Heads of Departments', the new Statutes raise the number of non-professorial members to one third of the total composition of the Senate. That means that in 1970–1 the Senate of forty-two members included fourteen from the non-professorial staff.[1]

[1] The relevant Statute prescribes that two of these members shall be Wardens of Halls of Residence, one man and one woman. The Ordinance associated with the Statute provides that about one half shall be elected by the non-professorial staff of the Board of Studies to which they belong and the remainder by the non-professorial staff as a whole. In effect this second half is elected by the Lecturers' Association, a body which had for years been campaigning for increased non-professorial representation on the Senate.

Seven

College and University II: General

THE GROWTH OF STUDENT NUMBERS AND STAFF

Keele was conceived and planned as a small institution which would have an annual intake of 150 undergraduates and a total enrolment of about 600. Even though by 1970–1 its numbers of first degree students had risen to 1,611 and its full-time research and advanced students to 252, making a total of 1,863, its rate of growth has been less than that occurring elsewhere and it is still one of the smaller British universities. Three things have contributed to this aspect of Keele's development. In the first place there was a strong conviction among many at Keele that a small institution has an educationally valuable homogeneity which would be destroyed if the numbers of students were allowed to increase beyond some vaguely apprehended limit: 'it might be 1,000, just possibly 1,500, certainly not as high as 2,000'; and consequently proposals for expansion were looked at askance by the upholders of this 'college' concept. The second consideration is that the pattern of studies for a degree at Keele makes it necessary for expansion to be on a broader front than elsewhere; no single subject or group of subjects can grow without involving a parallel, though not necessarily equal, growth in other fields: to take the simplest example, provision must be made for students taking two principal sciences to offer a subsidiary of their choice in one of the other two groups and that could mean additional staff in departments where the college would not otherwise have planned for expansion. The third check on growth is the most serious of all. From the earliest negotiations with the UGC the promoters of the new College had argued that it must be 'to a predominant extent residential' and with the acquisition of Keele Hall a policy of residence for all became feasible. But every increase in student numbers would need therefore to be matched by an increase in residential accommodation—and furthermore it was a course of four, not three, years that was involved. This ideal would be expensive to sustain even in the very best of circumstances.

Keele's first problem, however, in relation to student numbers was not whether it should expand beyond its original target but how it could manage to accommodate even the 150 freshmen a year it was expecting. Something has already been said about the condition of the site as it was taken over in 1949.[1] Apart from Keele Hall itself there were some one hundred structures of one sort or another and it was decided to convert forty-eight of the army huts for student accommodation, one group being named Lindsay Hall and the other Horwood Hall. With five rooms to a hut, single study-bedrooms could thus be provided for 240 students, which was more than the first year's intake; but because of delays in converting the huts some students had at first to share rooms in conditions of discomfort. Lord Lindsay apologised: 'I am sorry that you are cramped in your living quarters, that your huts are so far without heat, and that you cannot yet do your washing—but it is fun to be in at the start of a show like this.'[2] But 240 rooms would not easily cope with the intake of an additional 150 in October 1951; and the eventual replacement of the huts by more permanent and more suitable accommodation was clearly a matter demanding attention. All that the UGC was able to provide immediately was a single three-storey building for 40 women (Sneyd House); a further application for a Hall for 150 students to be built in 1951–2 had to be deferred because of cuts in licensable building work. The prospect therefore for October 1952 was disquieting; for the next year it would be alarming. Few of the remaining huts were suitable for conversion and the UGC would not agree to the purchase of additional ones. Should some students therefore be sent into lodgings? Could some large houses in the district be purchased or rented and used as hostels? Fortunately the total number of students registered in October 1952 was only 417 instead of 450, since some students had withdrawn at the end of each of the first two years; Sneyd House was now ready for use and 'The Hawthorns' in Keele village had been taken over;[3] but even so, a gardener's tool shed had to be

[1] See pp. 84–6.

[2] Address to students as reported in the *Birmingham Gazette*, 18 October 1950.

[3] The house and its thirteen acres of land purchased for £7,400 proved to be

converted to accommodate twelve students and the device of 'doubling-up' again proved to be the means of salvation. But a lodgings solution had been avoided.

The real crisis occurred during the 1952–3 session when the College had to decide to limit new admissions in October 1953 to 130 and the total number of students to 526. The number of new students admitted was in fact only 108[1] and the total enrolment 495; and it was not until October 1956 that the total reached 600, three years later than had been intended. But the policy of residence on the campus for all had still been maintained.

In the years following 1953 the problem of accommodation eased and the building of new residential quarters showed signs of proceeding steadily. Harrowby House for women, adjacent to Sneyd House, was opened in 1955; and the first additional units for men in the grounds of 'The Hawthorns' were begun in 1956. The College could now breathe more easily and the possibility of expanding numbers to 800 by 1962 began to be talked about.[2]

It was early in 1957 that the first major policy decision on deliberate expansion was called for. The UGC had been looking towards the future demand for university education and Keele was asked whether it would be willing and able to expand to 1,200 by 1965 on the assumption that two-thirds of an increase from 800 to 1,200 would be in science students.[3] The Senate, despite some misgivings, were clear that the challenge had to be accepted: in so doing the College would take its share in satisfying a national demand and at the same time could hope to secure staff, buildings and recurrent grants for which it would otherwise have to wait a long time.[4] But the acceptance of this

---

a very wise investment. Negotiations for Madeley Manor and Madeley Rectory fell through.

[1] A factor contributing to the fall in admissions was the reluctance of some Local Authorites to award grants for a four-year course to qualified applicants.

[2] The figure of 800 is sometimes mistakenly referred to as the 'original target'. The Memorandum of 11 November 1946 (see p. 101) spoke of 'a total of 500 to 600 students by the end of the first three years'. Certainly what the UGC agreed to in 1949 and 1950 in assessing its financial support was an annual intake of 150 for a four-year course, that is 600 undergraduates in all.

[3] It was eventually agreed with the UGC that anyone taking one principal subject from group C should be classified as a science student.

[4] In the course of the discussions in the Senate the idea was mooted that the Foundation Year might be divided into two, one course for intending arts

proposal by the College was made conditional on the maintenance of the policy of 100 per cent student residence, on the provision of staff residence on the campus, on preserving the existing staff–student ratio and on adequate grants for building and recurrent expenditure: the existing character of the College must be preserved.

But less than three years later consideration was being given to a further expansion, and again on the initiative of the UGC. What could Keele do in relation to a national target of 170,000 students (including postgraduates) by 'the late 1970s'? To this question the Senate directed its attention in the spring of 1960 when the College enrolment was only 732 and boldly suggested a figure of 2,400. The Chairman of the UGC suggested to the Principal (Sir George Barnes) that so great an expansion might unduly strain the existing organisation at Keele. And in what fields of study would expansion take place? Apart from the growth and development of existing departments, the College advanced the idea of research institutes and, within the field of applied science, the possibility of introducing nuclear and control engineering. The Chairman of the UGC stressed the development of the biological sciences, biochemistry, biophysics and genetics at undergraduate level. Without completely abandoning an eventual target of '2,400 in the late 1970s', the College therefore decided to raise the 1957 proposal of 1,200 students by 1965 to 1,600 or 1,700 'by the early 1970s', a figure which implied an annual intake of about 400 freshmen; but ultimately an intermediate figure of 1,470 for 1967–8 was agreed with the UGC.

So matters stood when the publication in October 1963 of the 'Robbins' Report on Higher Education forced the country to contemplate a degree and a rate of expansion in university education which had never previously been envisaged. This Report enunciated as a basic principle the doctrine that 'courses of higher education should be available for all those who are qualified by ability and attainment to pursue them and wish to do so'. In practical terms the Report recommended that the number of students in institutions of university status (including the Colleges of Advanced Technology which were to become

students, the other for science students. This abnegation of Keele's basic idea of a 'common core' was not pursued further.

universities) should be raised to 197,000 by 1967–8, to 218,000 by 1973–4 and possibly to 350,000 by 1980–1. The government immediately accepted the Report in principle and adopted the Robbins figure for 1967–8 as a firm proposal. Already by the middle of November 1963 universities were being told by the UGC that adequate funds would be available to enable them to expand by 1967–8 to as near the target previously set for the early 1970s as they could achieve. For Keele this seemed to mean 1,600 or 1,700 and the University resolved to aim at the higher figure; but to the chagrin of Keele the UGC took the figure of 1,470, previously agreed for 1967–8, as the basis on which they made a supplementary allocation from the 'Robbins money'. It could be that the UGC was still worried about the rate at which Keele as a fully residential university could expand: with 922 students in October 1963, a target of 1,700 within four years would involve almost doubling the number of residential places, and this at a time when some newer universities would have to house their students in near-by seaside resorts. Keele by this time had in fact not been able to erect permanent halls even for the students it already had.

The euphoria induced in all universities by the expansionist Robbins Report and the government's speedy provision of some additional funds was short lived. By May 1964 the Secretary of State for Education and Science was giving warnings about all forms of capital expenditure; it was also evident that no building work begun after March 1966 could effectively contribute extra places in 1967–8: it was therefore announced late in 1964 that building allocations for 1966–7 were to be drastically cut; and in 1965 there was an economic crisis for which all-round retrenchment was part of the cure. What was a cause of particular alarm to Keele, however, was the fact that the letter received in December 1964 from the UGC[1] regarding the 1966–7 building grant contained the ominous statement that 'the extent to which the growth in your student numbers should be matched by additional residential accommodation raises important issues of policy'. Keele's reaction to the student figure of 1,470, to the meagre building grant of £100,000 for 1966–7[2] and to the

[1] The Chairman (1963–8) was now Sir John Wolfenden, formerly Vice-Chancellor of Reading (1950–63) and subsequently Director and Principal Librarian of the British Museum (1969).

[2] The sum was specifically indicated by the UGC at this time as being for laboratory accommodation, not residences.

question of policy was resentful. The reply of the Vice-Chancellor (H. M. Taylor) pointed out that Keele had raised £220,000 for buildings by an appeal in 1956 and that the further appeal launched in 1963 and now approaching £200,000 had been for research. All this had been done on the understanding that the UGC accepted the basic assumptions on which Keele had been founded and the lines of its development. He continued:

> What future does the UGC see for Keele? Up to now we have been working to a particular plan on assumptions based on meetings and visitations over the last fifteen years: the basic premise being that the special features of Keele provided in combination something unique in United Kingdom university education today, and something which the current vast expansion made even more worthy of preservation. Can we have some summary of the Committee's views on this?

Early in 1965 there were consultations with the UGC and in March the Committee itself formally re-considered the position of Keele in the following terms:[1]

> The point which emerged clearly . . . was that the University was not committed to an expansion to any figure higher than 1,700, and that the study which had been made of the potential capacity of the site[2] did not reflect a policy decision to expand to 3,000, but was intended simply to provide information about the feasibility of such an expansion. In the circumstances, the Committee felt that it would be reasonable for them to continue to support the expansion of the University up to a total of 1,700 on the basis that the University would be fully residential. . . . If at any time between now and reaching its present target of 1,700, the University should begin to think seriously of a higher figure, the position should be open to review. . . . The Committee is not committed to any particular date for the achievement of the 1,700 figure. While we all hope that this objective may be

[1] Incidentally, the University was now asked whether they would wish to use the 1966–7 building allocation for teaching *or* for residential purposes.

[2] Early in 1964 Mr Peter Shepheard, the Consultant for development, had been asked, along with more immediate objectives, 'to advise on further expansion up to a total of about 3,000'.

> attained by the early 1970s, the pace of the development will depend on the amount of the allocations which can be made available from the resources at the Committee's disposal.

This was a parting of the ways for the University. Both total size and residence were involved, and these two factors could well be incompatible. Opinion in favour of expansion was now strong because it was realised, even more than before, that the number of students in a university must be an important consideration with the UGC in determining the size of the Committee's quinquennial grant, and without more money than they were now getting, Keele could not achieve the academic developments they had in mind: new courses and new subjects would have to be postponed, perhaps abandoned. Yet how far could the ideal of total residence be modified without changing the character of the University? Even from 1950 there had always been an insignificant handful of students living at home or in lodgings for special reasons;[1] but if such arrangements were to be extended, a definite policy would be called for. The first innovation was a scheme introduced in October 1964 for twenty-five day-students living at home in Newcastle or Stoke-on-Trent. When plans were formulated in 1964–5 for the 1967–72 quinquennium, a far more radical policy was adopted after much heart-searching; and the UGC were told in 1965 that Keele itself now made four assumptions:

(a) that by October 1967 they would reach the target of 1,470, almost all of whom would be in residence;

(b) that the minimum increase in the 1967–72 quinquennium would take them to about 2,150 in 1972 of whom about 1,700 would be in residence and 450 in lodgings;

(c) that, even though no undertaking had been given by the UGC, the necessary grants would be forthcoming to build up residences to 1,470 by 1967 and to 1,700 by 1972;

(d) that Keele envisaged itself as remaining a predominantly residential University, which would mean that up to 25 per cent of students, but not more, would at any time be out in lodgings.

The transfer in 1964 of the UGC itself from the aegis of the Treasury with direct access to the Chancellor of the Exchequer to that of the newly constituted Department of Education and

[1] See Appendix II, Table 2.

Science resulted in some delay in announcing the grants for the last four years of the 1967–72 quinquennium; but Keele was eventually told that its recurrent grants were based on an expansion up to 2,050 by 1971–2, a figure only 100 less than it had itself suggested for October 1972. The grants for recurrent purposes, however, were less than had been hoped for; and the capital grants allocated during the quinquennium did not permit the rate of increase in the number of residential places which Keele had suggested as desirable. A fourth Hall of Residence, however, Barnes Hall, was commenced in 1966; from April 1966 a Lodgings Officer was appointed; and as a practical measure it was decided that from October 1967 onwards each student entering the University would be assured of residence within the University for not more than three years of his four-year course.

How these changes of policy have shown themselves in operation can most easily be seen from Appendix II, Tables 1 and 2, where the details of student numbers and residence are set out year by year from 1950. Applications for admission are many times the number of places Keele is prepared to offer; and the admissions policy is related to the residential accommodation available. Even so, the number of students not in Halls of Residence has not yet reached the 25 per cent which was regarded in 1965 as the firm but acceptable limit. Incidentally it is worth noting that a sharp increase in the number of students in lodgings had already shown itself in October 1964 when the number of attractive applications for admission could not be matched by the number of places in Halls; and this pressure must have contributed to the formulation of policy in 1964–5. If we except St David's College, Lampeter, and Oxford and Cambridge where students in lodgings have a special and intimate association with their own colleges, Keele, with around 80 per cent of its students in residence on the campus, is still the most markedly residential university in the country.[1] It will of course be noted that whereas in 1950 half of the students came from within thirty miles of Keele, the proportion had dropped to one-quarter by 1954–5 and to one eighth in 1964–5, the last year in which this kind of distinction was recorded. Keele has never drawn its students predominantly from the Potteries or

[1] The current national averages, excluding Oxford and Cambridge, are 34·5 per cent in Halls, 46·4 per cent in lodgings and 19·1 per cent at home.

Staffordshire, whatever ideas on this score its early promoters had had in mind; and the progressively severe competition for university places in general has meant that academic achievement and promise had to be the main criteria in selection. Another feature of interest is the balance between the sexes which has depended to a great extent on the policy decisions relating to the provision of places in Halls of Residence. In 1950–1 there were 55 women to 102 men, or 35 per cent of the total. This proportion rose to 40 per cent in 1960–1; and in 1970–1 the figure of 38·5 per cent was still appreciably higher than that at most other universities.[1] On the other hand, overseas students, whether from the Commonwealth or other countries, have never been more than a very small proportion of the student population, rising from 3·2 per cent in the last year of the College (1961–2) to a peak of 4·5 per cent in 1969–70.[2] An interesting feature, however, has been the arrangement with Swarthmore College, Pennsylvania,[3] which from 1950 sent one or two students annually for a year at Keele; a similar scheme was introduced somewhat later by Reed College, Oregon. Though the numbers involved have been small, the existence of a definite link of this kind with these USA institutions has been worthwhile; but reciprocal arrangements to send Keele students to the USA have been hampered, though not wholly prevented, by financial difficulties.[4]

The pattern of events up to 1969–70 has been clear enough: the UGC agreed to an expansion up to 2,050 by 1971–2 on the basis of 1,700 residential places; and Keele for its part accepted the necessity for up to a quarter of its students living off the campus. A new quinquennium was due to begin in 1972; but though responsible estimates had been made which indicated that the decade 1972–82 would see a further expansion in all forms of higher education, the government had not announced by the end of 1970 an objective for student numbers in universities.

[1] Comparable percentages are found only at St Andrews and at the University Colleges of Aberystwyth and Bangor. The national average is 28·3 per cent or, excluding Oxford and Cambridge, 29·6 per cent.

[2] Nationally the figure is 7·4 per cent (3·7 per cent from the Commonwealth and 3·7 per cent from other countries.)

[3] See p. 132.

[4] The Leverhulme Trust made a grant of £400 p.a. for five years in 1961 to assist Keele students to go to Swarthmore; but Keele now relies on its own funds. Exchanges of staff between Keele and these institutions have also been effected from time to time, thanks in part to the interest and help of the Carnegie Foundation.

All that the UGC therefore could do to assist universities in the preparation of their quinquennial estimates was to provide for each university an indication of what the Committee itself regarded as a possible basis for planning. So far as Keele was concerned, the UGC expressed the view that expansion to 2,400 within the 1972–7 quinquennium was 'the maximum number possible under the existing condition of a four-year course for all undergraduates'. So the figure first suggested by Keele in 1960 for the late 1970s was acceptable as a target or limit for 1976–7; the restriction on UGC financed residences was presumably to be maintained;[1] but a new and disturbing factor—the length of the Keele curriculum—was now being introduced at the UGC level into the discussion of expansion.

The reactions of the Senate were first, to ignore the advice about numbers and include in their estimates the figures of 3,000 which had been envisaged in their 1964 development plan;[2] and secondly, to ask Heads of Departments under what circumstances, if any, they would contemplate a three-year degree course. Already in June 1969 a Working Party on Curricular Development had been set up and prior to the UGC's comment on the four-year course had discussed the question of a three-year course for a minority of students. Though no firm proposal was made by the Working Party, it was re-affirmed that, however necessary it might be to transpose Lindsay's principles into another key, Keele should feel itself committed to retaining a characteristic breadth in the curriculum whatever its length might be. Subsequent talks with the UGC have led to an agreement that Keele could increase to 3,000 in the 1972–7 quinquennium provided that the additional 600 places would be for students taking a three-year course.[3] The acceptance of this proposal means that Keele in the very near future will have to do some hard thinking about the nature of a three-year programme for 20 per cent of its students.

We turn now to the expansions which have taken place in the academic staff. During the course of the very first session the

[1] From 1969 the University itself embarked on a further residential development for students on 'The Hawthorns' site under a loan-financed scheme.

[2] See p. 218.

[3] In addition, the UGC would expect that the number of science-based students would not exceed 700 and the proportion of postgraduates would not be increased; and no new science buildings could be provided in the 1972–7 period.

College had to face something of a major crisis. The initial group of nineteen teachers could cope with the first Foundation Year; but for 1951–2 there were also subsidiary courses and the first year of principal subjects to be provided. A large immediate increase of staff was therefore imperative; yet, money was short and the UGC was alarmed by the possible cost of Keele's demands. Consequently, of the additional twenty-four members of staff appointed for the second session, eighteen were assistant lecturers whose presumed enthusiasms for the Keele concept could not be expected to compensate entirely for their inexperience; and for several years recruitment of staff had to be predominantly in that same grade. Inevitably there was competition and some friction between departments for such additional posts or promotions as could be provided year by year. Until about 1962 there were difficulties too in retaining staff, especially in science subjects; and though it might be gratifying to feel that Keele was a stepping-stone to higher posts elsewhere, the abnormal number of changes in staff not only made life difficult for heads of departments but militated against the building up of a solid cadre of Keele-orientated teachers. Since 1962, however, greater staff stability has been maintained; but the number of Chairs has markedly failed to keep pace with the increase in student numbers.[1] Table 10 shows the fluctuations in the staff-structure.

Table 10 Percentages of grades of staff

<table>
<tr><th rowspan="2">Years</th><th colspan="2">Professors</th><th colspan="2">Readers & S/Lecturers</th><th colspan="2">Lecturers</th><th colspan="2">Assistant lecturers</th><th colspan="2">Others</th></tr>
<tr><th>No.</th><th>%</th><th>No.</th><th>%</th><th>No.</th><th>%</th><th>No.</th><th>%</th><th>No.</th><th>%</th></tr>
<tr><td>1951–2</td><td>13</td><td>30·0</td><td>4</td><td>9·3</td><td>8</td><td>18·6</td><td>18</td><td>42·0</td><td>—</td><td>—</td></tr>
<tr><td>1956–7</td><td>15</td><td>17·0</td><td>7</td><td>8·0</td><td>37</td><td>42·0</td><td>29</td><td>33·0</td><td>—</td><td>—</td></tr>
<tr><td>1960–1</td><td>15</td><td>13·2</td><td>9</td><td>7·9</td><td>53</td><td>46·5</td><td>33</td><td>28·9</td><td>4</td><td>3·5</td></tr>
<tr><td>1968–9</td><td>21</td><td>7·8</td><td>34</td><td>12·7</td><td>135</td><td>50·4</td><td>31</td><td>11·6</td><td>47</td><td>17·5</td></tr>
<tr><td>1970–1</td><td>24</td><td>8·4</td><td>51</td><td>17·9</td><td colspan="2">171</td><td colspan="2">60·2</td><td>38</td><td>13·4</td></tr>
<tr><td>National average 1966–9</td><td colspan="2">11·6</td><td colspan="2">19·5</td><td colspan="4">65·3</td><td colspan="2">3·6</td></tr>
</table>

[1] As a high priority the Senate is recommending seventeen new professorships during the 1972–7 quinquennium.

DEVELOPMENT OF THE SITE

A reader who does not know Keele and may perhaps never visit the campus can scarcely be expected to be interested in the details of its physical growth. Nevertheless, the topic involves more than architecture and landscaping; for it is part and parcel of Keele's trials and tribulations. There is a daunting inevitability about what happened in regard to the site which merits a more sympathetic understanding than has generally been forthcoming. Given that the new College was to be residential, Keele Hall and its 154 acres turned out to be the one and only available location anywhere near Stoke-on-Trent; and with its main building and the huts and other army structures it offered accommodation in which the College could begin to function without serious delay. There was just no feasible alternative. But for nearly twenty years previously the estate had been neglected; British and American Forces had put in some drainage, a temporary reservoir, and a small sewage farm —and had set fire to the top floor of part of Keele Hall itself. Speedy makeshift conversions offered temporary solutions which had to be accepted; but practically nothing in the way of long-term planning could possibly receive any serious attention at that time. In the late 1940s most other universities which were facing problems of expansion appointed some prominent consultant to advise them on planning and architectural development; Liverpool, for example, secured the services of Sir William (later Lord) Holford. Keele had no money at all to spare from its UGC allocations for any such provident luxury: that harsh fact must be emphasised. In the early stages Keele had to rely, with gratitude, on the help which the City of Stoke-on-Trent could supply through the department of the City Architect, Colonel J. R. Piggott, FRIBA; and it is only fair to say that the amount of work which was accomplished in the first few years from 1949 is a tribute to the professional skill and above all to the goodwill and self-sacrificing co-operation of Colonel Piggott and his staff. They attended to the necessary services—water mains, gas mains, electrical substations, reservoirs, sewers, new roads and campus lighting, the adaptations of the existing structures, and the siting and building of staff houses; and J. A. Pickavance, for example, Piggott's Assistant Architect for Further Education, did all the work on the first stages of the chemistry, physics, geology and biology departments after normal office hours. Mr. F. G. Drummond of the Staffordshire Education Department also gave help in the laying-out of playing fields and in general landscaping. The need to convert and use existing structures was so pressing that few of them could be sacrificed to facilitate planning; the undulating contours of the terrain made some sites far too costly for development when money and building materials were so scarce; such roads and services as did exist were too useful to be diverted or modified immediately; and even the height of buildings was restricted by the risks of subsidence should the Coal Board decide to exploit the untapped coal seams underlying the campus. It was all very, very difficult. Yet here for the first time in Britain a university institution was being located on an extensive and potentially very attractive non-urban site. If only there had been more time to think, if the site had not been cluttered up with marginally usable buildings, if the possibilities of expansion had been envisaged, if it had occurred to Lindsay that, however the expense was covered, the part-time help of a hard-pressed local government architect ought to be supplemented by the advice of an expert in large-scale planning, then the Keele estate would not now be described as 'one of the least distinguished campuses in one of the most naturally beautiful of university parks in the country'.[1] Of all the lessons learned by the newer universities of the 1960s from the Keele experience, not the least important was the need to avoid from the very outset piecemeal planning and development.

The problems arising during the first two sessions and the sheer volume of work involved decided the College to set up its own Architects' Department and after the post had been advertised Mr J. A. Pickavance, FRIBA, was appointed as full-time Architect to the College and took up his duties in January 1952. It was now possible to undertake at least a full and methodical survey of the campus and to begin to think in terms of a master development plan; but some of the important planning decisions which had been hastily taken within the previous three years in regard to the siting of academic buildings, student accommodation and staff residences were by now virtually irreversible. In the spring of 1956 the distinguished

[1] H. J. Perkin, *New Universities in the United Kingdom*, p. 60.

architect Sir Howard Robertson, RA[1] accepted an invitation to assume consultant responsibilities as Development Architect, a part-time office he held until 1961; and in 1962 Mr Peter Shepheard[2] succeeded him. The majority of the individual buildings on the campus have in fact been designed and their construction supervised by the Architects' Department; but from 1960, as will be noted later, commissions for a number of important buildings have been entrusted to outside architects.

The completion in 1971 of a ring-road within the campus will effectively obscure the original lay-out of the site and dim the memory of the conditions which in 1949–50 determined the original development. It is, however, worth while to attempt to recall at least the outlines of the earlier situation. Think of a letter 'Y' lying approximately with its tail at the south-east and the two arms diverging where the Library–Chapel–Union roundabout was formed, one arm going to the right in a winding northwards direction to the Newcastle-under-Lyme entrance over half a mile away, and the other to the left leading almost west for rather less than half a mile to Keele village. Two hundred yards below the fork towards the tail of the 'Y' was Keele Hall itself with lawns, a series of small lakes and stretches of woodland beyond it. A subsidiary road ran between the two arms of the 'Y' some three hundred yards or so from their junction and so with them enclosed a roughly triangular area. It is within this area that many of the major academic buildings have been erected. The first four such buildings were sited along the road leading to Keele village: chemistry and physics within the triangle, and biology and geology immediately facing them on the opposite side of the road. Each member of this cosy cluster was designed for the needs of a small College and their proximity to each other has created problems when anything more than small extensions were needed.

Where should student accommodation and staff residences be sited if one was to avoid a sprawling development in a new institution? For students two major areas were selected. Three groups of converted huts within the academic triangle were used until a permanent Hall (Horwood) was eventually erected

[1] President of the RIBA, 1952–4. Among his many important commissions was the Faculty of Letters at Reading University, 1956.

[2] President of the RIBA, 1969. His works include the master plan and buildings for the University of Lancaster.

on a site to the north-east of Keele Hall. The other main groups of student huts, which became Lindsay Hall, lay to the west of Keele Hall and to the south of the Biology and the Geology buildings. The general effect has been that Horwood Hall, Keele Hall, the Clock House (the Principal's residence) and Lindsay Hall form a rough semicircle around the tail of the 'Y'. The accommodation for the staff was sited in another semicircle which wrapped itself around the western fringe of the academic triangle. Of the three sub-areas concerned, the Larchwood group of semi-detached staff houses lay to the south of the road leading to Keele village and adjacent to the Lindsay Hall site, the Church Plantation group of detached houses and the later blocks of single staff flats occupied a larger plot which was bounded by the link road and the western arm of the 'Y', and the Covert group of mostly semi-detached houses completed the semicircle on the north-west side of the link road. This disposition of staff residences was a very reasonable solution of one of the problems of accommodation for a College which did not expect to expand to anything like the kind of figure which is being talked of in 1971; but combined with the location of the Halls of Residence, it now presents an expanding University with a choice of a still higher density of buildings within the academic triangle or the siting of future buildings away from the central complex. An intrusion into the spacious playing fields in the north-west part of the campus would rightly be resisted. The remaining possibility is a development to the north-east outside the ring-road on the slope which leads to the Newcastle Road boundary.[1]

There is little point now in recounting the discussions which took place about priorities for building projects; but for historical record we must give a brief survey of the major schemes undertaken, commencing with the permanent academic buildings and then passing on to other more general buildings

[1] Since 1949 when the original 154 acres were purchased, Keele has acquired much more land adjoining the main campus, though most of it is still in agricultural use. The chief purchases have been 13 acres and 'The Hawthorns' in Keele village in 1952; 25 acres at Gateside to the south-west in 1953; 380 acres of the Home Farm to the north-east in 1954, 1955 and 1959; the Springpool area of 49 acres to the south-east in 1957; and 9 acres of the Paddocks Farm in 1964. These acquisitions ensure that Keele's rural setting will not be disturbed. All told the land belonging to Keele now amounts to 654 acres and, with Keele Hall and other buildings included in the purchases, has cost approximately £111,000.

and finally to student and staff residences. As will be seen, many of the projects had to be spread over several years.[1]

Preliminaries. The initial adaptations to Keele Hall, the huts and the Clock House, together with a preliminary layout of playing fields occupied most of the years 1949 to 1951 and involved an expenditure of £250,000.

Physics. The first two stages began in 1951; stage III in 1959; stage IV, a research block designed by Architects' Co-Partnership, in 1964; and the last stage was completed early in 1967. The total contract price over the years was £325,650.

Chemistry. As in the case of Physics, the first two stages began in 1951; stage III in 1959; and the final stage IV, designed by the firm of Robertson Young which had special experience in planning chemistry laboratories, was begun late in 1964 and completed by Easter 1967. The total cost was £381,500.

Biology. Stages I and II began in 1952 and were completed in 1954; but it was not until 1962 that the third and final stage was commenced. The total cost was £261,100.

Geology made do with a temporary laboratory until 1953 when stage I of a permanent home was begun; two further stages were begun in 1956 and 1968. The whole scheme cost £156,700.

Geography. The first two stages of this building next door to Physics were spread over the years 1952–7 and the final stage, begun in 1964, was completed in 1966. The total cost was £117,600.

Communication. A building designed, like Physics IV to which it is adjacent, by Architects' Co-Partnership was begun in early 1964 and finished in 1966. It cost £140,340.

Science Workshop. Sited to the north of Chemistry, this service building was erected between September 1964 and late 1965 at a cost of £52,530.

Computer Centre. This, the latest of the scientific buildings, was constructed in 1970 at a cost of £119,640.

R. H. Tawney Building. This was the first specially designed unit of teaching accommodation and now houses Mathematics and Modern Languages. Sited within the academic triangle, it was begun in 1954 and completed in June 1956 at a cost of £36,680.

Walter Moberly Hall, near the fork of the 'Y' provides a large hall suitable for lectures, concerts, recitals and for drama also since it

[1] The locations of the buildings are indicated on the map of the campus which forms the end-papers to this volume. The figures of cost which are given refer to the contract prices for the constructional work and do not include any professional fees, general overheads or expenditure on equipment.

contains a proscenium-arch stage with full lighting and green-rooms. Building was commenced in 1954 and completed at the end of 1956 at a cost of £53,000.

Chancellor's Building. This building, designed by Mr Peter Shepheard, lies near the northern corner of the triangle and accommodates History, American studies, economics, politics, psychology, sociology, law, education (including the Institute) and adult education. It also contains the large Foundation Year lecture theatre. Intended to facilitate the expansion of student numbers, its erection began in 1962 and the scheme was completed in stages by 1966 at a cost of £366,300.

The Library. Designed by the firm of Sir Howard Robertson, this important building was sited in a prominent central position to the south of the point where the two arms of the 'Y' diverge. Commenced in 1959 it was eventually completed in four stages in the summer of 1966 and cost £549,200.

Students' Union. Almost directly facing the Library at the fork of the 'Y', the Union was designed by Messrs Stillman and Eastwick Field. Construction began in 1961 and when finished rather more than a year later the building work had cost £171,100.

The Chapel. Designed by Mr G. G. Pace and built in 1964, this interdenominational focus of religious worship was sited at the junction of the two arms of the 'Y'. It cost £84,400 to build and the UGC provided £9,967 towards the cost of the organ and furniture. With the Union to the north-east and the Library to the south, it is one of a triad of buildings each of which is of special significance in the life of the Keele community. The completion of the ring-road will divert most vehicular traffic from the existing roundabout and the three buildings will then, even more than now, share the one definite focal point in the whole campus. Each was the commission of a different outside architect and the total result is, in the opinion of most visitors to Keele, a misfortune: in style, design, materials, texture and notably in colour, this group of buildings has a glaring lack of harmony and relationship.[1] Plans, however, are in hand for modifications and additions to this area which, beginning possibly in 1972, will provide a satisfactory remedy for the problem.

Health Centre. Erected on the fringe of the campus a little to the east of Horwood Hall, the first stage of this building was begun in 1961 and an extension in 1968. The total cost was £52,850.

Sports Centre. Lying to the north-west of the academic triangle,

[1] It is worth remembering that vital decisions about all these three buildings were being taken in a very awkward period when Sir Howard Robertson was ill and when, after an interregnum, Mr Shepheard had only just been appointed. A pamphlet sent out by Keele to prospective students describes the Chapel as being 'built in a striking blue Staffordshire brick'.

this building was designed by Mr Peter Shepheard, begun at the end of 1963, and completed early in 1967 at a cost of £246,050.

Halls of Residence. The first permanent residence was *Sneyd House*, a small hall for women erected in 1952 at a cost of £26,000; and a similar hall nearby, *Harrowby House*, was built for £56,000 in 1954–5: both now form part of the Lindsay Hall complex. The development of the *Hawthorns* site in Keele village began in 1953 and by 1958, £67,000 had been expended. After a few years a very much larger scheme, including a refectory and a general block, was undertaken in 1965 and by 1967 the further sum of £520,000 had been expended. In addition, since 1969, flats for student accommodation costing £152,400 have been erected. The permanent buildings of *Horwood Hall* were not commenced until 1958 but by the end of 1965 the scheme had involved a cost of £388,000, to which should be added £28,000 for the extension of the Keele Hall refectory to meet the needs of Horwood Hall students. On the *Lindsay Hall* site, the first building was the refectory begun in 1961 which was soon followed by the main residential blocks; the total cost of the scheme added up to £548,600. The most recent project of this nature is *Barnes Hall* which is sited opposite the playing fields beyond the academic area and fronts on to the road leading to the Newcastle entrance. The six units so far built are costing £207,500.

Staff Residences. The first twenty permanent houses for staff were built on the *Church Plantation* site in 1951 and including road works they cost £75,000. In 1959 and again in 1968 the site was further developed by the provision of staff flats, the total additional cost being £105,700. The comparatively small *Larchwood* site was used in 1953 for staff houses at a cost of £42,000. In 1953 also the first group of houses was erected on the *Covert* site; with further additions in 1958, the total cost of development was £57,500. Away from the main areas of staff residences, additional flats for staff were built adjacent to Horwood Hall in 1963 at a cost of £131,200.[1]

Summary. All told, between 1949 and the summer of 1970 Keele has been committed to the expenditure of £6,374,000 on the construction of buildings and the provisions of the necessary basic services associated with them. How this sum has been allocated among the various activities which make up the total pattern of life at Keele is a matter of special interest at a time when the future of the University is under consideration. The largest single category of expenditure has been on academic buildings, including the Library, which to date have cost in

[1] For residential provision being made through the Keele University Staff Housing Association, see p. 239.

bricks and mortar the sum of £2,560,240. Very close to this comes the sum of £2,463,500 which represents the cost of Halls of Residence, the Union, the Health Centre and the Sports Centre; and no clearer indication is needed of how expensive a policy of full student residence has proved to be. A further £854,460 has been spent on a wide variety of minor works including the preliminary conversions of 1949–50 and the ring-road of 1970–1. £411,400 has been devoted to the provision of staff residences, most of which sum has been obtained through special Treasury loan arrangements approved by the UGC. The £84,400 which was the contract cost of the Chapel was in large part secured by a special public appeal for funds. Apart from the last two items, over 90 per cent of the sums indicated above has been covered by capital grants made by the UGC. These grants, however, have taken into account not only the building costs with which we have just been dealing, but also the purchase of sites, furniture, professional fees and scientific equipment. That explains why the total of capital grants received from the UGC[1] between 1949 and the end of the 1968–9 session had amounted to £8,397,000. It is this last figure which most clearly represents the investment from public funds in the development of Keele.[2]

A visitor to the Keele site in its early days could find little to rouse his enthusiasm and in 1955 something of a public controversy broke out regarding the way in which the site was being handled. After an Easter conference of headmasters there, an editorial in *The Times Educational Supplement* voiced some current misgivings:[3]

[1] See Appendix II, Table 3, p. 307.

[2] In his introduction to the *Civil Appropriation Accounts, Classes VI and XI, 1968–69* (published in February 1970), the Comptroller and Auditor-General, who since January 1968 had had statutory access to the books of account of the UGC and the universities, drew attention to 'over-provision' of accommodation at Keele and Essex. Keele's target of student numbers for 1971–2 is 2,050; but using UGC 'models' as his standard, the Comptroller estimated that by that session Keele would have academic buildings for 2,600, library, administration and maintenance services for over 5,000, dining and catering facilities for 4,700 and social and recreation provision for well over 3,000. The UGC 'models' are not 'standards' or 'norms' but figures which assume the maximum use of accommodation. Keele is not alone in thinking that such figures make too little allowance for local difficulties in securing optimum use.

[3] 22 April 1955. By this time the first stages of the science buildings and

> A visitor to Keele, though he may approve its system, will be upset by the look of the place. Keele threatens to be hideous. The site is favourable; it has a hill, trees and lakes; Keele Hall itself is not without merit, in spite of its period. But the place seems to be going up without any master plan, and the design of the permanent buildings is lamentable. One building alone, the new hostel for women students, has a touch of elegance and grace. All else is monstrous.

The local *Sentinel* in editorials and in its correspondence columns joined in the fray; and equally unsympathetic was the *Architects Journal*:[1]

> Apparently buildings were going up . . . in a casual sort of way and no real attempt has been made to relate one block to another. . . . the pity of it all is that Keele Hall is a rousing piece of Victoriana of the kind that, with sympathetic handling, could have been exploited to create a fine collegiate atmosphere.

To such mixtures of legitimate criticism and witch-hunting, the Acting Principal, Professor Blake, replied in his address at the June Graduation.[2] He pointed out that the laboratories were all unfinished buildings and that to save money and because of brick rationing many of them had had to be constructed from the unprepossessing prefabricated 'Orlit' material: 'We are fully conscious of the fact that there is a need to site buildings well, to co-ordinate architectural styles. In this context we are probably our own most sensitive and demanding critics. We agree that a master plan is desirable. Had we waited for such a master plan before opening in October 1950, we would probably not exist today.' The College had in fact been drawing up an overall plan from the end of 1953 and, as we have already seen, Sir Howard Robertson was appointed as consultant in 1956. Since that time, much has been done to rectify the unsatisfactory architectural aspect of the campus. The later stages of the science laboratory buildings have masked the ugly earlier stages with new frontages which do at least

Sneyd House had been completed and the R. H. Tawney Building was well on the way.

[1] 16 June 1955.

[2] Reported in the *Sentinel*, 29 June 1955.

aspire to some kind of architectural style; and the newer lecture-room blocks and Halls of Residence have won positive commendation.[1]

A glimpse at least of what the future may have in store was provided by Mr Peter Shepheard when he gave an address in February 1970 on the problems confronting the University should it wish to expand to 3,500 or even 5,000 students in the next ten to twelve years. He pointed out that when he presented his own first development plan in 1964 the way in which the campus could develop was already largely decided—neither Keele Hall nor the lakes beyond could now be regarded as central. For this reason amongst others he had devised the ring-road which would keep traffic largely out of the 'restful academic area' in the centre, whilst the Halls of Residence would continue to be developed outside the ring-road. It would be possible to have a university of 4,500 students without extending the academic area beyond the ring-road but for a larger number than that, or if a new faculty needing a lot of space were founded, academic buildings would have to be sited on the hill towards the Observatory. The siting of the Chapel had not been in accord with his own scheme for development. The area between the Library, Union and Chapel, the 'natural gravitational centre' of the University, 'The Forum', could have more buildings than at present: the Library could have a one-storey extension forward, there could be a large University Hall in front of the Chapel, and a block of shops roughly in the area between the present drives leading to Horwood Hall and Keele Hall.

FINANCE

In chapter 3 a summary was given of the financial arrangements which were made to enable the College to begin work and see it through to the end of the 1947–52 quinquennium;[2] and at other points in our narrative passing reference has been made to the financial considerations which have influenced the formulation or implementation of Keele's policies for development. We must now trace in a more methodical manner the broad outline of Keele's financial record.

As one reads through the Annual Reports of the first Honorary

[1] See e.g., *Daily Telegraph*, 20 June 1967.

[2] See pp. 90–4.

Treasurer, Mr A. P. Walker, and successive Principals and Vice-Chancellors, three dominant themes continually recur: first, disappointment at the size of UGC allocations for general recurrent purposes and for buildings; secondly, an emphasis on the need for the strictest economy in every sphere of the College's activities; and thirdly, a great concern to secure endowments and to build up the meagre general reserves. The early years were full of anxieties and forebodings; but it was particularly from 1958 onwards when efforts to expand were being contemplated, that financial stringencies were most keenly felt and at times the expressions of disappointment could scarcely be distinguished from feelings of indignation at what appeared to Keele to be harsh and unjust treatment. Yet rarely, if ever, does any university think that the Treasury as advised by the UGC has been generous enough; and ever since the end of World War II the ups and downs of the national economy have meant that university development has proceeded disconcertingly by unpredictable fits and starts. Everywhere, and not at Keele alone, the scaling down of quinquennial academic programmes and the revision of building schedules are necessities which from time to time have had to be faced. This is no place to go into details, but from the published accounts of the UGC it could fairly be argued that, in comparison with institutions of similar size and range of activities, Keele has had few, if any, legitimate grounds for serious complaint, and that in the matter of student resident places up to the limit now approved by the UGC and in the provision of loans for staff residences it has indeed enjoyed privileged treatment.

There is no better way to grasp the financial vicissitudes of Keele than to take as a basis the Tables of Income and Expenditure in Appendix II.[1] Starting with a total *Income* of £75,651 in 1950–1, the revenue of the University passed the £1m. mark in 1965–6 and two years later was in excess of £1·5m.—a growth partly explained by a ten-fold increase in student numbers, partly by changes in the value of money, and partly by a

[1] The financial year of the UGC itself ends on 31 July. The accounts of individual universities are published at varying dates within the following twelve months to coincide with the annual meeting of the governing body. The UGC's own returns are published only at a still later date. The most recent UGC figures available at the time of writing refer to 1968–9.

significant widening of the scope of teaching and research activities over the years. The separate sources of income justify a few brief comments. UGC *Grants*: After the first two years the Exchequer grants have represented between 70 per cent and 75 per cent of the income; in the mid-1950s the percentage for Keele was in general rather higher than the national average and in 1968–9 at 71·1 per cent it was fractionally higher than the national average. *Local Authorities:* Support from the Local Authorities was one of the prerequisites of the UGC's approval of the foundation of the College and for the first two years this source provided about 25 per cent of Keele's total income. The amount of grant, however, which a Local Authority can provide out of its own revenues cannot be expected to keep pace with the requirements of a developing institution. In the early years Stoke-on-Trent, Staffordshire and Burton-on-Trent had agreed to step up their contributions to £32,000 in the proportions of 9:9:2; this sum was generously increased in 1955–6 and again in 1958–9 and in 1959–60; special contributions were made from 1963; and in 1964 Cheshire also began to make an annual grant of £5,000 rising to £7,000. The Cheshire grant, however, was withdrawn for the year 1969–70; and Staffordshire found it necessary to reduce their grant by £10,000 in 1969–70. The significant fact is that although the total of Local Authority grants in 1968–9 was three times the original sum, it had come to represent less than 4 per cent of the income of the University. Nevertheless, in that same year, only Essex and Stirling were deriving a larger proportion of their income from this kind of source and the national average had fallen to 0·9 per cent. *Fees:* Tuition, registration, examination and graduation fees constitute an area in which all universities, in consultation with the UGC, endeavour to keep in step. The amount and the percentage attributable to this source depend, of course, both on fluctuations in the number of students and on the scales of fees which are charged; and it is evident that it was mainly an increase of fees which raised Keele's percentage in 1957–8. The figure of 7·7 per cent for 1968–9 is near the national average of 7·4 per cent. *Research grants:* It was not to be expected that for the first few years there would be any appreciable income from grants and contracts for research; but from 1954–5 onwards the actual amounts received under this heading have steadily increased year by year.[1] For 1968–9, the figure of 9·2 per cent, though below the national average of 11·0 per cent, was higher than that of a dozen or so older institutions;[2] and if we bear in mind that Keele has only a small number of pure science departments and little applied science, the situation is one which may be taken as an indication of Keele's growing prestige in the activities on which it had concentrated. *Endowments and Donations:* This item shows only the sums actually used as income in any given year and is related only indirectly to the total capital value of endowment funds. The Keele figure of 1·9 per cent for 1968–9 was better than the national average of 1·6 per cent in that year.

In the matter of *Expenditure* and the way in which it is apportioned over various categories there are considerable differences between one university and another, arising in the main from the kind of activity to which a university is committed: a large technological faculty or a medical school will in general be more expensive to run than a faculty of arts or social science. After the first two exceptional years, Keele's expenditure on teaching and research, including provision for the Library, has fluctuated around 60 per cent of the total, a somewhat lower figure than the comparable national average which in 1968–9 was 67·0 per cent. At first the cost of administration was very high indeed;[3] it has fallen fairly steadily since 1954–5, and at 6·5 per cent is slightly below the national average of 6·7 per cent for 1968–9. The cost of maintaining premises, which include a high proportion of residential accommodation, has been one of the most intractable of Keele's problems and throughout the years this item has claimed one-sixth and even one-fifth of the total expenditure, whereas the national average has been around 15 per cent.

Apart from special allocations which are made from time to time, as in the case of the 'Robbins' expansion, the UGC makes its grants to universities on a quinquennial system, so that an institution knows in advance what income it will be receiving

[1] Almost three-quarters come from various government departments and agencies.

[2] Including Durham, Exeter, Hull, Reading, Wales and all the Scottish universities except Edinburgh and Strathclyde.

[3] A similar phenomenon occurred in the early years of the newer universities of the 1960s.

from the Treasury for each of the five years of the period. This makes it possible for a university to plan its finances with prudence and to compensate, if necessary, for over-spending in one year by economies in another. A comparison of the annual income and expenditure given in Tables 3 and 4 of Appendix II shows that even in its difficult first decade Keele managed to achieve on average a surplus of about 1 per cent of its income. After the years 1961–2 and 1962–3 when two successive deficits were incurred, the annual surplus has averaged 3 per cent of the income before making allocations for renewals and reserves.

On a number of occasions Keele has invited the support of industry and commerce by making special *Appeals* for funds. The first was launched early in 1951 but, not being expertly organised, its result was very disappointing. Other Appeals with a more satisfactory response were made in 1953, 1956, 1960 (for the Chapel) and 1963 (Expansion Fund).[1] The proceeds of these Appeals, mostly by way of seven-year covenants, were variously applied, some part being devoted to buildings for which UGC funds were not available, some part to provision for research, and some to general reserves. The extent of the overall success of these efforts is reflected in the *Balance Sheet* of 1969–70 which shows £350,705 still remaining in *Endowment Funds* and £221,614 in Renewal Funds, which with some smaller items bring the unexpended balances and reserves up to a total of £688,418. As against an annual expenditure now approaching £2m. this sum still does not allow Keele much elbow room; but it does represent a considerable determination on the part of the University to pay heed to the continued insistence of Mr A. P. Walker on the necessity for strong reserves. In this connexion a word should be added about the Halls of Residence. It has always been the policy of the UGC that, apart from capital costs, Halls should be self-supporting: it is no part of that Committee's function to defray even indirectly the cost of maintaining students. Keele fortunately has great attractions for vacation conferences. It is rural, has

[1] The 1951 and 1953 Appeals together brought in a little over £50,000. The 1956 Appeal (for £500,000) achieved £150,000 in the first year but no considerable sums thereafter. The Chapel Appeal (for £70,000) brought in £53,800 by 1962. The Expansion Fund Appeal (for £1m.), organised by professional advisers and launched by a special supplement of *The Times* on 9 October 1963 produced £300,000 by 1969. An Anniversary Appeal projected for 1971 was deferred (see pp. 251–2).

plentiful residential and refectory accommodation and has in the Walter Moberly Hall and the Chancellor's Building spacious and conveniently situated places where large meetings can be held. In 'The Hawthorns' too there is a useful self-contained complex of facilities. Consequently the gross revenue from conferences has increased year by year and in 1969–70 reached £70,735. The resulting net surplus on Halls of Residence account has therefore been considerable; and whereas many other universities find it difficult to make ends meet on Halls accounts, Keele has so far been able from this source to add to its reserves. A final point of special interest is that as soon as Keele had any money to put aside it invested it in mortgage loans and short-term loans with the Corporation of Stoke-on-Trent. This policy, which should gratify local sentiment, has been continued in preference to a wider range of investments and at the present time three quarters of the University's balances and reserves are handled in this way.

ON CAMPUS

It is not the purpose of this section of the present chapter to attempt to draw a composite picture of life on the campus. It is only those who have lived in that community who can assess in depth the quality of their experience. It suffices here to allude to a few obvious points. The environment and social pattern are congenial to many but unsatisfying for others; some, but not all, may positively enjoy the close and continuous proximity of colleagues or fellow students and the cloistered freedom from the distractions of a large city; the delight and enthusiasm of the freshman may turn into boredom by the final year; the junior and unmarried member of staff may well look at the scene with different feelings from those of a professor who, with his family, has spent many years there; and the Keele of 1971 is itself a very different place from the small College of 1950.

What we shall here be concerned with is a number of topics affecting staff and students which in a variety of ways have contributed to the making of Keele as it exists today. First, perhaps, should come the question of residence. We have already seen how the problems of student accommodation have been resolved.[1] *Residence for staff* has been scarcely less of an anxiety.

[1] See pp. 214–16, 230.

The first permanent houses were not ready until April 1952 and as the staff has increased there have been several periods, particularly around 1960, when the number of houses and flats has not fully met the need. But that is only half of the problem; the other half is financial and sociological. Virtually all staff accommodation up to 1969 was provided by Treasury loans due to be repaid in forty-five years[1] and made on the basis that the rents would be strictly economic: there was to be no indirect housing subsidy for the staff residents. Yet as building costs increased, an economic rent on later houses and flats could rise faster than academic salaries. Here indeed was a possible source of misunderstanding or friction between the College and its staff.

As early as October 1954, in the Annual Report he wrote during the illness of Sir John Lennard-Jones, Professor Vick drew attention to the difficulties: 'The first occupants are in fact buying their houses for the College, though they have no security of tenure, and nothing to show for it at the end of even a long tenancy. The rents are high in relation to salaries and this, combined with the absence of choice in housing, makes for a landlord-tenant relationship not altogether devoid of grievance.' A formal Residents' Association, which came into being in 1959 to consult with and advise the housing sub-committee of the Council on the financing, size and design of staff accommodation, has been of great value in minimising tensions. The problem, however, of finding capital to purchase a house of one's own on retirement still remained. A new line of approach was found in 1968 when the Keele University Staff Housing Association was formed to take advantage of statutory housing subsidies; the University sold three acres on the estate to the Association and a Building Society gave financial backing. It thus became possible for some at least of the members of staff to acquire the ownership of a house which they could dispose of within the rules of the Association when they left Keele.

Nevertheless, as the address list in the 1970–1 Calendar shows, almost one third of the academic staff now live elsewhere than on the campus; but of the professors, readers and senior lecturers four out of five are still faithful to the ideal of residing within the University itself. How much and in what ways the

[1] It was because of the vigorous insistence of Lord Lindsay that the period was not fixed at thirty years.

situation will change as student numbers and staff expand is an imminent problem.

The general welfare of students and the provision of amenities were matters of immediate concern to the early Senate and Council: a Union and playing fields were obvious requirements and no less important were religious needs and medical care. Although the 1949 Charter made no mention of a *Students' Union*, the existence of such a body was assumed in the Statutes;[1] and a home for it was at once provided in temporary accommodation which had on several occasions to be extended. As an organisation the Union became responsible for social and common-room amenities, debates, dances and the College shop. Within the Union there was a partly autonomous Athletic Union; and a wide variety of student societies quickly came into being. Many of these societies had a departmental or subject basis; but there were others equally lively, such as the Film Society, Music Group, Drama Group, and a Rover Crew; and very soon debates were arranged with other universities. From 1954, too, the students made contact with the Stoke Council of Social Service and began a tradition of helping in social work in the area. The first 'rag day' was held in 1956: 'Press and the general public were unanimous in praise of student conduct'[2]. Everyone who knew Keele in its early days testifies to the vigour of student activities and to the strikingly happy relationship then between students and staff. The Senate needed no prodding from the students in giving quite a high place in their priorities to a permanent Union building, which ultimately was erected and came into use in 1962.

Very closely connected with the Union activities have been the *lectures, recitals and exhibitions* arranged within the College and University, often on the initiative of student societies themselves. Regularly from 1950 many distinguished members of other universities and of cultural organisations have visited Keele to address students and staff; and one very good effect of the Foundation Year is that the audiences have been drawn from the whole student body. The Choral Society and the College Orchestra have existed from the early years and were

[1] See p. 83.

[2] Sir George Barnes, Annual Report, 1955–6. He adds: 'One direct result was the gift from the Borough of Newcastle-under-Lyme of a handsome silver mace which will be used by the College on all ceremonial occasions.'

greatly encouraged by Sir George Barnes. They have given public concerts of major works and lunch-hour performances for campus residents. Among the visiting artists many famous names are to be found: as examples only, we may mention the Amadeus and Allegri string quartets, Benjamin Britten, Peter Pears, Joan Sutherland, Sotan Kodaly, Gina Bachauer. Since 1967 the resident Lindsay String Quartet has greatly strengthened the musical life of the University by its own performances and the coaching of student players. Exhibitions of pictures have been a prominent feature. Organised with the help of several members of staff, and assisted by the Arts Council from time to time, they have drawn upon public and private collections and have included examples of the work of Paul Nash, Stanley Spencer, Paul Klee, Epstein, Kandinsky, and Japanese prints. A picture loan scheme for study-bedrooms has also flourished. All in all, whatever disadvantages there may be in Keele's geographical situation, its students have not suffered from educational or artistic isolation; indeed residence on campus has made it more easy for them than for students dispersed in a large city to take advantage of the opportunities offered.

At this point it is appropriate also to mention the *Keele Society*, which was founded in 1954. Such an Association of Past Students was adumbrated in the 1949 Statutes and empowered to elect one representative to the Court, a number which was increased to ten in the 1962 Statutes. Not all former students join, a fact which has sometimes caused anxiety; but a London Branch was formed in 1957 and one in Oxford in 1961, by which time the Association membership had reached six hundred. An annual newsletter keeps members in touch with the activities of the University and a Reunion at Easter is generally well atttended by 200 or so who come to renew associations with each other and with the University.

Almost equal in importance to the prompt accommodation for the Union was the provision of *recreational facilities*. A Director of Physical Education (H. W. B. Hayley) was appointed full-time from September 1951 to organise instructional classes and sustain an interest in games and athletics. Twenty-six acres were earmarked for playing fields and fixtures were arranged with other universities; but though the area was levelled and it was hoped to have pitches ready in early 1951, poor drainage and a succession of rainy seasons thwarted the plan. A field adjacent to 'The Hawthorns' had to be used and other pitches rented or loaned. Not until the summer of 1953 were games continuously possible on Keele's own pitches. Even so it was not until the summer of 1955 that a small brick pavilion was built and in 1959 visiting teams were still complaining about the poor facilities for changing and washing. In response to Mr Hayley's sustained pleas for a properly equipped Sports Centre, Mr Peter Shepheard was commissioned to design a suitable building; and when the first two stages were taken into use in 1966–7, Keele students had no longer to apologise for the inadequacy of their sports quarters. But the third stage which was to include a swimming pool ready by 1965, is still a hope for the future.

In contrast to Oxford and Cambridge where the pious founders of Colleges had taken it as self evident that a *Chapel* would be an essential part of their foundation and where reasonable attendance at services used to be compulsory for undergraduates, very few of the university colleges founded in the nineteenth century took any positive action as institutions to provide for the religious side of their students' development.[1] For this there were two main reasons. Most of their students at first lived at home and so needed no specially provided centre for corporate worship. In the second place, a struggling institution which drew its support from many quarters could not risk the damage to its well-being if denominational antagonisms should be aroused by an issue of this kind. Even now several civic universities give no official status or recognition to chaplains appointed by denominations to undertake the pastoral care of students. But for Lindsay, and for Horwood too, it would have been inconceivable that the College they were founding should lack a chapel. For many years a Nissen hut had to suffice until the permanent Chapel was dedicated in 1965; but it served its purpose well. Three chaplains, Anglican, Free Church and Roman Catholic, were appointed early in 1951 on a part-time basis, all three posts becoming full-time during the 1960s. The interior design of the new Chapel is such that simultaneous services can be held. At the Sunday morning University service the Anglican and Free Church chaplains co-operate and

[1] A notable exception is King's College, London, founded in 1829 as a counterblast to the 'godless institution' of University College in Gower Street (1826).

conduct the worship together, and united services are also held from time to time at which the chaplains of all three denominations officiate jointly. A great feature of the Chapel from the earliest years has been the participation in its services of distinguished visiting preachers, both ordained and laymen: the long list of such visitors is an impressive catalogue of eminent theologians, philosophers and educators.[1]

The requirements for *medical care* were at first covered by the part-time appointment of Alderman Dr A. P. Spark who in 1953 was succeeded by the present Medical Officer, Dr J. S. Scott, whose post became full-time in 1967. A sick-bay with a fully trained nurse in charge was equipped in one of the huts until the Health Centre was commenced in 1961. There is now a woman Assistant Medical Officer also, two part-time consultants, and three nurses. For general *academic guidance* each staff member of a Foundation Year discussion group accepts responsibility for two students as a general tutor to exercise a broad oversight over academic progress which continues throughout the student's four years. For the discussion of their *personal problems* students can seek the help of their general tutor, the warden and resident tutors of their Hall, the University's counselling service or any member of staff in whom they have confidence. An appointments office was launched on a small scale in 1953 by A. H. Iliffe[2] and substantially developed by H. R. Leech[3] until 1962 when the Appointments and Counselling Service was established with Miss A. Newsome as its full-time head. Since then both sides of the work have expanded vigorously and the success of the counselling service in particular has attracted much attention from outside.

YEARS OF TROUBLE: 1968–71

In the early days of the College *staff–student relations* were exceptionally close and visitors to Keele were struck by the intimacy and *camaraderie* which seemed to be on the way to becoming a Keele tradition. No doubt the difficult physical conditions under which the work of the College was conducted induced a general pioneering feeling and a strong sense of

[1] A still thriving Sunday School for the children of staff was started in 1951 by Miss Mary Glover, Director of Social Service Training.

[2] Lecturer in psychology, later senior tutor until he left Keele in 1970.

[3] Senior lecturer in history. His death in 1967 was a great sorrow to Keele.

common purpose; and the fact that Keele did not expand rapidly also helped to ensure the continuance of this happy situation until it was marred, though far from being destroyed, by the events of the late 1960s.

A study of what is sometimes called 'The Students' Revolt' and which eventually made its impact on Keele would require a book to itself; and only the briefest outline can here be given of the world-wide student unrest of the 1960s which is the general background to what happened at Keele. The traditional sense of a corporate identity among students became intensified in the 1950s as universities in every country expanded at an unprecedented rate; effective communication between students and the university hierarchy became more difficult to maintain; in an increasingly permissive society the claims of authority were challenged; students' dissatisfaction with the broad patterns of their education and many of its details went unheeded; and alongside all this was the youthful idealism of a bewildered generation which, in the atmosphere of the 'cold war', distrusted the ability of their elders to fashion a better world: where, it was asked, did the universities stand—were they not the willing handmaidens of governments and the agencies of a brutal industrialism? Opposition to the Vietnam war and to all forms of racial apartheid also had a prominent place in students' thinking. The more militant and politically conscious elements in the student population became the spearhead of protest; even a minor incident could spark off a large-scale revolt; and injudicious or provocative reactions on the part of authority could easily result in the involvement of large sections of moderate and otherwise acquiescent student opinion. Demonstrations, boycotts of lectures, and peaceful occupation of university buildings led with increasing frequency to the disruption of public meetings and the denial of freedom of speech for opponents, to physical violence and even to conflict with the civil power. The first major manifestation of student rebellion occurred in 1964 at the Berkeley campus of the University of California; and subsequently serious troubles broke out intermittently in many universities throughout the USA. West Germany, Spain, Italy, Holland, South America and Japan had to face similar outbreaks and in May 1968 the uprising at the Sorbonne shook the French government itself. Though some of the activists in the various countries had contacts with each other and some leaders (Cohn-Bendit, Rudi Dutschke, Tariq Ali) acquired an international notoriety and the influence of Marx and Mao was evident enough, it is too facile an explanation for these happenings to attribute them to a world-wide plot organised by radical extremists; they occurred because of the general climate of student opinion, of which extremists may well have taken advantage but without which they would have had no fertile ground for their ideas. Sheer imitation also played its part in the dissemination of slogans and plans of campaign; and the presence in a university of a handful of ring-leaders could make all the difference between academic calm and rioting. In Britain, student action, though by no means free from disruptive and violent incidents, was in general less excessive than elsewhere; but from 1967 onwards few universities escaped embarrassing situations with their students.

At Keele the Senate had always valued and fostered good relations with the Students' Union. In 1964, as numbers reached 1,000 a joint Deputy Vice-Chancellor's Committee was set up with strong student representation to discuss matters of common interest; in 1965 it was agreed that the President of the Union might be invited to attend Senate meetings for specific items of business; by 1966 the students were allowed to have representatives on the important Discipline and Welfare Committee of the Senate and within the next two years on a number of other committees as well. Nevertheless a sense of frustration grew among students as requests for an increase in representation and a widening of its range were rebuffed. Other causes of discontent began to emerge: the allegedly paternalistic attitude of the Senate to student opinion about various aspects of the curriculum; the examination and assessment procedures for academic performance; the hours at which the Library was open; restrictions on the visiting hours in Halls of Residence for members of the opposite sex; University rules for the approval of student lodgings; and, as an ultimate challenge, the structure of authority within the University.[1]

[1] Some of these matters were politely but firmly ventilated in a Memorandum prepared by the Students' Union for discussion with the UGC when that Committee visited Keele in the autumn of 1966. A correspondent who was well placed to comment on later happenings from the student point of view writes: 'The disputes of the 1960's reflected the restlessness with the academic system in operation at the time; they were also encouraging signs that the

The first significant rumblings of the storm occurred during the summer term of 1968. A small fully 'committed' group of twenty to twenty-five students calling itself Action for a Free University (AFU) and supported by up to 150 others, organised meetings early in June to campaign against the examination system but quickly broadened its scope to 'an attack on the existing power structure within the University'.[1] There was a 'sit-down' at High Table in Keele Hall to engage members of staff in conversation, a noisy mass march of 100 to the Vice-Chancellor's House, and a short 'sit-in' at the Library. The Vice-Chancellor and some of his colleagues saw representatives of the AFU at an early stage but refused to pass on their 'demands' to the Senate on the ground that the Students' Union Committee was the official channel for student requests. When the Senate met on 12 June what it had before it, therefore, was not a manifesto from the AFU but a set of recommendations previously prepared by the Deputy Vice-Chancellor's Committee, and the President of the Union was present to speak on some of them.[2] So far the Students' Union Committee had taken no effective line about the AFU; but there was a marked change when the results of the Senate's deliberations became known.[3] The Senate stated that it had 'always accepted that participation by students in the University's governmental processes is desirable'; it listed the ten committees or sub-committees on which students were already represented; it revised the composition of the Disciplinary Panels on which there would be student representation; it extended the opening hours of the Library and modified the lodgings regulations; and it extended 'permitted hours' for visiting in Halls of Residence. On the basic issue, however, the Senate yielded only a little: 'The case for participation by students in each sphere of University government needs to be considered on its

idealism which had kept Keele going had remained, that people were sufficiently concerned about Keele to want to fight pretty hard to make it a "better" place. The events of the summer of 1968 started as a campaign for a better *academic* climate, to stimulate a debate about the quality and excellence of Keele as an academic and social community.'

[1] The student newspaper *Concourse*, 28 June 1968.

[2] A petition was also received from some members of staff asking for the recommendations of the Deputy-VC's Committee to be given sympathetic consideration.

[3] *A Statement on behalf of Senate* was issued on 13 June and widely circulated on the campus.

merits. There will be matters . . . in which it is not desirable that students should take part.' Nevertheless the Senate agreed to establish an Exploratory Committee 'to consider participation of students in University and staff in Union affairs', including student representation on the Senate; it was to consist of five members of the academic staff and five students, one being a postgraduate, with the Deputy Vice-Chancellor (Professor D. J. E. Ingram) as Chairman.

Within a few days by a vote of 306 to 160 with 40 or more abstentions a Union General Meeting 'mandated direct action'. The President of the Union promptly resigned. On 18 June about 100 to 150 students took over the University Registry for two whole days and nights and then left it 'in excellent order and without any damage to or interference with property or papers'. Some members of staff continued to talk with students occupying the Registry, for the most part advising an early end to the insurrection; but more than half of the non-professorial staff signed petitions which while deploring direct action indicated a general sympathy with the students' desire 'to improve the quality of life of the academic community'. The Vice-Chancellor's address to a meeting of 500 students and staff on 23 June neither improved nor worsened matters; and there was no further direct action for the rest of the term. But the wide press publicity given to the events of June damaged the prestige of Keele; the whole campus community was sorely shaken: was Keele, after all, turning out not to be so very different from other universities?

The following session was one of comparative calm;[1] indeed the only incident was a 'sit-in' at Keele Hall on 4–5 February 1969

1 Nationally tension was eased by two things. First, in October 1968, the Vice-Chancellors' Committee and the National Union of Students issued a joint statement setting out in carefully phrased and reasonable terms the areas of agreement and disagreement. Secondly, early in 1969, the House of Commons Select Committee on Education and Science (Sub-committee A) concerned with student matters visited universities (including Keele) and had meetings with representatives of the student bodies, the teachers and the authorities. Its Report (15 October 1969) stated: 'Student representation on governing bodies should be accepted. Student members should be considered as representative and not as mandated delegates'. Later, in June 1970, the Privy Council let it be known that when any university proposed a revision of its Statutes to provide for student participation, the Council would need to be satisfied that student opinion as a whole was genuinely represented and that the areas of 'reserved topics' were clearly defined in accordance with principles acceptable to the Privy Council.

in 'support' of the students at the London School of Economics[1] and the Keele authorities refrained from taking disciplinary action. Everyone was in fact waiting to see what the new Exploratory Committee would do. Its first interim action was conciliatory; for it recommended in January 1969 and the Senate approved that there should be an experiment: 'designed to show how effective the administration and enforcement, in residences, of disciplinary regulations by students might be, in order that, if the experiment should be successful, it could point the way to a development of the existing system on the lines of the American "honour" system.' Furthermore, the Senate agreed that the 'visiting hours' rules, a long-standing student grievance, could be suspended for the course of the experiment—a stupendous concession which has not subsequently been withdrawn. The experiment in 'self-government' was launched at 'The Hawthorns' and in 1969–70 the system by which student residential blocks could frame and enforce their own regulations was extended to the rest of the campus.[2]

The Exploratory Committee met nineteen times between 1 November 1968, and 12 May 1969; over seventy memoranda were received and much oral evidence was given; some of the meetings were in open session, but the attendance of observers was small. At its meeting on 11 June 1969 the Senate had before it a Majority and a Minority Report and for the first part of its deliberations all members of the Exploratory Committee, including students, were present and spoke on both reports. The 'main premises, purposes and conclusions' of the Minority Report, signed by two students, were overwhelmingly rejected; but this did not mean that the Majority Report was going to fare very much better.[3] As regards assessment, the Senate rejected recommendations that 'variations within the range of (degree) classifications should be explored, and that consideration be given to whether classification could be omitted for those who so wish'; and while agreeing that information should be given about 'the factors involved in policy decisions on assessment procedures', the Senate did not approve of students taking part in discussions leading to such decisions. As regards

[1] Serious disorders had led to the closing of the LSE for three weeks.

[2] Such regulations, however, are subject to the general oversight and agreement by the wardens.

[3] The Committee had deferred consideration and recommendations on (a) discipline and welfare; (b) the rôle of staff and students in student affairs.

appointment of staff, the Senate rejected a well-meaning but feeble recommendation that 'Departments should be encouraged to provide opportunities for candidates to meet informally with students if the candidate so wished', and accepted instead a motion that 'students had no rôle to play in the selection of academic staff'. On the subject of departmental government, the Senate rejected a proposal requiring each department to review arrangements for 'consultation with students in appropriate academic matters'. A far more important recommendation, namely, that eight students should be appointed to the Senate, was rejected and a compromise motion that the number should be four suffered the same fate. The institution or increase of student representation on eight Senate committees was recommended by the Exploratory Committee; but the Senate approved of only four such proposals—none of them affecting major committees. The Senate thus rejected virtually everything proposed by the Exploratory Committee to increase student participation in University affairs. The only tenuously constructive suggestion it made of its own accord was that the possibility should be investigated of setting up a General Purposes Committee of the Senate with student representation; but the Senate refused to be rushed into any definition of the functions or composition of such a Committee.

The students were enraged and it was fortunate that examinations were in progress and the end of term was in sight. There had been a strong student representation on the Exploratory Committee and the general tenor of the recommendations the Committee was likely to be making had become generally known on the campus. Hopes and expectations of a 'progressive' policy had consequently risen high and the resentment at the Senate's rejection of the Committee's proposals was correspondingly great. The state of feeling was expressed in the resolution passed by the Union:

> This Union considers that the decision of Senate on June 11th to reject the major recommendations of the Exploratory Committee is an insult to this Union. In the light of progress made in other universities, such high-handed action by this authoritarian body constitutes an abominable and total repudiation of any pretence this University has to being a liberal institution.

When the 1969–70 session opened it was unmistakable that student grievances were now concentrated on the Senate's rejection of the proposals of the Exploratory Committee and throughout the Autumn term there was picketing of Senate meetings and lobbying of individual members of the Senate.[1] In the Spring term, however, the issue was complicated by the intrusion of a new one. In February the students at Warwick had laid their hands during a 'sit-in' on what were said to be 'secret files' on students' political opinions. Like wildfire a demand spread among students everywhere that they should be told what confidential documents about them were being kept: otherwise they would find out for themselves. In the evening of 10 March the Vice-Chancellor and some of his colleagues addressed students in the Union and made it clear that a request for 'a student file-searching committee' would not be granted. Left to themselves the students drew up an inflammatory manifesto of demands and voted in favour of direct action. During the night a group of them broke into Keele Hall, forcibly entered the office of the Vice-Chancellor's Assistant to search for files and occupied the Senior Common Room until the next afternoon. A phase of overt violence had begun. Relatively mild disciplinary penalties imposed on four of the students involved in the Keele Hall break-in further inflamed student opinion. The summer term was the most unhappy in Keele's history. On the night of 2 May there was uncontrollable noise and uproar at an outdoor party; on 3 May two fires of unascertained origin occurred in the Registry and the Horwood General Block; on 6 May a 'Festival of Peace' resulted in considerable damage to the Union Ballroom; on 20 May the Registry and Keele Hall were daubed with paint; on 7 June paint was thrown through the windows of the Registrar's house; two days later a petrol bomb was thrown into the Architect's department; and a little later windows in Keele Hall and the Library were smashed. These events, described by *The Times*[2] as 'the most violent acts yet seen on a university campus in Britain', were vigorously condemned by the Students' Union Committee. The incidents posed a much more immediate threat to the proper running of the University than all the bad feeling which had preceded them; but they were brought under

[1] Among the pickets were eight persons 'elected to Senate' by the students.
[2] 23 June 1970.

control by joint patrols of staff and students to guard the campus by night.[1] Public opinion at large was shocked by these exhibitions of vandalism and hooliganism on the part of extremists; it was outraged still further by an amazing incident on 19 June. It was a very warm sunny day and some twenty or more students, men and women, lounging in the area near the Union divested themselves of all their clothes to sunbathe and walked about naked. Popular newspapers[2] somehow managed to secure photographs of the scene and the reputation of Keele fell to its lowest ebb. For the Local Authorities this was the last straw and Staffordshire announced that they would withhold their grant at least until the authorities at Keele had control of the situation.[3] Stoke also considered taking similar action.

The University had, of course, already done what it deemed wise to do in asserting its control. Disciplinary action (fines, and in some instances the barring of students from residence) had been taken in regard to the events of 10 March and later. The Union invariably protested at the sentences. In most cases an appeal was made to the Council, rarely with success. One case arising from the nudity scenes of 19 June went as far as the High Court,[4] where the judge, while rejecting the appeal, held that the way in which the University's own discipline regulations had been applied constituted 'a failure of natural justice': such are the pitfalls which beset any university in the exercise of 'control'.

There was a recrudescence of trouble in October 1970 at the beginning of the new session: a 'sit-in' at the Walter Moberly Hall, a forcible entry of the Registry and a noisy demonstration at the Clock House; otherwise the first term passed off quietly. But the events of the previous session and these new evidences of unrest forced Keele to take a bitter and frustrating decision, which the Vice-Chancellor announced at the end of January 1971:

> We had expected to help ourselves by launching an Appeal in our 21st year (1971–72) but the bad record of Keele in

[1] Actually, as the Vice-Chancellor repeatedly pointed out, 'not one hour of teaching time was lost, none of the main University committees was affected in any way and no examination was disrupted'.

[2] *Daily Mail*, 20 June, and *News of the World*, 21 June 1970.

[3] The grant was restored after a meeting with the University in September.

[4] See *The Times*, 18 December 1970.

> the Spring and Summer of 1970 produced such adverse publicity that our experts advised us that there was no point in starting. We shall have to build up public confidence over a period of years before we can expect support from the public; and the next quinquennium will be crucial for that purpose.

We must, however, not lose perspective. After all, Keele was by no means the only university which suffered from unreason and violence; as elsewhere, it was a determined minority which fomented trouble; as elsewhere, the problem facing the university was to sift the wheat from the chaff of students' requests and demands: the emergence of 'the student estate' could not now be ignored.[1] The events of 1968–71 did indeed strain the good relations between the Senate and the student body and brought Keele into serious disrepute, as similar events had done elsewhere. But the lines of communication were never wholly disrupted. So far as the students are concerned it is important to put on record that the Union Committee, though it had not always been in control of its own situation, eventually made clear its opposition to the extremist elements and recognised that 'mutual trust must be re-established' and that its own policies must be pursued 'through democratic and non-violent means'. So far as the Senate itself is concerned, the appointment of the Deputy-VC's Committee as early as 1964 had recognised the wisdom of bringing students into consultation in areas where the students' individual and corporate interests are unmistakably concerned and where their experience and consequently their opinions are of value; and that has been the broad line of Senate policy throughout. Under very considerable provocation in the stormy years 1968–70, the Senate as a whole kept cool heads: they neither imposed vindictive or unduly severe sentences on any of the students concerned in the disorders; nor, when the recommendations of the Exploratory Committee in June 1969 seemed to them to be going too far, did they abdicate from their own responsibilities for the conduct of University affairs.

Nothing apart from injurious public notoriety was achieved by violence; but much has been achieved by quiet deliberations

[1] See E. Ashby and Mary Anderson, *The Rise of the Student Estate in Britain*, 1970.

and consultations in which Senate committees and student representatives have participated. Even before the events of 10 March 1970, the Senate, albeit with some dissentients, had reported to the Council that they supported student representation on the Council and its main committees provided that the proportion of academic representation was not adversely affected and personal and academic matters were 'reserved areas'. Actual student membership of the Council, however, would be contrary to the Statutes and for the time being at least it has been agreed that the President of the Union and another student officer should be invited to attend meetings of the Council without the right to vote but should withdraw when 'reserved areas' of business are discussed.[1]

Membership of the Senate was also precluded by the existing Statutes; but early in 1970 the Senate proceeded further with the idea advanced in May 1969 of setting up a General Purposes Committee of Senate. By the end of the autumn term 1970 the composition and functions of the Committee were worked out and despite the intransigence of a very small minority of students, the Union's co-operation was apparently assured.[2] This new Committee is to consist of all members of the Senate, ten persons elected by the student body, the President of the Union and the Chairman of the Keele Research Association of postgraduate students. Its field of discussion includes discipline, welfare, library matters, physical education and off-campus lodgings—the Senate reserving to itself academic matters and the appointment and promotion of staff. Since the Senate could not, without a change in the Statutes, devolve its powers and responsibilities to another body, the decisions of the General Purposes Committee need to be formally ratified by the Senate itself, but there is an understanding that such decisions will not be challenged. The Committee may come into fully effective operation during the 1971–2 session.

[1] The papers relating to 'reserved areas' are not made available to students.

[2] In May 1971 the Union withdrew from the Committee pending discussions in October about the 'reservation' of academic matters.

Eight

Views on Keele

THREE LAME HARES

The main purpose of this chapter is to present to the reader a body of responsible comment on the extent to which Keele has been able to achieve the educational purposes its founders had in mind. Before dealing with strictly educational matters, however, there are a few things recurring with some frequency in public and private comment on Keele to which some attention should be given. The first of these is the accusation that Keele has turned its back on the Potteries which gave it birth. It is erroneously assumed that out of a wide range of possibilities Keele deliberately chose to 'put itself in the country'; that it has been disloyal to the early concept of a 'local university'; that it plays little or no part in the educational or social life of the area; and that in its choice of title it disowned both Stoke and North Staffordshire. The siting is one of the scarcely avoidable accidents of history, and from that much else follows: people in the Potteries cannot be as conscious of the physical presence of the University as the inhabitants of Manchester, Leeds or Sheffield are of theirs; they do not see so much of students in their streets or have many of them lodging among them; they do not have professors as neighbours mowing lawns and going shopping: psychologically as well as geographically, Keele is remote for them. That the curriculum should have turned out to have little direct bearing on the local industries is due not to a positive rejection by Keele of the needs of the area but in the main to the insistence of the UGC and the sponsoring universities that ceramics and physical chemistry with social studies were not an adequate basis for a university institution; and for its part Keele, though welcoming and achieving some measure of co-operation in special fields with the College of Technology,[1] avoided trespassing on ground

[1] *E.g.* a course in 'Fundamentals of Ceramic Technology' is offered jointly

that was already being well tilled. The proportion of local students coming to Keele has indeed fallen; but that is in accord with the national pattern of student migration and if a lad from Stoke proposes to get his university education away from home he may himself well prefer to go further afield than Keele. Even in the matter of adult education, a sphere which loomed large in the early discussions about a College and one in which the College could be expected to make an impact, Keele's hands were tied until it had its own organisation and its own department: the Potteries' link with Oxford deflected attention from Keele. In a similar way the delay in setting up an Institute of Education denied to Keele many opportunities of local participation and influence. On the other hand, it tends now to be forgotten that in the early years, though the local authorities did not falter in their support of Keele, popular opinion looked askance at the 'socialist' institution nearby: aloofness was not all on one side. By 1971, however, there is much that is positive in the relations between Keele and its area. Annual 'open days' of one sort or another, university concerts in Keele itself or in Stoke and Newcastle, art exhibitions, Arts Festivals of music and drama, extra-mural classes held on and off the campus; all these things now bring the University into closer contact with the general public; and from 1953 when Professor Finer became Chairman of the Stoke Council of Social Service and a member of the Staffordshire Education Committee, an important contribution to the life of the area has been made by members of staff and their wives who serve as magistrates and on the committees of local societies, the governing bodies of schools and Education Committees, and participate in a wide variety of social and charitable work.

There are some snide aspersions which are distasteful to repeat and embarrassing to comment upon. One such is the statement that Keele has never had on its staff a Fellow of the Royal Society, as if it were a quite common occurrence for a small institution with only a few science departments to be able to boast of several. Apart from the fact that some former members of staff have in fact been so honoured after leaving Keele, the overtones of the remark are unfair to the staff as a

by the department of chemistry and the College of Technology (N. Staffs. Polytechnic).

whole, both past and present. Of former members, six have become Vice-Chancellors: F. A. Vick at Belfast, Bruce Williams at Sydney, J. W. Blake in Botswana, T. G. Miller at Salisbury, Rhodesia, A. J. Earp at Brock, Ontario, and W. A. C. Stewart at Keele itself. Sixteen of the Keele departments have between them provided forty-five professors for other universities, including ten in mathematics and six in education. Most of them hold Chairs in the old, civic and new universities of the United Kingdom, a few in the older Commonwealth and the USA, and one in Louvain. For a small institution this is a very impressive record. Among the present staff of under 300 there are 90 who took their initial degrees at Oxford or Cambridge, 50 at London, 105 at civic universities, 15 in Scotland and 25 at Keele; and of the 110 doctorates held by staff members 25 were awarded by Oxford or Cambridge, 16 by London and 40 by the civic and Scottish universities.

We can deal briefly with the third misunderstanding about Keele, namely, that its most evident achievement has been to produce school teachers and that its curriculum has otherwise been a handicap to its graduates. It is true that something like a third of its former students have taken up school teaching as a profession though not all of these have followed the Keele course for the Certificate in Education. Yet almost 1 in 6 of Keele graduates now goes on to further academic work for higher degrees in other universities or for vocational training; and the posts held by former students cover as wide a spectrum as would be expected from graduates of other institutions: we find them in appreciable numbers as senior lecturers and lecturers in universities, heads of departments and lecturers in Colleges of Education and Colleges of Technology; many others hold administrative positions in the Civil Service and the BBC, in planning departments of Local Authorities, in social and welfare work, and—quite notably—in managerial, development and research posts of considerable responsibility in industry and commerce.

There is something quixotic in any attempt to probe into and assess the value, effectiveness and 'success' of a continuously developing educational institution which has an organic life of its own. Nevertheless the experiment to which Keele was committed is of an importance which justifies an essay in evaluation, hazardous and uncertain though such an enterprise may be. The plan which has been adopted is to seek the opinions, not of casual or doctrinaire observers whose transient pronouncements carry little weight whatever harm, hurt or pleasure they may cause, but of those who are in the best position to know what Keele is really like and what it actually does. We shall start, therefore, with the students who have been to Keele and see what they have to say. Those who teach at Keele and have an immediate concern with its educational practice will form the second line of enquiry. In the third place come the opinions of those who visit Keele as external examiners and provide a standard of comparison with other universities.[1]

A FORMER-STUDENT ENQUIRY

This enquiry was designed to elicit confidential information about the opinions held by former students in regard to various aspects of their academic course at Keele and their life as students. The main survey covered selected groups from the whole range of students who had graduated at Keele by July 1969. A questionnaire was sent out to people who fell within one or other of three groups. The first group (*f*) consisted of all the 123 who had taken a class I degree; current addresses were known for 99 and 89 replied. The second group (*p*) consisted of all the 114 who had been awarded a pass degree; current addresses were known for 95, but only 28 replied. The third group (*x*) consisted of 165 selected at random[2] from those whose degrees were II(i), II(ii) or III and to them were added the 19 Presidents of the Union, making a total of 184; current addresses were known for 153, of whom 70 replied. This group (*x*) was intended to provide a quick comparison with the opinions of groups (*f*) and (*p*) who are at the two extremes of academic achievement; and a preliminary analysis of the results suggested that the broad picture would not be appreciably modified by an expansion of group (*x*). Indeed, the opinions expressed by

[1] The opinions of those who employ Keele graduates would be of interest too. But an enquiry along such lines would be almost insuperably difficult to organise and its results unreliable. What can be said is that many who have recruited staff from Keele come back for more.

[2] From a consolidated and alphabetical list of each of these three classes every fifteenth name was selected. The total population of these degree-classes was 2,473.

all three groups are quite remarkably consistent and in the paragraphs which follow it has generally been possible to treat the 187 replies as a whole without distorting the evidence of any of the three separate groups; but where there is some discrepancy of importance or interest the fact has been noted. To avoid needlessly confusing the reader, no account is taken of any differentiation by sex or by the principal subjects taken in the Final examination or by modifications which have taken place over the years in the Foundation Year or the degree course; it is only when one or other of these considerations seems to be pertinent that further reference is made to them. At the end of the questionnaire room was left for general comments and these have been taken into account in considering the replies to the individual questions. The number of those who did not answer a question is given in brackets with a plus sign at the end of each analysis. At a number of points A. H. Iliffe's study, *The Foundation Year* (1968), which deals with the 497 students who entered Keele in October 1962 and October 1963, provides a useful check and is frequently cited below. This present enquiry makes no claim to statistical refinements; and it must be borne in mind that what were asked for, in the main, were opinions rather than facts and that these opinions are often based on recollections only. What the survey does is simply to suggest the kind of things which would be said about Keele by any reasonably representative group of former students whom one happened to encounter. Even this, however, throws some light on the success and value of the Keele experiment and might provide some hints for the future.

1. FOUNDATION YEAR LECTURES

(a) Did they appreciably improve your understanding of:

- (i) the development of Western civilisation: 'yes' 135, 'no' 47, (+5).
- (ii) the nature and methods of the experimental sciences: 'yes' 102, 'no' 73, (+12).
- (iii) the nature and methods of the social sciences: 'yes' 100, 'no' 74, (+13). The answers in group (*f*) were almost equally divided.
- (iv) the major problems of the modern world: 'yes' 66, 'no' 103, (+18).

The comment that more frequent reference should be made to current problems was a feature of the replies of the more recent half of the graduates and was particularly notable in group (*f*).

(b) Did they have any lasting effect in broadening your intellectual interests: 'yes' 154, 'no' 30, (+3). The general comments confirm Iliffe's finding that graduates feel they have gained confidence in tackling books and articles on topics outside their special fields, and in understanding the problems and attitudes of colleagues with whom they have to work.

(c) Did the lectures affect your later choice of principal subjects: 'yes' 59, 'no' 125 (+3). The answers to this question should be compared with those given later in regard to sessional and terminal courses in the Foundation Year.

(d) Did you feel that there were too many Foundation Year lectures: 'yes' 65, 'no' 120, (+2). Group (*p*) were particularly emphatic in saying 'no'. The most frequent complaint was that there was not enough time for a student to pursue by his own reading a topic which he found had a special appeal to him: the kaleidoscope turned too fast.

(e) Did you think the classes were too large: 'yes' 29, 'no' 158. The increasing size of the annual intake up to our datum line of the 1965 entry seems not to have affected opinion at all.

(f) Were the lectures on the whole well prepared: 'yes' 164, 'no' 12, (+11).

(g) Were the lectures on the whole well delivered: 'yes' 142, 'no' 35, (+10).

The answers given by all groups to questions (f) and (g) are in sharp contrast to opinions frequently expressed by students and by graduates in general about the quality of university teaching. Keele can take great credit for this.

(h) In so far as the amount of time devoted to major topics is concerned, did you think the general plan of the lectures was well balanced: 'yes' 146, 'no' 36, (+5).

(i) Were there any topics not included in the Foundation Year lectures which you now think should be included: please specify: The answers to (h) and (i) are best considered together. Some of the criticisms were based on the earlier lecture programmes, some are due to faulty recollections of what was included, some to misapprehensions of the purpose of the course, and some to unrealistic expectations. As A. H. Iliffe remarked: 'Given the ambitious aim of the Foundation Year, the list of topics which might with value be included is virtually endless. . . . It is thus no criticism of the course that omissions can be detected with ease.' Nevertheless some of the more frequent and serious comments should be recorded: Western civilisation occupies the centre of the stage (as Lindsay intended it should) to the virtual exclusion of other civilisations; Greece and Rome have a liberal allotment of time, but Russia, for example, is treated very cursorily; colonialism and its heritage of problems are insufficiently prominent; there is too little of art, music, comparative religion and anthropology; recent history from 1920 and world problems of today should be more continuously related to the whole course of lectures; the three areas of the humanities, natural and social sciences are not adequately related to each other; and in a technological and managerial age there is need for a greater emphasis on the applications of science and economics. A number of these criticisms have been taken account of in the later lecture lists.

2. FOUNDATION YEAR DISCUSSION GROUPS

Only 170 of the 187 indicated that they had attended these groups which did not begin until October 1954.[1]

(a) (i) Were they well related to the lectures: 'yes' 89, 'no' 74, (+7).

(ii) What degree of benefit did you derive from them: 'much' 33, 'little' 110, 'none' 25, (+2).

(b) State briefly in what ways you think they could have been made more useful: The problems of organising and conducting a seminar group even within a single department are well known. Keele attempted an analogous operation over a dauntingly wide field; and the difficulties soon became apparent. It was originally intended that the seminars should bear directly on the content of the Foundation Year lectures; but the staff members had rarely attended the lectures; often enough none of them was sufficiently expert in a particular topic to guide a discussion fruitfully, or alternatively one of them was so expert that the seminar became a supplementary lecture. Inevitably, to ensure active and lively discussion within the group, strict adherence to the original purpose was tacitly abandoned by many chairmen who, as Iliffe remarks, 'were properly reluctant to take on the rôle of the blind leading the blind'. The facts of the situation were faced in 1963 when the Senate redefined the purpose of the discussion groups as providing 'systematic coverage of a large and balanced proportion of the matters covered in the lectures, while still allowing considerable latitude for the discussion of other subjects'.[2] Some quotations from the present set of replies will show

[1] See pp. 153–4.

[2] The booklet now issued to Foundation Year students contains lists of suggested topics for group discussions.

the trend of opinion amongst those who have experienced the discussion groups. 'Everything depends on the skill with which the Chairman co-ordinates the group, the interest he has in the particular topic, and his general firmness.' 'All staff members of the group should turn up regularly and not give the impression that attendance is a bore; they do not seem *committed* to the idea of discussion groups.' 'Relevant experts are needed at every meeting.' 'The staff should show more knowledge of and (at least) interest in subjects which are outside their special fields.' 'Periodic changes in the staff membership of a group would give a new stimulus.' 'Too many students make no preparation for the discussions.' 'It is too easy for the shy or lazy student to avoid participation entirely, while the articulate "know-alls" are allowed to pontificate.' 'The groups are dominated by those whose interest is in the particular topic of the day and the others learn nothing.' 'Keele expects more broad-mindedness from students than is common among staff.' No doubt criticisms of this kind would be heard about seminars in every university; but the overwhelmingly unfavourable opinions expressed in the responses to this question show that Keele has not yet solved the problem of the discussion groups which in theory ought to play at least as great a part as the lectures in broadening the students' outlook.

3. FOUNDATION YEAR ESSAYS

Since these essays were not a regular feature until 1963, only 99 of the 187 could assess their value.[1]

(a) (i) What degree of benefit did you derive from them: 'much' 57, 'little' 36, 'none' 6.

(ii) Were too many essays prescribed: 'yes' 18, 'no' 79, (+2).[2]

(iii) Were the essays carefully marked: 'yes' 51, 'no' 44, (+4).

(iv) How often were they discussed with you individually: 'always' 5, 'often' 7, 'sometimes' 56, 'never' 19, (+12).

As a necessary preparation for the writing of the essays, there was reading to be done and for this a suitable range of books was suggested for each topic. The essay by itself is therefore not the whole of the story and Iliffe's judgment is that the scheme was 'valuable in raising the amount of work done by students and in giving them

[1] There always was some essay work expected in connexion with discussion groups and sessional and terminal courses. What the 1963 scheme ensured was that the amount of essay work was more uniform in relation to the discussion groups and that each of the three main subject groups was covered. Each department gives a choice of essay themes (listed in the handbook) and a date for completion.

[2] Fifteen was the number first prescribed; it was reduced to nine in 1964.

confidence that their work was relevant; in developing unsuspected interests; and in providing some sense of achievement and progress'. From the present enquiry it is evident that a majority of students felt the essays were worthwhile. The weakness of the scheme clearly lies in the lack of regular discussion of a student's efforts with the member of staff who marked the essay; and this must be in part, perhaps mainly, a question of logistics. Any one topic could result in the production of a hundred or more essays; by the time they are marked the individual student's attention has become focused on something quite different; and the finding of times for the serious personal discussion of every essay of every student is out of the question in the existing or foreseeable staffing situation. But an explanation does not dispose of the problem.

4. FOUNDATION YEAR SESSIONAL COURSES

(a) What degree of benefit did you derive from them: 'much' 114, 'little' 55, 'none' 10, (+8). Every student took two sessionals; and the full questionnaire asked for opinions about each course separately. The figures given above are averages for the two subjects. The actual figures for the subject first mentioned, which presumably is the one which made the greater impact, are 127, 43, 10, (+7); for the second subject 100, 68, 11 (+8). The distribution of favourable comment is the same in all three groups (f), (p) and (x).

(b) Did these Sessional Courses affect your choice of Principal subjects: 'yes' 67, 'no' 111, (+9). The courses were planned to introduce students to subjects they had not studied in school and they provide the first taste of continuous organised study at university level. That 67 students out of 187 should have changed at least one of their previously intended principals is evidence of the value and effectiveness of the sessionals.[1]

5. FOUNDATION YEAR TERMINAL COURSES

(a) What degree of benefit did you derive from them: 'much' 47, 'little' 90, 'none' 41, (+9). Each student takes three terminals; and opinions were asked for in regard to each of the three. The figures here given are averages for the three subjects. The actual figures for the subject first mentioned were 49, 92, 40 (+6); for the second 51, 90, 40, (+6) and for the third 42, 86, 43, (+16). The distribution of

[1] In regard to subsidiaries taken in the second (or third) year, Iliffe also points out that the number of students choosing as a subsidiary subject one which they had taken as a sessional in their first year is almost exactly three times what random allocation would produce.

favourable and unfavourable comment is very similar in all three groups (*f*), (*p*) and (*x*).

(b) Did these Terminal Courses affect your choice of Principal subjects: 'yes' 89, 'no' 93, (+5). Terminals were at first intended as 'bridge' courses to keep students in touch with subjects they had done up to 'A' level at school and two of which they expected to pursue as principals; but terminals are also available in some subjects not taught in schools, such as philosophy. Our figures show that for the 187 graduates the choice of principal subjects was affected in 67 cases by sessionals and in 89 by terminals; and a more detailed analysis showed that in 47 cases the choice of principal was affected by both.[1] So far as a change in principal subjects is concerned, sessionals show a positive and attractive influence, while that of terminals is negative and repellent; and both have a more significant effect in later choices of principal subjects than the Foundation Year lectures. The opportunity to change one's mind during the Foundation Year about principal subjects was not stressed or perhaps even contemplated when the curriculum was first being devised; but it has become an important facet of academic life at Keele; a student is not irretrievably bound by a choice made by him or for him at the time he entered the sixth form. It has, however, one awkward effect in that the changes are predominantly away from science: it is much more possible for a chemist to become a good historian than for a historian to become a good chemist.

6. FOUNDATION YEAR: GENERAL

(a) Did you regard the Foundation Year as a whole:

(i) As a valuable part of your training: 'yes' 155, 'no' 29, (+3).

(ii) Mainly as a 'hurdle' to be surmounted: 'yes' 49, 'no' 104, (+34).

The discrepancy between the answers to (i) and (ii) is probably not as great as it seems; for all the 34 who did not answer (ii) had given 'yes' to (i) and presumably implied 'no' to (ii).

(b) (i) Do you now think that 'general education' should form part of a university course: 'yes' 176, 'no' 9, (+2).

(ii) If 'yes', do you think it could be more effective if it were not concentrated in a Foundation Year: 'yes' 53, 'no' 118,

[1] Iliffe's finding from his group was that 'in the reasons given for choosing new Principal subjects, experience in Terminals appears only half as frequently as experience in Sessionals'. But: 'Terminals appear over three times as frequently as Sessionals in the reasons for giving up subjects originally chosen; the position is reversed in the reasons given for taking up new subjects, where Sessionals are mentioned twice as often as Terminals.'

(+5) = 176, see (i). Group (*p*) was particularly emphatic in answering 'no'. The conclusion to be drawn from the answers to 6 (a) and 6 (b) is clearly that the Foundation Year has justified itself in principle in the opinion of those who have been through it.

7. DEGREE COURSES

(a) If there was any significant change in regard to your Principal[1] subjects from your original intention, please specify the reasons: Out of the 187 in the three groups, 100 answered. The question was intended as a cross-check on the answers given in regard to the Foundation Year lectures, sessionals and terminals[2] and the broad pattern is the same in all the groups (*f*), (*p*) and (*x*). In many cases several reasons converged to determine the choice. 'I hated the subject at school but the lectures showed me its value.' 'I had never done the subject before and the lectures roused my interest in it.' 'The Terminal showed me that I did not really have the capacity to pursue the subject further.' 'I discovered I was no good at laboratory work.' 'I became bored with the subject in the Sessional.' 'The teaching in the Sessional was so good and stimulating.' 'I formed a poor opinion of the quality of the Department.'

(b) Do you in retrospect wish you could have offered only one Principal subject: 'yes' 17, 'no' 165, (+5). This decisive response is noteworthy in view of the fact that in a preliminary question regarding the students' motives in coming to Keele, only 58 of the 187 gave a two-subject Final as one of their reasons.

(c) Do you consider that taking more than one Principal subject has affected your career: 'favourably' 100, 'adversely' 13, 'neither' 71, (+3). By and large, of course, graduates would tend to obtain posts with employers who themselves regarded two principals as an advantage.

(d) Have your career expectations since leaving Keele been reasonably satisfied: 'yes' 150, 'no' 15, (+22). An odd question to ask, perhaps; but who would have expected to find Keele graduates so contented a lot?

(e) Apart from career prospects, do you consider that the study of more than one Principal subject has been worthwhile for you: 'yes' 175, 'no' 12.

[1] No specific item about subsidiaries was included in the questionnaire: the possible and actual combinations of subsidiaries with each of the principal subjects are so multifarious and the factors affecting choice (including timetable problems) so intricate that the topic would demand a separate survey based on a much wider population.

[2] See 1(d), 4(b) and 5(b) above.

8. LIFE AT KEELE

(a) (i) Did you have a General Tutor: 'yes' 157, 'no' 20, (+10).

(ii) If 'yes', were your contacts with your General Tutor: 'close' 14, 'sporadic' 54, 'minimal' 89 = 157, see (i). Iliffe's findings for his group were along the same lines and only 23 per cent of them said they would go for help in the first instance to their general tutor, another 30 per cent would go to some other member of staff, 23 per cent would go to student friends or write home, while the remaining 24 per cent would not know where to go.

(b) Did you have any significant contacts with other members of staff (apart from your General Tutor and the staff of your Hall): 'yes' 130, 'no' 55, (+2). Group (*p*) was almost equally divided. 'It seemed a pity', wrote one student, 'that there wasn't out-of-hours contact with staff; what *do* they do in the evenings?' Staff who have been at Keele for many years often remark that informal social contact was much freer and more frequent when Keele was small.

(c) (i) Did you have any sense of isolation from the outside world while you were at Keele: 'yes' 117, 'no' 70. In groups (*f*) and (*x*) 2 out of 3 answered 'yes', but in group (*p*) the same proportion gave 'no'. Iliffe's remarks on this topic suggest that the sense of isolation or claustrophobia was much less marked in his group.

(ii) If 'yes', what steps did you take to counteract this feeling: A 'sense of isolation' is too subjective a feeling for too much stress to be laid on the answers; but it is perhaps significant that 'yes' was distinctly more frequent in the replies of the more recent graduates. As Iliffe remarks: 'in a small community it is possible to feel that one knows, and is known by, every other member; beyond a certain point this is no longer possible; an increasing number of the group are strangers.' He also suggests that this psychological process may be responsible for the frequency of couples who 'go steady' for the major part of their four years. It was interesting to find within the present survey that about 1 in 3 found the 'isolation' congenial: 'I loved it and concentrated on being a student'; 'I'm not sure I wanted to cure it'; 'I enjoyed it—rather like a retreat'. A common remark was that the isolation became more burdensome in the last two years of the course. As for cures, most found the vacations a sufficient antidote, many went away for an occasional weekend, others made the effort to get out frequently into Newcastle or Stoke for relaxation or social

> service, and one laconically placid individual 'bought a newspaper daily'.

As one reads through the questionnaires it becomes evident, despite criticisms of this or that aspect of the academic or social organisation, that from the point of view of the majority of those who replied life at Keele has been a satisfying experience; and in the general comments which graduates were invited to make, the sense of loyalty to Keele, gratitude for the kind of experience it provided, and concern for the way Keele may develop are remarkable. By way of illustration, a few quotations from replies, mostly by former Presidents of the Union, are worth putting on record:

> I regard the Foundation Year as probably the most important part of my education; but it was not until I left that I realised how valuable this had been.
>
> The Foundation Year provides brief encounters with subjects which will never be looked at again. There is no harm in this and the advantage of just *feeling* the breadth of things is enormous. But there is a real need for something to counterbalance the instructional side of the course which is too encyclopaedic.
>
> At present Keele students spend their first year learning the inter-relatedness of human experience and knowledge; and spend their next three years in Departments which are jealously upholding the sanctity of disciplinary barriers. The Faculty at Keele have on the whole been less faithful to the 'idea' of Keele than have many of the students.
>
> The value of Keele lies less in the structure of the courses than in the nature of the community. There can be no doubt that Keele is much more demanding personally and emotionally than academically. From visits back to Keele I regret the destruction of the Union as a central focus of student life and the fragmentation of the student body in large Halls of Residence. The central concept of Lindsay's plan was the single cohesive community and everything possible should be done to get back to Lindsay's ideal. Keele has become less informal and less experimental, more institutional and more traditional.

There were other students too: the 661 who prior to October 1969 had entered Keele but had withdrawn before finishing their course. Of these, 380 left during or at the end of the Foundation Year, 185 in the second year, 80 in the third year and 16 failed in their Final examination. The official records show that 422 were marked as having withdrawn because of academic failure at some stage in their course, while 239 did so for other reasons. It seemed worthwhile to send the questionnaire to this large group also, in order to discover whether their experience at Keele and their opinions about Keele diverged markedly from those of students who had been successful. The response was better than had been expected and 221 replies were received. It turned out that two-thirds of these replies were from people who had passed in the Foundation Year examination and most of these had remained at Keele for a further year or so more.

The questionnaire contained an item in which this group of 661 students were invited to place a mark against any one or more of twelve possible factors which might have affected them in their university course and room was left for them to add further comments. There were few indeed who attributed their difficulties to a single cause and the average number of reasons given was about three; 130 added further comments, either to expand what they had marked on the list or to mention other points. So far as the list is concerned, the frequency in descending order was as follows: emotional difficulties (100), insufficient personal effort (95), loss of interest in the course (81), school preparation inadequate (79), excessive time spent on non-academic activities (60), the making of a wrong choice of subjects at the University (54), content of University course overloaded (53), poor teaching at the University (39), family problems (38), illness (31), personal financial difficulties (18), marriage (12). About one-half of our 221 expanded their markings of the list and a number of comments often recurred: 'I was far too immature when I came to Keele'; 'I did not know how to study properly, no one helped me in this, and so I did not divide up my time to best advantage'; 'I made a completely wrong choice of university'; 'Perhaps I ought not to have gone to a university at all'. Readers who are acquainted with studies of students' problems which appear from time to time in the educational press will find all these frank introspections very familiar. But the most interesting feature among the 'other reasons' was transfer to another university, almost always in the case of students who had not failed the Foundation Year. The usual reason given was that the student found that he now preferred to do a single-subject honours course; and since, by making a grant to send him to Keele, his Local Authority had already committed itself to a four-year course, there was generally no financial reason why he should not be allowed to spend his last three years elsewhere if that was thought to be educationally advantageous for him. Within our group of 221, there were 50 such transfers recorded; but one should not assume that the same proportion applies to all the 661: those who had proved their worth elsewhere were presumably more likely to answer a questionnaire than those whose academic career had ended in their failure at Keele. In addition to those who transferred to another university, there were almost as many who went either to a college of education or to another institution of higher education where they obtained a professional qualification. We do not know what happened to the 440 who did not reply; but of the 221 who did, almost one-half eventually had some academic or professional achievement to their credit.

It is evident from what has just been said that the opinions of our 221 are likely to be worth consideration as representing in broad terms the views of a reasonably serious and responsible sector of Keele students. In what ways then do their recollections of Keele differ from those of groups (f), (p) and (x)? Let us briefly take the topics in the same sequence as before, noting only the important changes of emphasis in the replies. The *Foundation Year Lectures* were found less successful in regard to an understanding of Western civilisation and definitely unsuccessful in the matter of the experimental sciences; their lasting effect, though widely acknowledged, was not as strikingly attested; their effect on the choice of principal subjects, where applicable, was less; the number of lectures and the size of the classes were much more frequently criticised; but the answers about the preparation and delivery of the lectures were just as favourable as those given by the other groups. In short, the general impact of the lectures was feebler for this group; and partly in keeping with this, fewer suggestions (none of them novel) were made for the inclusion of additional topics or changes of balance.

As for the *discussion groups*, the same small proportion found them of 'much' value, but a greater proportion wrote them off as of 'no' rather than 'little' benefit. Their criticisms followed the same general lines as the other groups, with somewhat more emphasis on the need for all staff members to be as interested in a topic as the students are supposed to be. The *essays* were not thought to be too many; but only half of the group were satisfied with the marking and more than two-thirds of those who did essays alleged that they were 'never' discussed personally. Rather less than half the group found the essay work of 'much' benefit. The judgments of this group about the value and influence of the *sessional courses* corresponds almost exactly with those of groups (*f*), (*p*) and (*x*): about 2 in 3 considered them to have been of 'much' benefit. The *terminal courses* were thought to be of 'much' benefit by only 1 in 4 of the other groups but for this group the figure is distinctly more favourable at 2 in 5.

It is in the *general assessment* of the Foundation Year, however, that this group of 221, heterogeneous as it may be, differs most clearly from the other groups. The proportion of those who regarded it as a valuable part of their training is only 5 to 2 as compared with 5 to 1 in (*f*), (*p*) and (*x*); and a majority of the group were prepared to say that, whatever its value, they thought of it as a hurdle. They have rather more frequent doubts about the inclusion of 'general education' in a university course and quite contrary to the views of the other groups they think it would be better if it were not concentrated in a Foundation Year.

The opinions expressed about *principal subjects* by this group are weighted by those who, as we have mentioned, went elsewhere after their first year to do single-subject honours. If these persons are excluded from our calculations, the majority of the remainder who went further than the first year favour the two-subject Final but with nothing like the same preponderance as the other groups. In regard to career expectations since leaving Keele, 4 out of 5 in the other three groups said they were reasonably satisfied; but, as would be expected, in this group only a half were satisfied and that half included most of the people who had eventually qualified elsewhere.

Finally, there is the question of life on the campus. Here the trend of opinion as compared with the other groups is significantly different. Contacts with the general tutor were appreciably less satisfactory than even the other groups found them to be; almost 2 in 3 recall no significant contacts with other members of staff, which is the reverse of the experience of the other groups: and the sense of isolation was in proportion much more frequently mentioned.

The purpose of this enquiry was to obtain a broad evaluation of 'the Keele experiment'. One should, of course, bear in mind that the student population at Keele tends to be made up of people who were consciously attracted there by one or other feature of the Keele pattern: provided their expectations were not utterly disappointed they would have a bias in favour of Keele. All the recipients of the questionnaire had been asked to say what factors had appreciably influenced their choice of university. Two-thirds of those who replied indicated that (apart possibly from Oxford or Cambridge) Keele had been their first choice and the predominant reasons they mentioned for selecting Keele were: first the Foundation Year, second the certainty of being in residence, third the two-subject Final and almost equally third, the possibility of reconsidering what subjects they would wish to study in the later years of the course.[1]

What is shown by our survey of these particular groups of students—note the limitation—may be summed up as follows. The Foundation Year as a whole is recognised by the majority as a valuable element in their education and one which has had a permanent effect on their outlook. The main criticism, and an important one, has been that there is a need for a still closer integration of the various elements of the Foundation Year as a whole. The course of Foundation lectures is a manageable assignment and admirably conducted by those who give the lectures; and it achieves its purpose of widening a student's horizons and improving his understanding of the Western heritage, of the social sciences and (less certainly) of the natural sciences. The discussion groups and essays, however, which are

[1] Iliffe reports that within his group, while almost all students gave the Foundation Year among the reasons for applying to Keele, only 16 per cent referred to any other feature of the curriculum. His evidence was a questionnaire completed by students on their first day in the university. Iliffe's findings suggest that some of the reasons given in response to the present enquiry may be very much *post factum* and are really experience masquerading as motivation.

associated with the lecture course are much less successful. The sessional courses are thought to be well worth while; but the terminal courses are unfavourably regarded and often do not achieve their prime purpose of maintaining a student's interest in the subject. The two-subject final has met the needs and expectations of most students and is not felt to have affected their later careers adversely. The relations between students and staff seem to be much more effective on an informal level than within the official scheme of general tutors; and it is in this matter particularly that the weaker students seem to suffer.

SOME STAFF NOTES

What the former students say about the quality and value of their undergraduate courses is something of which everyone interested in Keele must take serious notice. Yet, however responsibly expressed the opinions of graduates may be, they are not the only criterion by which the work of the University should be assessed. The members of the academic staff too have their own points of view; and it is to these we now turn.

The collecting and presentation of frank comments from members of a university staff about the institution in which they serve is a matter of some delicacy. Instead of a formal questionnaire, which would have been quite inappropriate in the circumstances, a personal letter was sent to everyone who had spent four years or more at Keele and so had seen at least one generation of students through their courses. Both present and former members of staff were included in the list. The letter invited personal and confidential comments on a number of suggested topics bearing on educational and social aspects of life at Keele and on anything else which it might be thought useful to raise. The letter was sent to 128 present members of staff, of whom 44 replied at some length; the comparative smallness of the response was to some extent compensated for by the fact that a majority of the replies came from professors and notably from senior lecturers; and the evidence was supplemented by personal conversations with some who did not write. Out of the fifty-eight former members of staff on the list, twenty-three replied; and more than half of these responses were from people who had known Keele from its earlier years and had had a long experience of its development. An undertaking was given that any use made of the replies received would be such as to preclude personal identification of the writers; the author therefore has to assume the responsibility for making a balanced selection in the summaries and quotations which follow.

Many of the replies were concerned mainly to stress the good features of the Keele system; and it may perhaps also be assumed that many of those who did not reply were not moved to express criticisms which they did not regard as fundamental. A few examples of laudatory comment may be cited:

> I have been impressed by the unanimity with which former students regard the Foundation Year as having been an extremely valuable experience not only in terms of personal development but also for their professional versatility and flexibility.

> I think the Foundation Year was a bold conception which on the whole is worth while. I think it would still be necessary (even if school education were broadened in the VIth forms) as a means of opening up horizons at a *University* level of thought. Certainly it did this for at least the brightest students.

> I still recollect that on arrival at Keele my impression was one of a very integrated and friendly academic community of considerable intellectual excitement. The first students I taught there were considerably more lively than those I had been teaching elsewhere. The Foundation Year was creating an awareness and alertness I had previously missed in students.

> The Foundation Year could be, and has been improved. What is impressive is the confidence and maturity our finalists achieve. I have a greater respect for the finalists at Keele than for those I have known at three other universities; they appear to develop more interesting personalities and are more tolerant and understanding than is usual with graduates.

> In my last years at Keele, and even more since leaving, I have been enormously impressed by its quality as a teaching university. I do not know any university in the country which exacts so very much from its students. The

> Foundation Year is a considerable intellectual hurdle. The two Subsidiaries which students have to take are not nominal by any means: they are dense courses and the standards that have to be attained are just as high as those in final honours: the only difference is that the Subsidiaries are short courses and not long ones. And then in addition to this they have to do a joint honours school without the benefit of a Part I. I will claim that Keele's products—or at least those who are in the II(ii)s and better—must be among the very best educated and trained undergraduates in the U.K.

It is only with assessments of this kind in mind that the more critical opinions are to be seen in perspective. The *Foundation Year*, taken as a whole, was generally regarded as sound in principle and there was only one writer who argued that it was basically misconceived. Some thought it would be more effective if there had been a break between school and university; others wondered whether it would be preferable if the course could somehow come at the end of university degree studies as a 'rewarding intellectual adventure'. Among the various constituents of the course, the main criticism of the lectures was that they attempted too much; both the discussion groups and the handling of the essays gave rise to misgivings; the sessionals found much more approval than the terminals.

> The comprehensiveness of the Foundation Year does not work and in particular non-science students do not really come to terms with science. I think the course tries to do too much and that, given the state of modern knowledge, the idea of comprehensiveness is an anachronism.

> The Foundation Year lecture course has dangers at age 18: it prompts a feeling of 'I know it all' and over-generalisation.

> The discussion groups scarcely justify the amount of staff time spent on them. The worst effect is that some students seem to think they can learn by swapping opinions.

> I am much in favour of the opportunity the Foundation Year gives to students to try out new subjects in the Sessionals but am entirely opposed to the Terminals which seem to me a waste of time for all concerned.

> It seemed to me that the superficiality of the multitude of topics covered in the Foundation Year lectures could not be educationally sound. As for the discussion groups, I was put in the position as Chairman of helping along a discussion with students on a subject about which my colleagues and I had often only the most superficial knowledge. I found marking masses of Foundation Year essays distasteful. I was expected to mark essays on topics in which I was poorly grounded, about which I was not consulted and based on lectures I had not attended. Two considerations seemed constantly to stand in the way of reform: (i) the system was that 'laid down by Lord Lindsay'; (ii) Keele must preserve some differences from other institutions at all costs.

Opinions about the *degree course* are divided mainly on the basic issue of a two-subject Final. An appreciable minority, particularly among members of scientific departments, hanker after a single subject which could be so pursued as to lead on directly to research. There are those, too, who would prefer a 'major-minor' arrangement which would permit not necessarily the dropping of one subject entirely at the end of the third year, but a greater concentration in the fourth year on one or other of the two subjects. Among the weighty majority opinion which would retain the present balance, there are many who, while agreeing that there is some measure of co-operation between departments, would like to see more of it and a closer integration of the two subjects offered by candidates; but it is realised that the provision of 'bridging' courses of lectures would, in view of the variety of possible combinations of subjects, impose a still heavier burden on the staff.

> I am convinced that the fourth year of study should be in one subject alone. In attempting to get a broad and general type education by introducing the Foundation Year and then following it with a two-subject Final, the pendulum had swung too far. I also had some doubts about the effectiveness of a double honours course leading to a research career in a particular subject. However, quite a significant number of my research students went on to university careers and have reached positions as Reader or Senior Lecturer at British universities.

> I definitely approve of the two-subject Final but wish it could be made more effectively a really interdisciplinary instead of a multidisciplinary course, integrated rather than parallel.

> Among the disadvantages of the two-subject Final are: (i) entry into a Department depends too much on the student's choice and too little on the Department's judgement of his capability to do good work there: this leads to marked unevenness of ability in the classes; (ii) one of the two subjects taken is too often a *pis aller*: this means that the level of interest is uneven; (iii) each Department overteaches its students.

> The effect of taking two Subsidiary courses in the first Principal year is very bad, sometimes disastrous. Students are grossly overloaded in this year and the quality of work suffers.

> I dislike the insistence that students must do a combination of Principal and Subsidiary subjects spread over both science and arts. One consequence has been that our Department has large Subsidiary classes of up to 100; many of the students are there by duty not desire.

What of *research*? The list of serious publications given in the Annual Reports and the increase in the number of research students show that this side of Keele's activities is expanding year by year. Some general comments on this topic were made in chapter 6;[1] and it is not surprising that most of the present replies, all of them critical, came from the scientific staff.

> A relatively small university is excellent in many ways; but it is not suitable for most of those teaching and researching in the physical sciences. It cannot hope to have the equipment and technical support which scientists are bound to need. Secondly, most scientists need the stimulus and opinions of a wide range of experts within their discipline if they are to flourish. At Keele I found myself heading for a *cul-de-sac* for want of stimulation. Not until I visited the USA did I realise how far behind I had slipped. The reason was of course that the Department at Keele was too small for novel ideas to be properly aired.

[1] See pp. 186–8.

> The inter-departmental competition for inadequate financial resources and the non-scientific bias in Senate have brought about a situation where scientific research, taken over all the scientific Departments, represents too small part of the University's impact on the outside world.
>
> Limited resources have been spread thinly instead of being concentrated for maximum effect.
>
> We cannot make substantial progress in research except to the detriment of undergraduate teaching. Apart from the activities of individuals (which will flourish even in the most barren soil), I think that we must have the courage to decide *where* we want to deploy resources which are bound to be slender and *there* make a substantial effort. We are too hesitant and tentative about new developments.

As for the *general aspects* of life at Keele, the following quotations will give an insight into the things which are thought by the staff to be worthy of comment:

> The 'isolation' of Keele is a subject on which almost nothing but nonsense is talked. Surely one should insist on answers to the questions 'of whom?' and 'from what?'
>
> Some families find the Keele community very satisfactory if they have small children. Some others complain of a lack of privacy: they feel they are living in a 'goldfish bowl'
>
> It is a very difficult undertaking to live at Keele as a member of staff: you have to learn how to live in the Keele world and yet not be absorbed by it; you need to exercise the sort of discipline about your coming and going and your speech that is demanded of a monk in a religious order.
>
> As regards the 'isolation' of Keele, the chief problem is not the fact that we are in the country but that culturally we are nowhere.[1]
>
> People were already lamenting the departure of the 'old Keele spirit' when I arrived in the late 1950s. What they

[1] Stoke is maligned by comments like this. It has its theatre, art gallery, concerts by first-class visiting orchestras, and plenty of societies in which local people participate.

> usually meant was that newly arrived people were unwilling to fall in with the old folkways or to recognise certain hierarchies of esteem. What marked the Keele ethos up to perhaps 1965 was the close network of personal relations which allowed controversies to be contained within certain general assumptions, *e.g.* that this was a peaceful place where people did not stop talking to one another. This ethos depended on total residence (nearly), a unified course structure, and a strong commitment to the place by a lot of people here.

EXTERNAL EXAMINERS AND OTHERS

So far in this chapter we have been concerned with the opinions of those who know Keele from the inside as students or staff. A third important group consists of those who as external examiners have been in a position to form a responsible outside opinion about Keele. All those who had acted in this capacity between 1956 and 1969 were invited to express their views on the understanding that if their opinions were quoted personal identification would be avoided. To the seventy letters so sent, fifty-five replies were received. In addition some confidential evidence was sought also from a number who had served as members of the Academic Council or as members of the UGC.

External examiners take no part in the assessment of the *Foundation Year* and their opinions about it must depend on the effect it may seem to them to have on candidates' written work in the Final examination and on impressions formed at *vivas*. It is not surprising, therefore, that only half of the examiners who replied felt that they could express a useful opinion. Nevertheless there was a quite considerable number of examiners both in arts and in science subjects who found a quality in Keele students which they believed was attributable mainly to the Foundation Year. Some of the more enthusiastic comments should be recorded:

> I had a distinct impression of the high quality of the students —a freshness of outlook, intellectual maturity and wide cultural background.

> In my experience what the Keele students lost in specialised knowledge they made up by breadth of interest.

> Talking to students at examination time and when I gave the odd lecture there, I thought they were a more exciting bunch than the general run of undergraduates elsewhere.

> The first year I examined at Keele I also examined at Birmingham and Cambridge. My impression was very clear. Although all papers by all students are much of a muchness, I felt that the Keele students are better than the others at sustaining an argument, and at presenting and discussing ideas. I believed at the time that if I were given some unidentified essays to read I could pick out the Keele scripts.

> I thought Keele students expressed themselves on average more ably than similar students at other universities.

> I regard the Foundation Year as a valuable experiment in university education which should not be lightly abandoned.

In their remarks on the *degree course* itself the examiners were naturally concerned first and foremost with students' achievements in their own particular subjects, though most of them appreciate that the compulsion to take two principals was an important doctrinal element in the Keele curriculum. Broadly speaking, examiners in the humanities and the social sciences found the two-subject Final acceptable from the point of view of their own disciplines; some, notably in philosophy and politics, thought it wholly admirable; and in groups A and B it was only a few examiners who were positively opposed to joint honours in any form. It was the scientists whose comments were almost unanimously critical. While they admitted that there was a place for broader courses, it was the complete exclusion of single subject specialisation at the undergraduate level which worried them. Let them speak for themselves:

> The two-subject Final leaves the average student with some rather large gaps in his knowledge of my subject. I do not think this is serious for the abler student who will at least know what he has left out; but some may be at a disadvantage in their careers.

> The two-subject Final was a mistake and should be abandoned. I have not found Joint Honours Schools really viable in any of the universities I have worked in, and

> with the present explosion of knowledge in the sciences it is becoming less and less possible for a candidate to attain an acceptable Honours level in more than one subject.

> For most students the double subject was far too heavy a load at the level expected and only a few of the bright students could cope successfully. I believe a good case can be made out for the broader final Honours degree course, but *not* for every student. The student from Keele is not well-equipped to proceed immediately to research in a specialised scientific subject but, on the other hand, he is well placed to go into some industrial jobs—sales, potential management, technical service, production, etc.—but *not* into research and development.[1]

> Even at Keele the double honours system does not seem to make any difference to *what* is taught; I think it should. The juxtaposition of subjects is purely mechanical and no effort seems to be made to encourage students to bring what they are learning in one subject to bear on what they study in the other.

The opinions of external examiners about *research* activities at Keele need to be interpreted cautiously. Almost all those who expressed views on this topic were scientists. They mostly came from large and relatively affluent universities where they are accustomed to have all the equipment they can reasonably desire, a large honours school and a steady supply of post-graduate students and where the staffing situation enables them and their colleagues to find ample time for their own investigations and to work in teams. One had the impression that their standards of comparison and their tacit expectations were often quite unfair to Keele. There were however many tributes to the amount and quality of original work being done by individual members of staff. What was particularly noted on the debit side was that in some instances the department at Keele is 'as yet' too small to nourish a vigorous research school and in others the department is not as a whole research-orientated. It is indicative, however, of the continuously widening scope of research at Keele that comments of this kind were much less

[1] The number of Keele graduates in science who have in fact gone into research and development in industry or to posts in universities belies this opinion.

frequently made by examiners who have acted at Keele in recent years.

What the *future of Keele* could be or should be was the last of the topics on which the opinions of examiners and others were invited. There was no mistaking the consensus of opinion that Keele had in broad terms justified its foundation and the hopes and policies of its promoters; equally clear was the view that change was not only inescapable but desirable and on a wider front than had hitherto been attempted. A few passages will illustrate the interest which examiners have in the possible development of the University.

> I am sure Keele has a very useful place in the university setup of this country. It will probably have to change, however, and adapt itself somewhat to the traditional pattern of provincial universities if it is to grow in size. I think there is a danger of its becoming a too inward-looking university if it keeps too rigidly to the original pattern.

> Keele set out to do for generalist education what the new universities have since done with a good deal more window-dressing; and events have now overtaken it.

> I would very much regret any reorganisation which meant giving up the Foundation Year entirely and would prefer its reorganisation in such a way (*e.g.* by a limitation to two terms) as might enable departmental staff to be convinced that their particular honours subject could be covered in a further six or seven terms. I can see that this would probably be acceptable only with a one-subject Final; but I think this is a cost I would be prepared to pay.

> I support the general Keele pattern apart from the compulsory two-subject degree. I feel confident that the institution is viable; certainly the university system has room for it. While pruning operations are needed, these do not require root and branch upheaval, only a remedial reappraisal.

> Keele has suffered in attractive power from a number of factors including its siting in separation from a cultural centre; the fact that it has always demanded a greater

investment of time and money to get a first degree there than one from other English universities; the changed attitude—and fashion—regarding residence; its lack of research facilities and research specialisms; and its bad luck in the short tenure of several of its Principals. But I must say all its old students known to me speak happily and gratefully of their time at Keele. It would seem to have done a specially good job with intelligent young men and women who did not want to specialise in the narrow way so frequent in this country and who came from schools which had not made them conventionally ambitious. Keele will have sooner or later to go over to a three year course for first degrees. Perhaps a compromise could be worked out and a system adopted by which each year had four quarters and ran from mid-September to mid-July. The first two quarters of the twelve might be the Foundation Course and replace the Foundation Year. Keele certainly needs to do something new and bold to get into the public eye favourably again as, say Sussex, Lancaster, Stirling are in it. I am not sure whether they are any more deserving than Keele: they have certainly been more lucky.

A BRIEF SUMMARY

From the three lines of enquiry we have pursued there emerges a picture which in its main outlines is remarkably consistent. The very great majority of students, staff, and examiners are in agreement that the Foundation Year taken as a whole has fully proved its effectiveness. The lecture course, though possibly too encyclopaedic, has been carefully thought out, is well balanced and is very well taught; apart from its relative failure to give non-science students a feeling for the methods of scientific thinking, it broadens the outlook of students and is regarded by graduates as a particularly valuable part of the curriculum. The students and some at least of the staff agree that the discussion groups and the handling of the essay work, both of which are associated with the lecture course, are much less good than they might be. There is a consensus of opinion that the sessional courses in the first year play an important rôle in opening up horizons and in helping students to find where their real interests and aptitudes lie; but the terminal courses have tended to cause an appreciable number of students to abandon their earlier intentions and this has on the whole been to the disadvantage of the science departments.

The degree course with its compulsory two-subject Final is very favourably regarded by the students who have opted to go to Keele and it is a negligible number who in retrospect would have preferred specialisation in a single subject. In contrast to this 'consumer opinion', however, there are many external examiners and some of the teachers at Keele, almost all of them on the science side, who remain unconvinced of the wisdom of excluding the possibility of a single-subject Final, on the ground that depth of study and standard of attainment are thereby restricted. That is a point of view one can understand and respect. It has to be accepted, however, that a spread of subjects within the degree course is one of the basic principles at Keele; and it would be fair comment that a student who knows that his interest is firmly fixed on a single subject would be well advised to go elsewhere. Within this framework two other criticisms are made. The first is that insistence on the taking of both a science and a non-science subject tends to be satisfied by the choice of a subject at the subsidiary level. Though a student is advised about this choice, it can involve some element of caprice or even some search for what it is easiest for the student to do. This leads to disparity of interest and aptitude within the subsidiary classes themselves; and if the subsidiaries are both taken in the first of the three years of the degree course, something, though not all, of the educational advantages of a continuous spread of subjects is lost. The second point is one raised by students, teachers and examiners alike. It amounts to a complaint that though there is a spread of subjects, not sufficient attention is paid to their integration with one another or to the development at the undergraduate level of inter-disciplinary courses apart from those in International Relations and Social Analysis. It is easy and indeed fashionable to profess a desire for a higher standard of integration and cross-fertilisation between departments; but every university teacher knows how intractable the practical problems can be and how much depends on having the right person to breathe life into a scheme which otherwise looks well only on paper. Certainly there is no easy solution when the possible combinations of subjects are as various as they are at Keele, when the number of students taking a particular combination is so unpredictable, and the number of staff not sufficient to meet every such requirement. Co-operation at the postgraduate level is easier to achieve, as is shown by such courses as the M.A. in Mediaeval Studies, Victorian Studies and Comparative Government. It may be that, because of its known stress on breadth of study, even *too* much is being expected of Keele. After all, at the end of his four-year course a Keele student is more likely than most to have gained a sense of the inter-relatedness of the branches of knowledge.

Finally reference has to be made to two impressions about Keele which are frequently voiced by people in university circles. The first is that Keele has been content to keep its numbers relatively small and has grown more slowly than it need have done. The second is that Keele's efforts have been concentrated too much on its admittedly excellent undergraduate teaching at the expense of its potentialities for research. Our earlier chapters, it is hoped, will have done something to put both matters in perspective. As regards the rate of growth, it will be recalled that in its early years Keele was fully occupied with the organisation of a quite new curriculum and when this was placed on a firm footing, consolidation within the scope of its agreed limit of size was a much wiser policy than a speedy expansion would have been. In this opinion Keele was in accord with the advice which the UGC offered. The policy of total, or near-total, residence coupled with restricted financial resources was in any event a check on rapid growth; and this factor has continued to operate. Nevertheless, when expansions of numbers were being generally discussed from 1957 onwards, the targets which Keele suggested were proportionately as co-operative as those of other universities. On every occasion it was the UGC which pruned the figures and proposed lower ones on which its financial support would be based; even for the end of the 1972–7 quinquennium it was only after long discussion that the UGC agreed, on condition of the limited introduction of a three-year course, to raise its own proposal for Keele from 2,400 to 3,000. Between October 1953 when it had its first full complement of students, and the last session of its existence as a College, Keele's numbers rose from 495 to 818 and between October 1962 and October 1970 from 853 to 1,863. In terms of percentage increases this is a rate which bears comparison with those of most well established universities.[1] The target of 3,000 for 1976–7 envisages an equally rapid rate of growth.[2]

In the matter of postgraduate and research activities there are two things to be said. The first is that for its first twelve years when it could award only a B.A. degree, there was little or no opportunity to build up research schools. Individually, however, members of staff were able from the outset to pursue and publish the results of their own researches and in chapter 6 we gave some indications of the number and kind of investigations being undertaken towards the end of the College's first decade. Since that time the range has been considerably enlarged (e.g., in the 1967–72 quinquennium, in communications, biochemistry, statistical sociology, computer development in association with Manchester, and in studies of curricula under the aegis of the Department and Institute of Education); and the lists of publications from the Charter year onwards show that every department has been producing a steady stream of learned and scientific books and articles which matches the lists of any institution of comparable size. The second comment to be made is that once higher degrees could be conferred the number of postgraduate and research students has progressively increased. Their numbers rose from 38 in 1962–3 to 252 in 1970–1971 and are now 12 per cent of all the students at Keele. The suggestion that Keele, having made a success of its undergraduate teaching, is only belatedly turning some of its attention to research, is refuted by the facts.

The results of an educational experiment are not to be assessed in the terms of the black and white of success and failure and those who are most closely involved in Keele would be the last to assert that ideal answers have been found for everything they have attempted to do; but if an accountancy of academic credits and debits is to be instituted, there is no doubt where the balance clearly lies. The founding of Keele was an act of faith. After twenty-one years Keele can fairly claim that its faith has been justified by the distinctive features of the curriculum it has evolved, by the influence its initial example of

[1] For academic developments taking place alongside expansion in numbers see pp. 166–75.

[2] For the suggested numbers of science students and postgraduates, see p. 222n.

forward thinking has had on university education as a whole, by the quality of its teaching and the development of its research, and not least by the kind of men and women who are its graduates.

Nine

Epilogue

THE NEWER UNIVERSITIES[1]

The main reason which induced the UGC to agree to the foundation of Keele was the experimental nature of its curriculum; as a small institution it was not expected to affect very appreciably the need for more university places which had been advocated in the 1946 Barlow Report. The need for expansion became still more evident in the early 1950s as the influence of two distinct factors made itself felt. The first, known as 'the trend', was the increase in the number of school pupils who stayed on to do sixth form work and so qualified themselves for admission to a university. The second, known as 'the bulge', was the increase in the absolute numbers of the age group concerned, resulting from the higher birth-rate which began in 1944 and reached a peak in 1946–8. The effects of these two factors were cumulative and by 1955 it was becoming a matter of urgency to plan for a further increase in university places. Up to that time the UGC had expected that the existing universities could cope with the situation up to the early 1960s; but the number of applications for university entry was rising steeply.

At this juncture the UGC received from W. G. Stone, the Director of Education for Brighton, a memorandum which revived an earlier proposal for the establishment of a University College in that town;[2] Brighton itself was prepared to offer a site at Stanmer Park; neighbouring local authorities supported the scheme; in February 1957 the Government authorised the UGC to support the foundation of the College provided that the capital required could be fitted into the general capital pro-

[1] On this topic there is already a considerable literature. The best comprehensive survey is H. J. Perkin's *New Universities in the United Kingdom*. For the formulation of policy, see the UGC's *University Development 1957–62*, pp. 90–113.

[2] In his memorandum Mr Stone clearly had Keele in mind as the prototype for newer universities.

gramme and the Committee was satisfied with the plans as they were evolved; and in July 1958 the Sussex scheme was formally approved. An important step was taken the next year when Mr J. S. Fulton (now Lord Fulton) was appointed as the first Vice-Chancellor. It will be recalled that Lindsay had hoped he would have been the first Principal of Keele;[1] he was now to play a crucial part in the establishment of the first of the newer universities and the discussions he had with the UGC and others about the nascent University did much to set the pattern of thinking for the next few years. The success of the Brighton proposal and the growing public awareness of the need for more university places encouraged other localities to stake their claims. Of the twenty in England and eight in Scotland who did so, six were successful: York and Norwich (East Anglia) gained approval for their proposals in 1960, Essex (at Colchester), Kent (at Canterbury) and Warwick (at Coventry) in May 1961, and Lancaster in November 1961. Sussex received its Charter not as a College but as a University in 1961, a year before Keele; the others between 1963 and 1965. The still further expansion recommended by the Robbins Committee in 1963 led to the designation of most of the Colleges of Advanced Technology as universities and their transference to the UGC grant list; and to the foundation of the University of Stirling in 1967. In 1965 the Government of Northern Ireland approved the establishment of the New University of Ulster in Coleraine which received its Charter in 1970.

From an early stage in their discussions with Sussex the UGC began to consider what policies should be adopted in regard to new universities. It was now axiomatic that governmental approval and central finance, as in the case of Keele, were essential and that responsibility for planning should be shared between the UGC and the local Promotion Committees. To this end Academic Planning Boards were set up in consultation with the UGC to advise on development, choose a Vice-Chancellor, draft a Charter, assist in the important initial academic appointments and later merge themselves into Advisory Committees which for the first few years of a new institution's existence would be a guarantee of academic standards. This was a refinement of the sponsorship principle which had been initiated with Keele; but it differs from the Keele arrangements

[1] See p. 59.

in that, first, the Planning Boards and Advisory Committees were smaller than Keele's full Academic Council and, secondly, their membership was in each case designed to cover a well balanced spread of academic interests and in fact brought in the experience of six or seven universities instead of only three. Nor did it remain long in doubt, in the light of Keele's experience, that the new institutions should have full degree-granting powers from the outset as universities; and this has meant that they could build up their postgraduate work much more quickly than Keele had been able to do.

The size and location of the newer universities were inter-related. The UGC 'felt strongly that any new institution should aim at not less than 3,000 full-time students as a minimum target', and should reach that figure within ten years—a more rapid rate of growth than Keele had achieved.

Table 11 Numbers of students at new universities—autumn 1970

University	*Undergraduate*	*Postgraduate*	*Total*
Keele	1,611	252	1,863
Sussex	2,760	864	3,624
E. Anglia	2,422	293	2,715
York	2,001	444	2,445
Essex	1,571	372	1,943
Kent	2,002	246	2,248
Warwick	1,698	311	2,009
Lancaster	2,353	451	2,804

Some of the new universities in fact envisaged a still higher eventual figure for themselves, notably Essex which had 10,000 or even 20,000 in mind. Institutions of 3,000 students would make an appreciable contribution to the number of places needed in universities; to plan for smaller numbers would be uneconomic. Academically they could plan immediately for a wide range of subjects and the staff to support them; the variety of what they might offer would, they hoped, attract students of high quality; and the prospect of having a good sized department of one's own, a staff with varied interests and the nucleus of a research school within a reasonable time would be an inducement—as proved to be the case—to well-established and well-known scholars to come and share from the outset the challenge and responsibility of setting a new institution on its feet. Opinion had changed since Keele embarked on its experiment: the academic world no longer looked askance at what Professor Asa Briggs (now Vice-Chancellor of Sussex) called 'redrawing the map of learning'; the public in general was now more alive than ever to the importance of universities; and the government was prepared to be more generous in the supply of funds than it had been in a position to be in the 1950s.

In choosing the locations for these universities several considerations were taken into account. Sites in the centre of large cities or towns would be too expensive to acquire: what was needed was an area of about 200 acres as a minimum to allow for future developments. Yet, though a campus was envisaged, it should not be too far away from a vigorous community with access to civilised amenities which would be attractive to students and staff alike and so not suffer from the reputed isolation of Keele. Emphasis was also placed, as it had been for Keele in 1946–50, on the measure of local enthusiasm which was being evinced, the financial support which would be forthcoming and the likelihood that local people would effectively contribute to the running of the university by serving on its Council and committees. In most cases the chosen site was in fact donated by the Local Authority. Another factor was the potential supply of lodgings for students since the UGC was now not prepared to provide student accommodation on any appreciable scale: Sussex, for example, relied entirely on Brighton, East Anglia on Norwich, and Lancaster on Morecambe to begin with, and still do so to a considerable extent.

For our present purposes the main interest lies in the kind of curricula which the new universities evolved. The UGC had declared that on the academic side their main concern was 'in the general broadening of the undergraduate curriculum, in the breaking down of the rigidities of departmental organisation and in the strengthening of the relationships between teacher and taught'—every one of which topics had been a major concern of Keele since 1950; there was a 'need for more experiment in the structure of degree courses, in the content of curricula, in methods of teaching and in university organisation'. The members of the Academic Planning Boards 'had been selected with a view to encouraging such experimentation' and the UGC 'was anxious that they should feel free to recommend major departures from the more orthodox pattern of academic development and organisation'.[1] Yet even if these Boards had wanted to base their proposals to any considerable extent on the example and experience of Keele, they could not have done so since the UGC made it plain that as a general basis a four-year undergraduate course was out of the question. The problem therefore was to secure breadth of study within the compass of a three-year curriculum, while at the same time providing such study in particular fields as would be appropriate to the students' future careers.

These seven new English universities together with Stirling and Ulster differ as much from one another as they do from Keele and the older foundations; but the broad principle underlying almost all their curricula is the concept of schools of studies, whatever title may be used for it. Related areas of study, for which the word 'department' is sometimes deliberately eschewed, are grouped together to provide an integrated curriculum and either in the first few terms or in a part I examination there is additional coverage for 'contextual' or 'supporting' courses common to all the students in one or sometimes more schools of studies. There are, however, few attempts—nor perhaps could there be—to provide a 'common core of knowledge' for the entire student body even on a less restricted scale than Keele's Foundation Year. In this Keele remains unique.

Space does not permit a detailed account of the variety of solutions which have been worked out; but a few illustrations will show the general trend. At *Sussex*, which has a special importance as the first of the newer universities to formulate its curriculum, there were at first four schools: English and American studies, social studies, physical sciences, biological sciences; to these there were added later: European studies, applied sciences, molecular sciences, African and Asian studies, cultural and community studies. The students reading for the B.A. take preliminary courses during their first two terms in three fields which generally include philosophy and history;

[1] It has been pointed out that no serving member of the staff at Keele served on any of these bodies; but F. A. Vick, Keele's former Professor of Physics, was appointed a member of the UGC's Sub-committee on New Universities in April 1959, and B. R. Williams, Keele's former Professor of Economics, was a member of the Planning Board for Lancaster.

and the contextual courses take up about half a student's time during his course. The B.Sc. candidate similarly has preliminary courses including mathematics and the structure and properties of matter. At *East Anglia* there are now eight schools, one of which is the fine arts (visual and music). At the end of his second term a student is tested in broadly based courses which introduce him to the main fields relevant to his chosen school; and the later work in a school covers a wide range. *York* is not so clearly organised in schools and departments are more clearly differentiated in the conventional manner; but a student's interests are broadened in two ways: he has the choice of studying two related subjects for his degree and if he elects to major in one of them he must spend at least a third of his time on the other; and there are 'open courses' on topics that may attract him or illuminate his major subject. *Essex* groups its departments in various combinations to form the schools of physical sciences, mathematical studies, social studies and comparative studies (which includes government, political science, literature and language). Each student's course is planned as a whole and no part of it is regarded as being merely subsidiary or ancillary. *Kent* is the only one which uses the word faculty in relation to the humanities, social sciences and natural sciences. The first four terms are, however, devoted in each faculty to an integrated study of several subjects with emphasis on 'the essential connexions between related topics'. At *Lancaster* the fields of study are variously combined into groups of related subjects, each group being controlled by a Board of Studies. A part I examination at the end of the first year covers three subjects and students are recommended to include one in which they did not specialise at school. The schools of studies at *Warwick* include engineering science and molecular sciences. Every student is expected to attend a common first year course on 'Inquiry and Criticism' consisting of a weekly lecture and a seminar in which 'the methods of the various branches of knowledge such as mathematics, the natural sciences, literary criticism, ethics, and politics are critically examined' with the object of giving the student 'a sense of the basis and limits of his own discipline and of its place in the universe of knowledge'. This is a kind of Foundation Year in miniature. At *Stirling*, where work is organised in two semesters of about fifteen weeks each, a general preliminary course entitled 'Approaches and Methods' was tried for a few years but was not thought to be sufficiently valuable academically to warrant its continuance; but the Keele-like integration of a degree course with a professional training for teachers has proved successful. At *Ulster*, too, which has its schools of physical sciences, biological and environmental studies, social science and humanities, there is a similar provision for an integrated professional training.

The successful launching and the rapid growth of the newer universities with their eagerness and freedom to try out and prove the value of new schemes of study have been to the good of British university education as a whole. It is sometimes remarked that not all their innovations in the curriculum are quite as novel and unprecedented, apart from nomenclature, as they profess them to be; but by and large they have moulded curricula which are flexibly adapted to the needs of the second half of the twentieth century. They were founded in quite a different climate of opinion from that in which Keele was born. In explaining this change of opinion too much must not be attributed directly to Keele itself; but the mere fact that Keele existed and had demonstrated that the plea for a broader university curriculum was more than idealistic theorising made it all the easier for the newer universities to develop along their own lines.

To fill in some of the details of the picture there are a few other points of interest to Keele which may be briefly summarised. With the exception of Stirling which follows the Scottish pattern and has a four-year course for honours and a three-year course for a pass degree, the newer universities assume that all students will be aiming at honours and, as at Keele, a pass degree is awarded only when a student falls below that standard. But the framework of the curricula is such that a student can generally opt to devote his major interest at least in his last year to a single subject. It was the policy of the UGC that as at Keele the new institutions should concentrate at least in their earlier years on the humanities, social sciences and pure sciences and a lower priority was given to technology. This has been the main trend; but Sussex is already developing a school of applied science, Warwick, because of its close proximity to a highly industrial area, has had a school of engineering science from the first, and Lancaster has set up a department of systems engineering. What has attracted public attention, however, has been the development of unusual departments or subjects of study in several places, such as Intellectual History at Sussex, Renaissance Studies at Warwick, and Operational Research and Marketing at Lancaster. It has also been possible to embark from the outset on postgraduate work; and instructional courses for Master's degrees have proliferated.

In the matter of constitutional organisation there are two points of interest. York, Kent and Lancaster, and to some extent Warwick, have evolved a college system in which there is an attempt to integrate residence and teaching. Each college houses from 300 to 600 students and provides the usual facilities of a hall of residence; but, in addition, teaching accommodation is incorporated and the college is host to a variety of non-laboratory academic departments. All students whether on the campus or in lodgings as well as members of the staff are associated with a college which rather than the Union is the focus of their social life and the centre of their allegiance. As at Keele, there is a generous representation of non-professorial staff on the statutory bodies and particularly on the Senate; and at East Anglia, Essex and Warwick there is an Assembly on the Keele pattern. In the development of their sites the new universities have not had to face the difficulties which beset Keele and in most cases the academic, administrative and residential buildings have been planned and designed by a single architect e.g. by Sir Basil Spence at Sussex, Mr Denys Lasdun at East Anglia, and Robert Matthew, Johnson-Marshall and Partners at York. Finally the public appeals for funds, especially for residences, have been much more successful than those made from time to time by Keele and targets of £1m. or £2m. have proved not too difficult to attain.

BEYOND 1971

It so happens that this book is being written just at a time when Keele is in the throes of considering what its future policy shall be and how its curriculum may need to be adapted to changing circumstances. It is no part of the historian's task to indulge in prophecy or even suggest solutions for problems which others have the responsibility for facing. But there are some things about which there can be little dispute. Two important changes from the original 1950 pattern have already been agreed upon with the UGC: the ideal of full residence for all students has been abandoned to the extent that 25 per cent will live off the campus; and from October 1973 a three-year course will be made available for 600 of the 3,000 students which is the present target for expansion. The modification of the residential requirement is the less serious of the two changes in policy. Whatever may be the educational and social advantages of residence in halls, there are some students who at some stage in their development undoubtedly do better work when they are less rigidly bound to the daily routines of a campus community; and it can be argued that this degree of relaxation from the residence requirement gives Keele a useful flexibility. Whether the proportion should or can be kept to 25 per cent is another matter. At that figure the residential principle is not seriously impaired; at double that figure there would be a significant change in ethos which many besides former students would regret. On the practical side much will depend on the way in which the provision of student accommodation can be financed for those who live on campus, on the availability of suitable lodgings reasonably nearby for those who do not, and on the measure of further expansion which Keele is prepared to contemplate. These are factors which interact with one another.

The proposed introduction of a three-year course poses fundamental questions.[1] If Keele stands for anything it is the concept of breadth of study throughout the whole course: the Foundation Year, the two-subject Final and the insistence on some science and some non-science have been basic to the unified Keele programme. From time to time, as we have seen in chapter 6, some radical proposals made for changes in the degree structure have been advanced and rejected. Now the nettles have to be grasped and the firmness with which the operation is conducted will determine the damage which is done to the principles which the Keele programme exemplifies. The worst and the least acceptable course of action would be to abandon for three-year students *both* the Foundation Year *and* the two-subject Final. That would mean that for such students Keele would be indistinguishable, apart from residence and size, from any one of two or three dozen other universities.

[1] For an earlier proposal of this kind, see p. 166.

Even a requirement that a subsidiary should be taken outside a student's main group of studies would do little to save the situation; and without some element of the Foundation Year and a requirement of 'spread', a formal tapering off to a single subject in the third and final year might be a cloak for virtual specialisation all through the course.

The crux of the matter would seem to lie in the Foundation Year itself. This, above all else, has been Keele's distinctive hallmark. It is, admittedly, not the only possible avenue to a broad conspectus of knowledge; but it is a programme which has been refined and elaborated with enormous care over the years; and the great preponderance of the evidence shows that it has been a successful venture and one which it is worth a great deal of effort to preserve in some form for all students. With increasing numbers and a prospective annual combined intake of 800 three- and four-year students, the organisation of the Foundation Year will in any event require consideration: a class of that size is a public meeting and will need to be broken down into small units. Neither the repeating of the same lecture to different groups nor closed-circuit television would be free from serious objections. It might be possible to cope with the sessional and terminal courses; but the logistics of the discussion groups and the essays are formidable. A separate kind of Foundation Year designed for different groups of students according as their interests lie in the humanities, the social sciences or the natural sciences, is a tempting proposal, and one which in essence but on a smaller scale has been adopted elsewhere. But it has two features which are contrary to Keele principles and experience. It rejects the concept that there should be a core of knowledge common to *all* students; and it virtually assumes that students will commit themselves to a major interest at the outset of their university course. This is not to say that for three-year students the Foundation Year element could not be in some way reduced; but the total disappearance of that element would have serious consequences not only for that particular group of students but for Keele as a whole.

A three-year course and a single-subject Final are not a single issue. If some appreciable element of a Foundation Year is to be retained for three-year students, the depth of study possible in each of two parallel subjects will be less than now obtains for Keele students; and if Keele sees the three-year course as a means of attracting more students in science, the option at least of a single-subject Final seems an inevitable consequence for this group of undergraduates. Yet once a single-subject Final is allowed for one category of students, the pressure to permit it for some four-year students as well may be irresistible. Joint honours degrees, however, are more popular and better regarded even in science than they were when Keele was founded; and it is not inevitable that the prestige of a single-subject Final would prove so attractive as to destroy utterly what Keele has stood for or that some kind of academic Gresham's law should operate to Keele's disadvantage. The essential problem for Keele is how it shall remain faithful to its doctrine of breadth.

The future of Keele cannot, however, be considered in isolation from the place which universities as a whole will occupy in the national system of education and the functions which they will collectively be expected to perform. The change in the status of the UGC in 1963 when it became responsible to the Department of Education and Science and the subsequent granting to the Comptroller and Auditor-General of access to university accounts have resulted in a much greater degree of national planning and co-ordination at all levels of university activity. When Parliamentary recurrent and capital grants made to universities are in excess of £250m. a year and over 70 per cent of the revenue of universities comes from the Treasury, it is inevitable that pressures to conform to norms and standards centrally determined should become more difficult to resist and that the limits within which universities are free to take their own decisions should be directly and indirectly curtailed. Among the questions now being raised we may mention: the size of the total university population and that of individual institutions; the minimum size in terms of student numbers of an acceptable department; the appropriate ratio of staff to students as a whole and in the different academic areas; the limited number of departments in certain subjects which on the grounds of national requirements it is proper to support; the proportion of postgraduate students to the student population as a whole and in particular universities; the amount of aid which should be given from public funds for student residential accommodation; and the relationships of universities to the developing polytechnics and other institutions of higher education, such as Colleges of Education. It is within this contracting framework of effective academic autonomy that Keele's decisions will have to be made.

In the world of universities there are many mansions. There is no conceivable curriculum which is universally valid: one may be preferable to others for some purposes, in some circumstances, and for some students. But there is no mistaking the fact that Keele, a pioneer, has carved out for itself a distinctive and enduring niche. Whatever expansion there may be in the university population as a whole, whatever may be the pressures for what is currently called cost effectiveness, whatever devices may be evolved for bringing the various sectors of tertiary education into closer relationship with one another, there must surely be a place for at least one institution where the kind of outlook and the pattern of existence which Keele has exemplified, are fostered and maintained. Keele is more than a page in a textbook of educational history. It is a living thing and its duty now to itself and to university education as a whole is to do all it can to ensure that its own distinctive quality is not lost amid a tide of uniformity.

The Officers and Professors of the College and the University

A. THE UNIVERSITY COLLEGE OF NORTH STAFFORDSHIRE

(Incorporated by a Charter dated 11 August 1949)

President

The Right Honourable John Herbert Dudley, Earl of Harrowby 1949–55
Her Royal Highness The Princess Margaret 1956–62

Vice-President and Chairman of the Council

Alderman the Reverend Allan Thomas Horwood 1949–56
Alderman Alfred George Beech Owen, C.B.E. 1956–62

Other Vice-Presidents

Alderman Lewis Davies, O.B.E. 1949–62
Alderman William Hutson 1949–52
Councillor Arthur George Appleby 1952
Councillor Dr Norman James Cochran, M.B.E. 1953–9
Alderman George Leonard Barber 1957–62
Alderman Mrs Ada Chadwick 1959–62

Principal

The Right Honourable Alexander Dunlop, Baron Lindsay of Birker 1949–52
Sir John Edward Lennard-Jones 1953–4
Sir George Reginald Barnes 1956–60
Harold McCarter Taylor, C.B.E. 1961–2

Vice-Principal[1]

Professor Francis Arthur Vick, O.B.E. 1950–4
Professor John William Blake 1954–7

[1] During vacancies in the office of Principal (see p. 146) when the Vice-Principal became Acting Principal, Acting Vice-Principals were appointed as follows: Professor A. E. Teale, 1952–3; Professor A. R. Gemmell, 1954–6; Professor H. D. Springall, 1960–1.

Professor Harold Douglas Springall	1957–9
Professor William Alexander Campbell Stewart	1959–62

Honorary Treasurer

Arthur Percival Walker	1949–62

Registrar

Walter Allen Jenkins	1949–53
John Francis Nicholas Hodgkinson	1953–62

Honorary Legal Consultant

Harry Taylor	1949–62

Academic Council[1]

Representatives of the University of Oxford

Miss L. S. Sutherland	1950–62
Sir Henry Clay	1950–3
Professor C. L. Wrenn	1954–62

Representatives of the University of Manchester

Professor H. G. Cannon	1950–62
Professor H. B. Charlton	1950–9
Professor G. L. Brook	1959–62

Representatives of the University of Birmingham

Professor J. G. Smith	1950–62
Professor L. J. Russell	1950–3
Professor M. Stacey	1953–62

B. THE UNIVERSITY OF KEELE

(Incorporated by a Charter dated 26 January 1962)

Chancellor

Her Royal Highness The Princess Margaret, Countess of Snowdon	1962–

Pro-Chancellor and Chairman of the Council

Sir Alfred George Beech Owen	1962–70
Sir (Edward) Humphrey Browne	1971–

[1] For the constitution of the Academic Council see p. 80.

Deputy Pro-Chancellors

Alderman Lewis Davies	1962–4
Alderman George Leonard Barber	1962–
Alderman Mrs Ada Chadwick	1962–71
Councillor Harold Albert Hawkins	1964–
Alderman Joseph William Parker	1971–

Vice-Chancellor

Harold McCarter Taylor	1962–7
Professor William Alexander Campbell Stewart	1967–

Deputy Vice-Chancellor

Professor William Alexander Campbell Stewart	1962–
Professor Samuel Edward Finer	1962–4
Professor David John Edward Ingram	1964–5
Professor Robert Joseph North	1965–6
Professor Edward Maurice Hugh-Jones	1966–8
Professor David John Edward Ingram	1968–71
Professor Ian Torrance Millar	1971–

Honorary Treasurer

Arthur Percival Walker	1962–8
Anthony George Hayek	1968–

Registrar

John Francis Nicholas Hodgkinson	1962–

Honorary Legal Consultant

Harry Taylor	1962–8
Leonard Keith Robinson	1968–

C. PROFESSORS AND HEADS OF DEPARTMENTS[1]

(*i*) *Board of Humanities*

American Studies

D. K. Adams (*Head of Department*)	1965–

Classics

J. M. T. Charlton (*Professor from 1953*)	1950–

[1] See also pp. 88–9, 176–7. Unlessotherwise indicated, the post held is a Professorship.

English	
J. J. Lawlor (*Professor and Head of Department*)	1950–
A. J. Smith	1971–
Modern Languages	
W. W. Chambers (*Professor [German] and Head of Dept.*)	1950–4
K. Brooke (*Professor [German] and Head of Dept.*)	1954–69
R. J. North (*Professor of French*)	1962–8
J. H. Broome (*Professor of French*)	1968–9
E. Lampert (*Russian Studies; Professor from 1968*)	1965–9
German	
K. Brooke (*see Mod. Langs.*)	1969–
French	
J. H. Broome (*see Mod. Langs.*)	1969–
Russian Studies	
E. Lampert (*see Mod. Langs.*)	1969–
History	
J. W. Blake	1950–64
W. M. Simon	1964–71
*	
Philosophy	
W. B. Gallie	1950–4
A. G. N. Flew	1954–71
*	
Music	
G. M. Pratt (*Director*)	1964–
Religious Knowledge (*Historical Theology from 1952*)	
R. B. Henderson (*lecturer*)	1950–4
T. A. Roberts (*lecturer*)	1954–61
A. W. Heathcote (*lecturer*)	1962–7

(ii) *Board of Social Sciences*

Economics	
B. R. Williams	1950–9

* Is not yet known.

L. Fishman	1969–
E. M. Hugh-Jones	1959–68

Education

W. A. C. Stewart	1950–67
S. J. Eggleston	1967–

Geography

S. H. Beaver (*Professor and Head of Dept.*)	1950–
H. B. Rodgers (*Social Geography*)	1970–1

Law

D. Thompson	1964–

Moral and Political Philosophy

A. E. Teale	1950–68

Political Institutions[1]

S. E. Finer	1950–66

Politics

M. Harrison	1966–

Psychology

I. M. L. Hunter	1962–

Sociology[2]

H. Jones (*Reader and Head of Dept.*)	1966–9
R. J. Frankenberg (*Professor*)	1969–

(*iii*) *Board of Natural Sciences*

Biology

A. R. Gemmell	1950–

Chemistry

H. D. Springall (*Professor and Head of Dept.*)	1950–
I. T. Millar (*Organic Chemistry*)	1966–

Communication

D. M. Mackay	1960–

[1] See p. 172. [2] See pp. 172–3.

Geology

F. W. Cope (*Professor from 1953*)	1950–

Mathematics

I. N. Sneddon	1950–6
D. S. Jones	1956–64
A. P. Robertson	1964–

Physics

F. A. Vick	1950–9
D. J. E. Ingram	1959–

(*iv*) *Departments Independent of Boards of Studies*

Adult Education

R. Shaw (*Director; Professor from 1968*)	1962–

Institute of Education

W. A. C. Stewart (*Director and Professor*)	1963–7
G. N. Brown (*Director and Professor*)	1967–

Computing Science and Computing Centre

H. H. Greenwood (*Director*)	1963–
R. McWeeney (*Professor from 1964*)	1963–6

Statistical Research Unit in Sociology

R. E. A. Mapes (*Director*)	1964–

University Library

S. O. Stewart	1950–

Appendix II

Statistical Tables[a]

TABLE 1: FULL-TIME STUDENTS AND STAFF

Session	*Students*[b]			*Staff*[c]						
	Men	*Women*	*Total*	*P*	*R*	*SL*	*L*	*AL*	*O*	*Total*
1950–1	102 (3)	55 (—)	157	13	3	—	3	—	—	19
1951–2	201 (3)	99 (—)	300	13	4	—	8	18	—	43
1952–3	274 (4)	143 (—)	417	13	5	2	16	30	1	67
1953–4	308 (6)	187 (1)	495	15	3	1	21	45	1	86
1954–5	324 (12)	209 (2)	533	15	3	1	26	39	—	84
1955–6	348 (14)	230 (1)	578	15	3	4	30	33	—	85
1956–7	367 (13)	240 (1)	607	15	3	4	37	29	—	88
1957–8	412 (17)	232 (—)	644	15	1	3	51	23	—	93
1958–9	432 (21)	257 (1)	689	15	1	3	55	24	—	98
1959–60	454 (30)	278 (2)	732	15	1	3	60	26	3	108
1960–1	463 (32)	306 (2)	769	15	1	8	53	33	4	114
1961–2	469 (42)	349 (—)	818	17	—	11	56	37	7	128
1962–3	488 (36)	365 (2)	853	18	3	14	59	24	26	144
1963–4	520 (36)	402 (5)	922	18	3	20	55	29	29	154
1964–5	627 (68)	456 (14)	1,083	21	4	23	76	34	17	175
1965–6	742 (93)	493 (15)	1,235	21	29		95	32	31	208
1966–7	822 (114)	588 (26)	1,410	21	29		104	31	32	217
1967–8	992 (123)	672 (29)	1,664	22	31		123	31	34	241
1968–9	1,096 (142)	719 (46)	1,815	21	34		135	31	47	268
1969–70	1,125 (174)	692 (50)	1,817	23	39		176		43	281
1970–1	1,145 (194)	718 (58)	1,863	24	51		171		38	284

[a] Sources: UGC: Returns from *Universities and University Colleges*, annually from 1950–1 to 1965–6 (HMSO); Dept of Educ. and Science: *Statistics of Education Vol.* 6 (*Universities*), 1966, 1967, 1968, 1969 (HMSO); later figures are from Keele records.

[b] The figures in brackets indicate the number of students (included in the preceding figures) doing research or attending courses for higher degrees.

[c] Members of staff are classified as P(rofessor), R(eader), S(enior) L(ecturer), L(ecturer), A(ssistant) L(ecturer), O(thers).

Appendix II

TABLE 2:
HOME AND UNIVERSITY RESIDENCE OF STUDENTS

Session	*Home*				*University*						
	Within 30 miles	*Other UK*	*Common-wealth*	*Foreign*	*Halls*		*Lodgings*		*Home*		*% in Halls*
					M.	*W.*	*M.*	*W.*	*M.*	*W.*	
1950–1	80	75	—	2	99	53	—	1	3	1	96·8
1951–2	116	178	—	6	199	96	—	1	2	2	98·3
1952–3	148	262	4	3	269	140	—	1	5	2	98·1
1953–4	135	351	7	2	298	183	1	—	9	4	97·2
1954–5	103	419	6	5	309	206	9	—	6	6	96·6
1955–6	83	484	5	6	330	230	13	—	5	—	96·9
1956–7	86	502	12	7	345	231	14	2	8	7	94·9
1957–8	93	535	6	10	389	231	21	1	2	—	96·3
1958–9	71	599	6	13	408	257	24	—	—	—	96·5
1959–60	66	647	7	12	424	277	19	1	11	—	95·8
1960–1	88	658	9	14	432	305	28	—	3	1	95·8
1961–2	71	721	22	4	456	342	4	—	9	7	97·6
1962–3	75	753	11	14	453	361	19	—	16	4	95·4
1963–4	85	807	12	18	486	394	15	1	19	7	95·4
1964–5	113	920	26	24	543	401	72	45	12	10	87·4
1965–6	1,178		31	26	644	446	71	35	27	12	88·3
1966–7	1,344		34	32	676	503	98	72	48	13	83·6
1967–8	1,623		20	21	800	561	137	88	55	23	81·8
1968–9	1,765		19	31	814	570	205	102	77	47	76·2
1969–70	1,735		28	54	871	568	225	106	29	18	79·2
1970–1	1,808		31	24	929	607	157	84	59	27	82·4

TABLE 3: SUM

Year No.	*Session*	*Exchequer grants*	*% of total income*	*Local Authority grants*	*% of total income*	*Tuition & other fees*	*% of total income*	*Research grants & contracts*	*% t in*
1	1950–1	48,500	64·1	20,000	26·4	5,799	7·7	—	
2	1951–2	65,000	63·4	24,000	23·4	11,375	11·1	—	
3	1952–3	115,000	71·9	28,000	17·5	15,417	9·7	—	
4	1953–4	127,000	70·7	32,000	17·8	18,484	10·3	—	
5	1954–5	153,250	73·6	32,000	15·4	19,234	9·2	2,521	
6	1955–6	170,240	72·5	38,666	16·5	21,460	9·1	3,634	
7	1956–7	183,540	73·3	38,666	15·4	22,293	8·9	3,862	
8	1957–8	221,860	72·6	38,666	12·7	34,942	11·5	6,791	
9	1958–9	234,344	71·7	40,593	12·4	36,487	11·1	11,020	
10	1959–60	278,425	72·3	44,445	11·5	38,619	10·0	20,105	
11	1960–1	315,918	71·8	44,445	10·1	39,829	9·1	36,915	
12	1961–2	345,636	71·0	49,445	10·2	41,417	8·5	44,767	
13	1962–3	429,040	70·9	44,445	7·3	55,712	9·2	68,923	1
14	1963–4	555,891	72·7	65,890	8·6	61,577	8·1	71,355	
15	1964–5	675,906	74·8	59,445	6·6	72,445	8·0	79,982	
16	1965–6	821,549	75·8	59,445	5·5	84,164	7·8	85,420	
17	1966–7	919,339	72·1	59,445	4·7	94,463	7·4	132,290	1
18	1967–8	1,100,730	72·7	60,112	4·0	114,633	7·6	139,159	
19	1968–9	1,178,842	71·1	59,111	3·6	128,789	7·7	151,855	
20	1969–70	1,402,620	72·5	44,870	2·3	139,116	7·2	154,154	

COME

wments & ations	*% of total income*	*Miscellaneous*	*% of total income*	*Total income*	*Capital grants*[a]	*Year No.*
25	—	1,327	1·8	75,651	235,464	1
347	0·3	1,757	1·8	102,479	378,000	2
230	0·1	1,242	0·8	159,889	220,159	3
598	0·3	1,597	0·9	179,679	168,868	4
246	0·1	1,020	0·5	208,271	121,843	5
175	0·1	713	0·3	234,888	120,599	6
285	0·1	1,942	0·8	250,588	163,222	7
432	0·1	2,750	0·9	305,441	104,302	8
727	0·2	3,827	1·2	326,998	174,215	9
1,134	0·3	2,468	0·7	385,196	223,206	10
1,046	0·2	1,862	0·4	440,015	371,129	11
1,639	0·3	3,771	0·8	486,675	645,512	12
5,049	0·8	2,274	0·4	605,443	536,927	13
7,437	0·9	2,380	0·4	764,530	715,019	14
),955	1·2	4,775	0·5	903,508	943,391	15
5,823	1·5	16,882	1·5	1,084,283	1,323,860	16
3,458	0·5	63,851	4·9	1,275,846	780,451	17
2,818	1·5	75,741	5·0	1,513,193	650,370	18
),777	1·9	107,961	6·5	1,657,335	475,692	19
2,619	1·7	159,654	8·3	1,933,033	248,138	20

e figures in this column refer to the sums actually paid by the UGC in the
ar concerned on schemes previously approved; there is no direct or easily
ntifiable relationship between these figures and the annual building
ocations and starting dates agreed from time to time by the UGC. The
ounts cover building costs, furnishings, equipment and professional fees.
e p. 231.

TABLE 4: SUM

Year No.	*Session*	*Teaching and research*				*% of total expendit*
		Salaries of staff	*Other departmental expenses*[a]	*Library*	*Total*	
1	1950–1	26,347	2,152	4,281	32,780	42·5
2	1951–2	46,824	6,929	6,907	60,660	54·2
3	1952–3	65,462	20,100	10,153	95,715	61·9
4	1953–4	77,979	21,646	10,118	109,743	61·5
5	1954–5	94,143	22,667	11,070	127,880	61·7
6	1955–6	100,698	26,818	12,914	140,430	60·8
7	1956–7	106,549	29,956	17,350	153,855	61·4
8	1957–8	138,108	31,236	17,692	187,036	61·6
9	1958–9	147,752	35,452	18,943	202,147	61·3
10	1959–60	170,545	41,864	22,836	235,245	61·4
11	1960–1	190,846	48,991	25,651	265,488	61·0
12	1961–2	205,958	52,649	27,889	286,496	58·6
13	1962–3	241,501	60,820	35,465	337,786	55·2
14	1963–4	320,414	114,567	42,683	477,664	66·3
15	1964–5	392,220	134,500	54,012	580,732	65·2
16	1965–6	397,074	204,781	59,749	661,604	63·1
17	1966–7	433,829	287,558	68,568	789,955	63·9
18	1967–8	483,711	289,431	86,294	859,436	58·7
19	1968–9	557,572	310,090	91,394	959,056	59·2
20	1969–70	635,404	351,048	104,880	1,091,332	57·7

[a] This column includes departmental wages and laboratory maintena together with expenditures covered by research grants and contracts.

XPENDITURE

inis-tion	*% of total expendi-ture*	*Mainten-ance of premises*	*% of total expendi-ture*	*Other expendi-ture*[b]	*% of total expendi-ture*	*Total expenditure*	*Year No.*
3,784	30·9	14,102	18·3	6,413	8·3	77,079	1
0,786	18·6	24,787	22·2	5,578	5·0	111,811	2
6,101	10·4	29,517	19·1	13,402	8·6	154,735	3
8,102	10·2	34,128	19·1	16,498	9·2	178,471	4
8,029	8·7	40,620	19·6	20,804	10·0	207,333	5
8,652	8·1	45,564	19·7	26,367	11·4	231,013	6
2,106	8·8	48,567	19·4	25,977	10·4	250,505	7
6,892	8·9	61,390	20·2	28,455	9·3	303,773	8
9,111	8·8	60,525	18·4	37,777	11·5	329,560	9
1,899	8·3	62,056	16·2	54,143	14·1	383,343	10
1,601	7·3	73,476	16·9	64,921	14·8	435,486	11
8,765	7·9	89,055	18·2	74,920	15·3	489,236	12
5,659	7·5	109,769	17·9	118,494	19·4	611,708	13
5,735	7·7	129,573	18·0	57,992	8·0	720,964	14
3,927	8·3	151,299	17·0	85,368	9·5	891,326	15
2,750	7·9	199,956	19·1	103,946	9·9	1,048,256	16
0,140	7·3	224,658	18·2	131,950	10·6	1,236,703	17
),140	6·8	309,940	21·2	194,675	13·3	1,464,191	18
5,192	6·5	293,603	18·1	262,519	16·2	1,620,370	19
4,857	7·1	354,142	18·7	312,348	16·5	1,892,679	20

This column includes expenditure on: student amenities and welfare; examination expenses, fellowships, scholarships and prizes; adult education; and (in the later years) computers and the Institute of Education. It includes also marginal capital expenditure defrayed from income but does not include allocations to reserves or provisions for renewals of furniture and equipment.

Foundation Year Lecture List, 1970–1

The broad scheme of the lectures is that which was adopted in 1966 (see p. 159). The lectures are given at 9 a.m. and 11 a.m. on Mondays to Fridays throughout the session. The setting-out of the list distinguishes typographically between: (i) the *Main Thread* with its sub-headings of major topics; (ii) the *Discursive Treatment*, indicated by a single indentation, which elaborates selected topics occurring within or related to the general framework of the lectures; and (iii) the *Friday Lectures* or *Recurrent Topics*, indicated by a double indentation, which deal with six areas in the general development of ideas and outlook: (A) Philosophical Questions and Presuppositions, (B) Politics and the State, (C) The Idea of Nature, (D) Creative Arts, (E) Religious Belief, (F) Social Change.

AUTUMN TERM

Lecture

1 Introduction by the Vice-Chancellor

The Earth as an Object in Space

2 Man's changing view of the universe
3 Methods of observation and measurement in astronomy
4 The solar system as we know it
5 The possibility of extra-terrestrial life
6 The stars, the galaxy and the universe

The Earth as an Object for Investigation

7 The structure of the earth
8 Denudation, deposition and earth movements
9 Relative displacement of continents
10 Fossils and organic evolution

Emergence and Development of Life

11 The stratigraphical record
12 Geological time
13 Cells and cell division

14 Mendelism
15 Evolution as a process
16 The whole geographical environment
17 Civilisation and climate
18 Are we controlled by our environment?
19 Language as a tool and its nature
20 The neolithic revolution

The Ancient World

21 Early civilisations of the Near East
22 The Greek city-states
23 Greek philosophy
24 Alexander and the Hellenistic empires
25 The growth of the Roman Empire I
26 The Barbarian peoples of Europe
27 The growth of the Roman Empire II
28 Roman Britain

Friday Lectures

29 (A) Philosophical Questions and Presuppositions (1) Plato's *Republic* and a utopian approach to politics
30 (B) Politics and the State: Methods and Scope (1)—Aristotle and the foundation of politics

31 The later Roman Empire
32 Greek and Roman art and architecture
33 Christian beginnings: I: Judaism and Jesus Christ
34 Christian beginnings II: The first-century church and the New Testament
35 The Christian Church and the Roman state
36 The significance of Greece and Rome

The Dark Ages

37 Christianity after the Fall of Rome
38 The 'Dark Ages'

Friday Lectures

39 (C) The Idea of Nature (1)—some basic thought-models
40 (D) Creative Arts (1)—some aspects of medieval art

The Middle Ages

41 Feudalism
42 The Roman Church and the West
43 The twelfth-century renaissance
44 The medieval synthesis

The Study of Language

45 The main topics of language study
46 Language across time and area I
47 Language across time and area II
48 Language in its social setting

Friday Lectures

49 (E) Religious Belief (1)—The changing patterns of religion in the West
50 Panel Discussion (1)

Renaissance and Reformation

51 The growth of urban society
52 Europe and the wider world
53 Renaissance humanism
54 The religious issues of the Reformation
55 Social aspects of the Reformation
56 The middle class and mercantilism
57 Absolute monarchy and limited monarchy
58 The scientific work of Copernicus, Galileo and Newton

Friday Lectures

59 (B) Politics and the State: Method and Scope (2)—The state as a work of art—Machiavelli
60 (A) Philosophical Questions and Presuppositions (2)—The state as a natural machine—Hobbes

The Enlightenment I

61 Descartes' programme for science: (i) systematic doubt
62 Descartes' programme for science: (ii) the ghost in the machine
63 The universe as mechanical: Galileo to Newton
64 The rise of empiricism: Bacon, the Royal Society and Locke
65 The challenge to Newtonianism: Leibniz and Berkeley

The Nature of Mathematics

66 Geometry from Euclid to Einstein
67 Notions of number
68 Applied mathematics

Friday Lectures

69 (D) Creative Arts (2)—Looking back at the Renaissance
70 Panel Discussion (2)

The Scope of Newtonian Physics

71 Mechanical models of heat and energy
72 Electricity and magnetism—the classical approach

Alchemy to Chemistry

73 Alchemy to chemistry I
74 Alchemy to chemistry II
75 Periodic Classification of the Elements

The Enlightenment II

76 Enlightenment scepticism
77 The idea of progress
78 Natural Law and society

Friday Lectures

79 (E) Religious Belief (2)—The condition of Religion at the end of the eighteenth century
80 (F) Social Change (1)—A Sociological perspective

Revolutions I—political

81 The American Revolution
82 The French Revolution
83 Romanticism, revolution and reaction
84 Liberalism and the revolutions of 1848

Right and Wrong

85 *Ought* or *is*
86 Objective and relative
87 Determinism and freedom
88 Morality and the law

Friday Lectures

89 (A) Philosophical Questions and Presuppositions (3)—The philosopher of the Glorious Revolution: John Locke

90 (B) Politics and the State: Methods and Scope (3)—The paradigm of revolution

SPRING TERM

English Law

91 The concept of law
92 Legal techniques I
93 Legal techniques II
94 The courts and the legal profession

Revolutions II—industrial

95 Introduction to agricultural and industrial revolution
96 Development of heavy industry
97 Development of transport
98 European penetration into other continents—The search for natural resources

Political Economy

99 The wealth of nations
100 The dismal science
101 Marxian economics
102 J. S. Mill and political economy

Friday Lectures

103 (C) The Idea of Nature (2)—The arrow of time

104 (D) Creative Arts (3)—Art and the French Revolution

Revolutions III—ideological

105 John Stuart Mill and utilitarianism
106 Charles Darwin and evolution
107 Karl Marx and socialism
108 Sigmund Freud and psychology

The Science of Politics

109 The nature of politics
110 The liberal democratic state

111 The authoritarian state
112 Government in the 'Third World'

Friday Lectures

113 (E) Religious Belief (3)—Belief and unbelief at the end of the nineteenth-century
114 Panel discussion (3)

Revolutions IV—scientific

115 The discovery of subatomic particles
116 The new radiations, X-Rays and radioactivity
117 Rutherford and the nuclear atom
118 Bohr and the quantum theory
119 The integrated spectrum—from γ-rays to radio waves
120 Unravelling the nucleus
121 The Periodic Classification of the Elements—The new approach
122 The building of molecules

Friday Lectures

123 (A) Philosophical Questions and Presuppositions (4)—Science and the philosophy of science
124 (B) Politics and the State: Methods and Scope (4)—Marx, revolution and the science of politics

The Chemistry of Life Processes

125 Carbon—The unique element I
126 Carbon—The unique element II
127 Chemistry and the treatment of disease I
128 Chemistry and the treatment of disease II

The Development of Social Concern

129 The idea of the Welfare State
130 Welfare State and affluent society
131 Education as a social institution
132 The state and education

Friday Lectures

133 (C) The Idea of Nature (3)—'Chance' and 'purpose'
134 (D) Creative Arts (4)—Art in an industrial society

The Population Explosion

135 Malthus and the significance of demography

The Biology of Food Production

136 Enzymes

137 Nutrition and diet

138 Food and food production

139 Elimination of food loss

Problems of Underdeveloped Countries

140 Rich and poor countries

141 The economics of underdeveloped countries (1)

142 The economics of underdeveloped countries (2)

Friday Lectures

143 (E) Religious Belief (4)—Aspects of religion in the twentieth-century

144 (F) Social Change (2)—historical and contemporary

The Growth of Planning

145 The extension of the role of the state

146 The planned society

147 The libertarian protest

148 Planning and democracy

Natural Resources and Planned Utilisation

149 Mineral and water resources

150 Fuel resources

151 Town and country planning—the growth of ideas

152 Town and country planning—in the context of an expanding economy

Friday Lectures

153 (F) Social change (3)—the country and the town

154 Panel discussion (4)

The Change in the Balance of Power in the 20th Century

155 The breakdown of the European order

156 The United States as a world power

157 The Russian revolution

158 The Soviet Union as a world power

159 The fascist revolutions

160 The twenty years' crisis

161 The development of total war and its social repercussions

162 The world since 1945

Friday Lectures

163 (C) The Idea of Nature (4)—Some open questions

164 (D) Creative Arts (5)—Art in the twentieth century

The Search for Stability

165 Keynes and positive regulation

166 From stability to growth

167 Stable and unstable political systems

168 Stability and instability in international affairs

Self-regulating Processes—Theory and Practice

169 Ecology as a science: cyclic processes in nature

170 Interaction of organisms

171 Self-regulating mechanisms

172 Computers, electronic and otherwise

Friday Lectures

173 (F) Social Change (4)—stability and order

174 Panel discussion (5)

Persons, brains and machines

175 The study of human individuals

176 The evidence of the senses

177 Interpreting sensory evidence

178 From perception to thought

179 Learning and remembering

180 The organisation of memory

181 Human limitations and accomplishments

182 Behind the eye

183 Mechanism and meaning

184 Brains and persons

Social Impact of Modern Technology

185 Modern Techniques in Psychiatry I

186 Modern Techniques in Psychiatry II

The Idea of the University

187 The medieval university

188 The development of the modern university

189 The future of the university

190 Higher education in a developing society

Form in Literature

Tragedy

191 Greek tragedy: Aeschylus, Sophocles and Euripides
192 Shakespearian tragedy
193 Shakespearian tragedy: *King Lear*
194 French Classical Tragedy: Racine
195 Ibsen and Chekhov
196 Brecht
197 Modern French drama: Anouilh, Sartre, Ionesco
198 Modern English drama: Eliot and Beckett

The Novel

199 The elements of fiction
200 The realist novel: Balzac, Flaubert and Zola
201 Psychological realism: George Eliot
202 Realism in Russia: Tolstoy and Dostoevsky
203 Changing perspectives I: Henry James
204 Changing perspectives II: Proust and Gide
205 Technique as discovery
206 The human condition
207 The elements of expression in music
208 Style in the Baroque
209 Stamitz to Schubert
210 Schumann to Schoenberg

Social Impact of Modern Technology

211 Fission and fusion—A new source of power
212 Nuclear weapons
213 Modern chemical industry I
214 Modern chemical industry II
215 The social impact of automation
216 The Technologist—What he is and What he does
217 Probability and statistics
218 Statistical decisions

The British Economy and World Poverty

219 Industry without empire
220 Co-existence and development

Recent Advances in Science

221 Beneath the Moho
222 Sediments of the deep ocean
223 Exploration of space
224 Global communications and their implications

225 Exploration of large molecules
226 The biological role of large molecules
227 The genetic code and genetic defects
228 The origin of life
229 Science in 1971
230 Conclusion by the Vice-Chancellor

Select Bibliography

ARMYTAGE, W. H. G., *Civic Universities*, 1955.

ASHBY, E., *Universities: British, Indian, African*, 1966.

ASHBY, E., and ANDERSON, M., *The Rise of the Student Estate in Britain*, 1970.

ASSOCIATION OF UNIVERSITY TEACHERS, 'Report on university development', *Univ. Review*, Vol. 16, No. 2, 1944.

ASSOCIATION OF UNIVERSITY TEACHERS, 'The university as a regional focus', *Univ. Review*, Vol. 17, No., 2 1945.

BARLOW, A. (Chairman), *Report of a Committee appointed by the Lord President of the Council on Scientific Manpower*, 1946.

BELOFF, M., *The Plateglass Universities*, 1968.

BERDAHL, R. O., *British Universities and the State*, 1959.

BIBBY, C., 'The general education of the specialist student', *Univ. Quarterly*, 1954.

BLAKE, J. W., 'The Sneyds of Keele, 1530–1949', *N. Staffs. Journ. of Field Studies*, 1962.

BROOK, G. L., *The Modern University*, 1965.

BROSAN, G. *et al.*, *Patterns and Policies in Higher Education*, Penguin Special, 1971.

BOURGES, H., *The Student Revolt: the Activists Speak*, 1968.

BROWN, A. W., 'Notes on the history of the college movement', *Staffordshire Sentinel*, 20 April 1914.

CHRISTIE, T., 'Contrary imaginations at Keele: an alternative interpretation', *Univ. Quarterly*, 1969.

COCKBURN, A., and BLACKBURN, R. (eds.), *Student Power*, Penguin Special, 1969.

COLE, G. D. H., 'The social studies in the universities', *Polit. Quarterly*, 1944.

COLE, G. D. H., 'The teaching of social studies in British universities', *Univ. Quarterly*, 1948.

CROSS, M., and JOBLING, R. G., 'The English new universities—a preliminary enquiry', *Univ. Quarterly*, 1969.

CROUCH, C., *The Student Revolt*, 1970.

DAICHES, D. (ed.), *The Idea of a New University: an Experiment in Sussex*, 1964.

DEPARTMENT OF EDUCATION AND SCIENCE, Statistics of Education, Vol. 6: *Universities*, 1966–.

DOBREE, B., 'Arts faculties in modern universities', *Polit. Quarterly*, 1944.

'DUNDONALD, J.,' *Letters to a Vice-Chancellor*, 1962.

EMERY, A. E., 'In the early tutorial classes: Longton', *The Highway*, April 1953.

FINER, S. E., 'The teaching of politics in the university', *Univ. Quarterly*, 1953.

FOREIGN OFFICE, *University Reform in Germany: Report by a German Commission*, HMSO, 1949.

FULTON, J. S., 'General education', *Univ. Quarterly*, 1950.

GALLIE, W. B., *A New University: A. D. Lindsay and the Keele Experiment*, 1960.

GREEN, V. H. H., *British Institutions: The Universities*, Pelican, 1969.

HALSEY, A. H., 'University expansion and the collegiate ideal', *Univ. Quarterly*, 1961.

HARTLEY, J., and BEASLEY, N., 'Contrary imaginations at Keele', *Univ. Quarterly*, 1969.

HARVARD UNIVERSITY, *General Education in a Free Society*, Report of a Committee, 1945.

HORWOOD, T., 'A new University College: a proposal for North Staffordshire', *Univ. Quarterly*, Vol. II, 1947, pp. 77–81.

ILIFFE, A. H., 'Student societies in the University College of North Staffordshire', *Sociological Rev.*, 1956.

ILIFFE, A. H., *The Foundation Year in the University of Keele*, Sociological Review, Monograph 12, Keele, 1968.

JAMES, D. G., 'New notions about universities', *Univ. Review*, 1943.

JAMES, J. and THOMAS, C. (eds.), *Keele: After Ten Years*, Students' Union and Keele Society, Keele, 1961.

JONES, J. LENNARD, 'Inaugural address', *Cambridge Review*, 7 March 1953.

KELLY, T., *A History of Adult Education in Great Britain*, 2nd ed., 1970.

KIDD, H., *The Trouble at the LSE, 1966–7*, 1969.

KOLBERT, J. M., *The Sneyds and Keele Hall*, 1967.

KOTSCHNIG, W. M., *The University in a Changing World: a Symposium*, 1932.

LAWLOR, J. J. (ed.), *The New University*, 1968.

LEAVIS, F. R., *Education and the University*, 1943; new ed. 1948.

LINDSAY, A. D., *The Essentials of Democracy*, 1929.

LINDSAY, A. D., *I Believe in Democracy*, 1940.

LINDSAY, A. D., 'A plan for education', *Picture Post*, vol. 10, No. 1, 4 January 1941.

LINDSAY, A. D., *The Modern Democratic State*, 1943.

LINDSAY, A. D., 'The relation of teaching and research in social studies', *Univ. Quarterly*, II, 3 May 1948.

LINDSAY, A. D., 'A dual task in higher education', *Listener*, 16 March 1950.

LINDSAY, A. D., 'The University College of North Staffordshire', *The Highway*, February 1951.

LINDSAY, A. D., *Selected Addresses*, Students' Bookshop, Keele, 1957.

LIVINGSTONE, R., *Some Thoughts on University Education*, 1948.

LÖWE, A., *The Universities in Transformation*, 1940.

LOWE, R. A., 'The development of adult education in the Potteries with special reference to the founding of a university in the area' (unpublished M.A. thesis, Keele, 1966).

LOWE, R. A., 'Determinants of a university's curriculum', *Br. J. of Educational Studies*, Vol. XVII, No. 1, 1969.

MACK, J. A. (ed.), *The History of Tunstall II Tutorial Class 1913–34*, Tunstall, Stoke-on-Trent, 1935.

MacMURRAY, J., 'The Functions of a University', *Polit. Quarterly*, 1944.

MALBON, G., 'Adult education in North Staffordshire and the foundation of a University College at Keele', *Rewley House Papers*, III, iii, 1954–5.

MANSBRIDGE, A., *University Tutorial Classes*, 1913.

MANSBRIDGE, A., *An Adventure in Working Class Education*, 1920.

MARITAIN, J., *Education at the Cross-roads*, 1943.

MOBERLY, W., *The Crisis in the University*, 1949.

MOBERLY, W., *The Universities and Cultural Leadership*, 1951.

MOUNTFORD, J., *British Universities*, 1966.

MURRAY, K., 'The development of the universities in Great Britain', *J. Roy. Statistical Soc.*, Series A, vol. 121, pt 4, 1958.

NUFFIELD COLLEGE, *The Problem Facing British Universities*, 1948.

PASCAL, R., 'The universities and social purpose', *Univ. Quarterly*, 1949.

PEERS, R., *Adult Education: a Comparative Study*, 1958.

PERKIN, H. J., *New Universities in the United Kingdom*, OECD, 1969.

PETERSON, A. D. C., 'The relevance of the liberal arts colleges', *Univ. Quarterly*, 1963.

PINK, M. A., 'Suggestions for a reformed university curriculum', *Univ. Review*, 1933.

P.E.P., 'The Keele experiment', *Planning*, October 1954.

RAYBOULD, S. G., *The English Universities and Adult Education*, 1951.

RIESMAN, D., 'Notes on new universities—British and American', *Univ. Quarterly*, 1966.

ROBBINS, LORD (Chairman), *Report of the Committee on Higher Education*, 1963.

ROSS, MURRAY G. (ed.), *New Universities in the Modern World*, New York, 1966.

SANFORD, N. (ed.), *The American College*, Wiley, New York, 1962; paperback, 1967.

SARMIENTO, E., 'Ortega y Gasset and education', *Univ. Quarterly*, 1952.

SLOMAN, A. E., *A University in the Making*, 1964.

SNOW, C. P., *The Two Cultures and the Scientific Revolution*, 1959.

STEWART, W. A. C., *The Adaptation of a University to the Changing needs of the Community*, Ghent, 1959.

STEWART, W. A. C., *Karl Mannheim on Education and Social Thought*, 1967.

STEWART, W. A. C., *British Universities: Dilemmas and Opportunities*, Keele, 1968.

STOCKS, MARY, *The Workers' Educational Association: the First Fifty Years*, 1953.

SWARTHMORE, *Critique of a College: Reports of the Commission on Educational Policy*, Swarthmore College, USA, 1967.

TAWNEY, R. H., 'An experiment in democratic education', *Polit. Quarterly*, 1914; reprinted in *The Radical Tradition*, 1964.

TEALE, A. E., 'The origin of the Keele experiment', *N. Staffs. J. of Field Studies*, Vol. I, 1961.

TEMPLEMAN, G., 'The modern universities', *Univ. Quarterly*, 1947.

THODAY, D., 'Halls of residence', *Univ. Quarterly*, 1957.

TROW, M., 'The idea of a new university', *Univ. Quarterly*, 1965.

'TRUSCOT, BRUCE' [E. A. Peers], *Redbrick University*, 1943.

'TRUSCOT, BRUCE' [E. A. Peers], 'The university and its region', *Polit. Quarterly*, 1944.

UNIVERSITY GRANTS COMMITTEE, *Annual Returns from Universities, 1949–65*; *University Development: 1935–1947; 1947–52; 1952–7; 1957–62; 1962–7.*

Victoria History of Staffordshire, Vol. 8, 1963.

WADDINGTON, C. H., 'The integral university', *Polit. Quarterly*, 1946.

WHITEHEAD, A. N., *The Aims of Education*, 1932.

Index

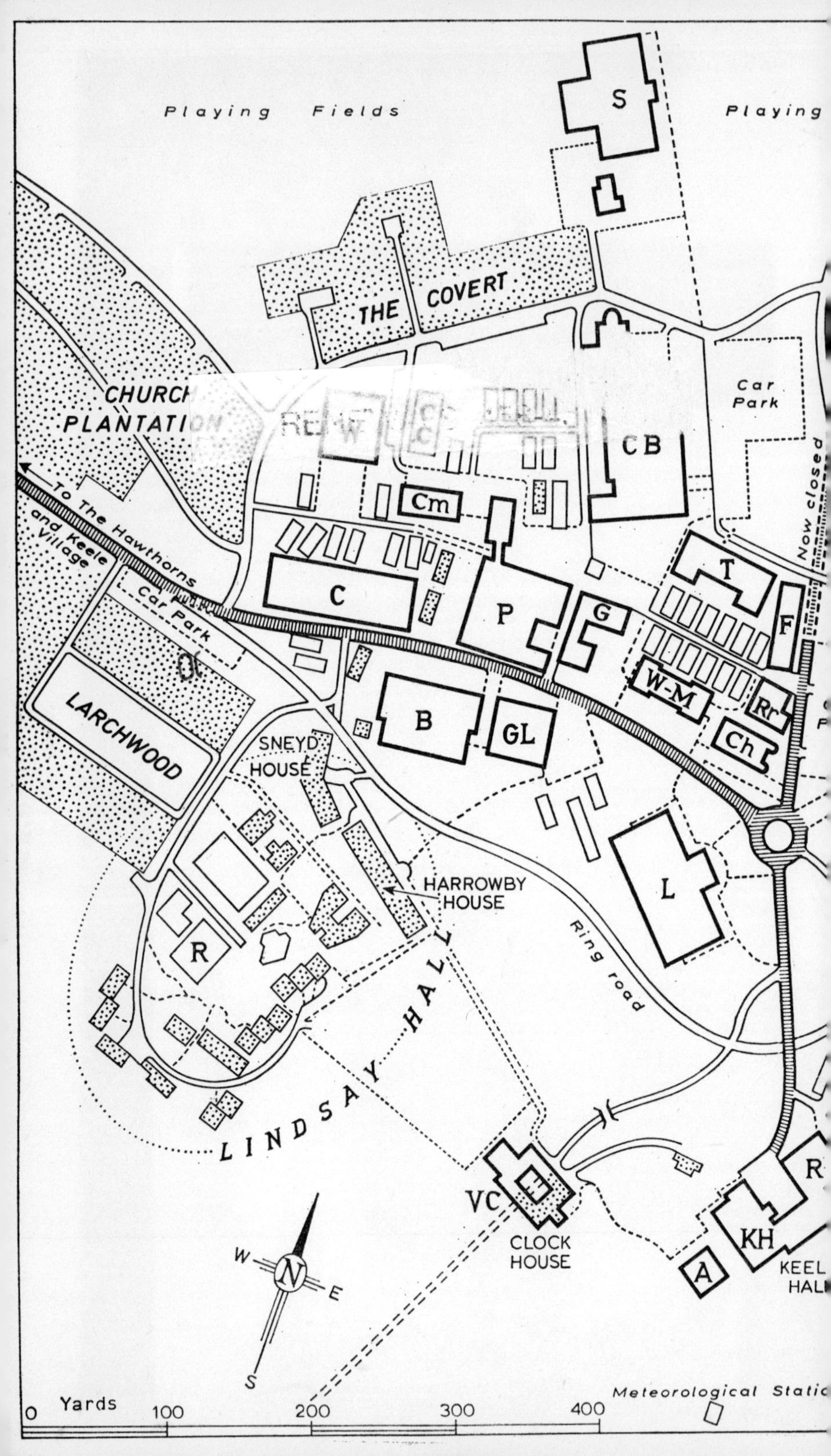

Playing Fields
Playing
S
THE COVERT
CHURCH
PLANTATION
Car Park
CB
Now closed
Cm
To The Hawthorns and Keele Village
Car Park
C
P
G
T
F
W-M
Rr
Ch
B
GL
LARCHWOOD
SNEYD HOUSE
HARROWBY HOUSE
L
Ring road
R
LINDSAY HALL
VC
CLOCK HOUSE
KH
A
W
N
E
S
0 Yards 100 200 300 400
Meteorological Statio